221819   24·99

Alternative Dispute Resolution in the Public Sector

**Published in conjunction with the
Policy Studies Organization**

Alternative Dispute Resolution in the Public Sector

Miriam K. Mills, *Editor*

Nelson-Hall Publishers/Chicago

Cover Art: *Balconies* by Connie Vepstas. Photocollage.

Library of Congress Cataloging-in-Publication Data

Alternative dispute resolution in the public sector / Miriam K. Mills, editor.
    p.   cm.
  Includes bibliographical references and index.
  ISBN 0-8304-1258-1
  1. Employee-management relations in government—Law and
legislation—United States. 2. Grievance arbitration—United
States. 3. Collective labor agreements—Government employees—
United States. I. Mills, Miriam K.
KF5365.D57 1991
344.73'0189041353—dc20
[347.304189041353]
                                     91-6474
                                     CIP

Manufactured in the United States of America

10 9 8 7 6 5 4 3 2 1

TM The paper used in this book meets the minimum requirements of American National Standard for Information Sciences—Permanence of Paper for Printed Library Materials, ANSI Z39.48-1984.

CONTENTS

INTRODUCTION

Miriam K. Mills

IN CONSIDERING the increasingly litigious nature of combatants in the United States, the litigation process has been stretched out of shape by the inclusion of many types of cases that are not appropriately located in the courts (McKay, 1985). This symposium considers conflict resolution approaches in labor relations, environmental issues, rule making, and related conflicts. The use of dispute resolution within administrative agencies and in contract formulation is also examined. Analysis of the practice and promise of Alternative Dispute Resolution (ADR) is analyzed within a number of settings. The policy implications of resolution models are assessed.

The ADR system comprises the various processes and mechanisms all of us have been hearing about. They range from negotiation and mediation to rent-a-judge plans, mini-trials, administrative agency processes, and ombudsmen. They include also the courts, arbitrators, and many other agencies. Together these mechanisms comprise a dispute resolution system, however unsystematic the mechanisms may be.

ADR is the resolution of disputes by means other than litigation. Its advocates claim that it will reduce court dockets by resolving cases more quickly, at less expense, and with more attention from the judiciary than the traditional system. Mostly, ADR involves methods of encouraging early settlement. In theory, a case settled is a case resolved. More significantly, the provision of alternative dispute resolution methods is itself an important preventive measure. Simply knowing that responsive in-place mechanisms exist helps to bring warring factions together.

There are two major categories of dispute resolution. One is adjudication by third parties and the other is joint decision making by the disputing parties (Kheel, 1985). While one may regard alternative dispute resolution procedures as a means of saving litigants time and money, the process may indeed provide a better model of conflict resolution.

Very slowly, the view is beginning to crystalize that ADR may in fact be the best place to conclusively reach settlement, rather than simply being a precursor to more "official" mechanisms.

Goals of ADR

The intent of ADR is to help assure that individuals receive just treatment in a manner consistent with their preference. In general terms, individuals may need to more specifically understand the range of dispute resolutions that are possible and then to select the most appropriate one.

In looking at ADR, there are clearly many efforts under way to institutionalize alternative ways of dealing with civil disputes that would otherwise be litigated. A second approach to dispute resolution deals with the ways in which public resources are allocated, that is with supplements to the legislative, administrative, and judicial processes for resolving differences over the allocation of public resources or setting of public policy. The third strand of dispute resolution has to do with interpersonal or intra-organizational conflict, not necessarily conflict that would go to court, but disputes between individuals and within families, groups, and private organizations (Susskind, 1983).

There are three major routes by which to improve the dispute resolution system: changing the law, using alternatives such as court-related mechanisms, and channeling disputes to non-adjudicative tribunals. The insistence on parity is at the root of many approaches to conflict resolution. There is an underlying presumption that right may indeed exist on both sides. One must also exercise caution that restrictions and barriers imposed in an allegedly power-sharing mode do not preclude widespread use.

What should the goals of alternative dispute resolution be? ADR should be more expeditious than the courts in resolving disputes. ADR should be informal and less technical than court procedures. The process should be more economical than court litigation. It is a private forum where hearings are closed and the proceedings are not a matter of public record. Parties to the dispute select their own expediter who has specialized knowledge in the field of the dispute. Unlike a court action, the informal atmosphere of the process works to promote good will in a dispute. This allows a long-term relationship to continue. Except for narrow grounds of appeal, the decision of the resolver is final and binding on the parties. This ends the dispute so that parties can concentrate on other matters.

Where there are long-term on-going relationships between the parties, where a lawsuit would be particularly disruptive, and where the participants know they are obliged to remain together, dispute resolution is becoming increasingly acceptable. In personal areas, for example, such as child custody, divorce, and with neighborhood disputes, people are finding ways to deal with problems themselves and avoid the inadequacies of court systems. Even prisoners now call for external assistance in dealing with conflicts with prison authorities.

Shortcomings of ADR

Over the years, however, the extension of ADR to newer issues has had some unexpected consequences. As the work force becomes more sophisticated, there is an increasing reliance on third party tryers of facts to resolve the issues that formerly lay between only the two parties. It is in the nature of ADR to aim at specific solutions to specific problems. Because of the lack of precedent, decisions that are made in one location may not necessarily be transmitted to related areas.

Although the goal of expeditious and private resolution is achieved, one may legitimately question whether such private resolution does not in fact negatively impact upon the common good. The shortcoming is that the solution may be applicable only to a single specific circumstance and may not necessarily have an impact on future difficulties. Others argue that the participants to the dispute may not be informed as to all their legal rights. They are required to settle based on what they know, rather than on the basis of what they are entitled to.

The principal thrust of recent criticisms of ADR has been also aimed at mediation, perhaps because that process blends third party facilitation with disputant control of outcome, and hence, is inherently imprecise and manipulatable. In theory, mediation is a voluntary process whereby two or more disputants arrive at a mutually acceptable solution with the help of a neutral third party.

> It is sometimes claimed that there are those who subscribe to the ADR movement because they view efficient and inexpensive dispute resolution as an important societal goal without regard for the substantive results reached. . . . This is not to say that private settlements can never produce results that are consistent with the public interest; rather, it is to say that private settlements are troubling when we have no assurance that the legislative or agency-mandated standards have been followed, and when we have no satisfactory explanation as to why there may have been a variance from the rule of law. . . . Inexpensive, expeditious, and informal adjudication is not always synonymous with fair and just adjudication. The decisionmakers may not understand that values at stake and parties to disputes do not always possess equal power and resources. (Edwards, 1986:678)

In many instances the disputes are private. What emerges from them is maintained within the boundaries of the specific locations. Another point that has been made is that expeditious ad hoc settlement may in fact be inappropriate for some issues altogether. The litigants may not know the extent to which the law protects them. Altogether too much approval has been given to the benefit of cost reduction and timeliness. Paradoxically, it may be in the best interests of the parties to resort to more time-consuming and costly mechanisms, especially if one thinks of the common good as a greater benefit than individual issue resolution.

There is further the distrust that often accompanies processes that are new and unfamiliar and that appear to be unaccompanied by the legal protections that disputants value so highly. A related deterrent may be the absence of mechanisms for ensuring high standards in the provision of alternatives (Goldberg et al., 1986:291).

For disputants unfamiliar with arbitration or mediation, the informality may invite mistrust. The cumbersomeness, delay and formality may for some individuals be more desirable because it conveys a ceremonial and ponderous pace. Can informal adjudication ever give the same degree of satisfaction as traditional mechanisms? There is also the issue of the ceremonial aspects of law. If the issue is critical to the participants, they may demand the full regalia of as legalistic a forum as possible with as professional a level of service as can be obtained.

Public Policy Implications

One of the basic issues raised for public policy is the problem of interruptions of functions that interfere with production considered essential to the general welfare. In the case of labor, a strike will also affect the goals or desires of others in the community—persons who are neither strikers nor struck employers—by depriving them of desired services, products, or commodities, by interfering with national defense activities, or by indirectly putting them out of work.

A subsidiary question is how to establish the socially approved norms of behavior to be followed by contending factions. The substance of these norms will be affected by economic circumstances, public attitudes and beliefs, and the balance of power among contending interest groups.

This volume examines two critical areas which generate conflict, labor relations and the environment. Considering employment relations and the land, there could be no two more significant issues that call for informed analysis and resolution.

The introductory chapter by Max O. Stephenson, Jr., and Gerald M. Pops examines the broad role of public administrators in handling public sector disputes. They suggest that conflict resolution and rule-making do not necessarily guarantee democratic processes. Outsiders to the process sometimes assume that if the mechanisms are carefully enough established, that political implications need not be addressed. For conflict resolution to be effective, it must also be acted upon in real life. This implementation is only possible if the approaches taken give due weight to democratic theory. Yet, even this view is open to considerable interpretation. The authors examine the area of negotiated rule-making as the starting point for their discussion of democratic process. They emphasize the criticality of political bargaining which will still be necessary regardless of structure. They conclude that there are ultimately three roles that must be highlighted within negotiation—the political generalist, the political professional, and the career professional.

The next broad section contains five papers dealing with various aspects of labor relations. There is discussion in this portion, not only of the activity, but also of the participants' perceptions. Vern Hauck and John South consider how arbitration has been used in disposing of discrimination cases in contrast to the more conventional labor dispute settlements dealing with problems explicitly covered with a labor contract. Many litigants in issues dealing with employment discrimination tend to support using the courts or civil rights agencies, rather than labor arbitration. The authors highlight the distinctions between conventional decision-making for labor disputes, as contrasted with cases dealing explicitly with discrimination. They illustrate diagrammatically the additional strands of authority that are used by the arbitrators. The arbitrators, by and large, tend to utilize arbitral decision rules, as well as legal precedents, in dealing with employment discrimination. They also tend to emphasize a higher decree of procedural fairness. They note that some arbitrators have assumed authority equivalent to that of federal judges in utilizing all aspects of applicable law.

When the parties are obliged to negotiate within settings open to the public, it has been widely assumed that bargaining would be hindered. Arbitrators have always been quick to contend that any constraint on candor would limit the effectiveness of the process. The chapter by Richard Feiock and Jonathan West suggests that these apprehensions may not be fully justified. Citizen participation in what had ordinarily been a private process has enjoyed greater benefit than initially anticipated. The authors provide an empirical analysis of public participation. The approach has been to provide structural access rather than direct participation. Evidently, materials prepared for the purposes of negotiation which might include strategy notes is exempt from legislation supporting sunshine laws. They scrupulously examine earlier research on this topic and find that a majority tended to find public involvement effective. While there are certain negative aspects, they are not significant for the ultimate output. The agreements reached within a more open forum are not of significantly different quality than those occurring within more traditional closed chambers.

The chapter by Paul Clark, Daniel Gallagher, and Thomas Pavlak examines the perspective of public employees, vis-à-vis the grievance procedure. Their findings are derived from an extensive survey of postal workers. The grievance process is probably one of the most visible aspects of union intervention. Whereas structural negotiations are generally time bound by external deadlines, interpretations of the contract continue over the duration of the agreement. The authors develop a scale to precisely measure union member attitudes. There are many functions to the grievance process, yet the most critical is the provision of due process. The survey set out to measure general reactions to grievance procedures, as well as the specific implementation within their own workplace.

Douglas McCabe looks at the role of the mediator within federal sector disputes. He derives his findings from an analysis of the viewpoints of 50 federal mediators. One of the key difficulties is that there is a conflict between the participants regarding their individual interests, as contrasted to complying with formal policies. It appears that the federal government stressed the concept of modern labor relations without providing the necessary preparatory training and motivation. An additional confounding factor was that mediators used within governmental issues were unprepared for the different nature of issues that they would face. Not only were the parties to the dispute unprepared for the process, so, too, were the mediators. The inescapable consequence of this study is that the planning of the implementation of a process is as important as the institution of the process.

In chapter 6 Matthew Silberman considers the topic of grievance resolution within prisons. Such an approach can ideally provide alternatives to violent self-help. His approach centers on the importance of internalizing social control. Critical to the maintenance of peace within the prison is an involved and consistent correctional staff. The continuity of an established relationship seems to help counter prison violence. The general trend in American penology has been a tilt towards a punitive rather than a rehabilitative model. He concentrates on those conditions which contribute to prison violence. Through his survey analysis, he determines that there are a number of responses to the threat of violence. He points out that avoidance is not a useful response, since it would be interpreted as weakness or lead to further victimization. On the other hand, violence seems to be diminished where correctional counselors work to establish a relationship with even the most difficult of inmates. The more consistent and long-term the relationship between staff and inmates, the more limited is the outbreak of violence. Silberman stresses that informal mediation mechanisms are very effective, inasmuch as they bypass hierarchical levels of bureaucracy. He also notes that permitting access to lawyers also helps to lower the level of violence.

The next major portion of this book deals with environmental issues. There is a broadly accepted view that environmental dispute resolution is a necessary approach today. Each of the authors in this section accepts the necessity of environmental dispute resolution, but see its benefits and limitations from varied perspectives.

J. Walton Blackburn regards environmental mediation as an alternative to customary courts. He notes deficiencies, including the absence of precedent and the lack of professional guidelines for mediators, but believes there are grounds here for further analysis. Does the process provide equivalent levels of equity to that of the courts? The characteristics of mediation practice within the environment is assisted from the viewpoint of the practitioners. He describes a ten-stage model for environmental mediation. Whereas the process itself has applicability to many settings, the emphasis here is especially on steps necessary for a successful outcome on issues dealing with the environment. The major weaknesses are the absence of full recognition of all affected parties, the complexities of the type of dispute, the number of interests affected by settlement, and lack of a knowledge base to deal with specific and highly technical issues. Given the consequences of an ill-informed decision on substantial people and resources, necessary steps must be taken, Blackburn argues, to ensure more effective choice and development.

Barry Rabe, in chapter 8, assesses some defects in policy formation in the area of environmental dispute resolution. He suggests that the nature of American politics may serve as a barrier to the broader use of informal mechanisms. The expectation is that informal mechanisms will lead to greater cooperation and efficacy. While the tradition of dispute resolution has long existed in labor relations, the process is newer within the environmental area. Rabe cautions that environmental dispute resolution should be viewed as a possible regulatory reform, rather than a proven alternative. Congress has sometimes chosen to avoid battles with its constituents by referring disputes to the judicial realm. The easy access to adjudication has led to an increasing number of pressure groups. Yet, as the number of issues and the numbers of players increase, there needs to be established an objective measure of implementation success. Rabe concludes that, although environmental dispute resolution as presently practiced cannot be seen as the total remedy, it may, in fact, be a precursor to a more fully realized and successful environmental dispute resolution mechanism.

Continuing on this theme, Michael Hamilton addresses requirements for the formalization of environmental mediation. He points out the relationships between environmental and labor disputes. He raises the issue of what conditions must be met to facilitate institutionalizing environmental mediation. Secondarily, he inquires as to the components of successful mediation. Hamilton recognizes the value of conflict. Through such friction, new constituencies may form, leading to social change.

He stresses the value and benefit of encouraging voluntary negotiation. This is in conformity with the democratic approach. He raises, also, the issue of open meetings and suggests the combination of open meetings for public officials and private caucuses of nongovernmental people. The approaches used in environmental mediation build upon the tradition within labor management. Some of the key differences, though, relate to sharply unequal power resources, the existence of many disputants, less clarity on the issues, and the lack of an accepted framework for negotiation. He concludes with a seven-part plan for effectively institutionalizing the mediation process.

Chapter 10 by Greg Protasel provides a useful case study of negotiated rule-making within the timber/fish/wildlife coalition in the state of Washington. He contrasts negotiated rule-making with administrative rule-making and terms the former as neo-corporatism and the latter as pluralistic policy making. He emphasizes the successful results of the timber/fish/wildlife coalition without the rancor usually seen in multi-party conflict. Protasel examines the quandary of trading off between technological expertise and public participation. He describes the coalition of 1986 within the state of Washington. Initially, conflict was engendered by administrative rule-making, but was replaced by negotiated rule-making, and within a few months, a framework was established for effectively managing forest resources. Forty individuals representing almost a dozen separate entities were welded together. The effectiveness of the approach underscores the importance of an understanding of a process that incorporates interest groups. The involvement of industry, Indian tribes, and environmental groups led to an unprecedented degree of consensus. Protasel suggests that this can become a useful model for other complex issues.

The various authors have examined the concept of conflict quite broadly. In some cases, the resolution has come about through a modification of traditional litigation and in others, the courtroom played no part at all. There have been both formal and informal approaches to resolving differences of position. The emphasis has been on conflict in the broadest sense, with specific approaches to satisfying the needs of adversarial partners.

These chapters have examined circumstances of conflict within many settings. What becomes clear is that, despite the best intentions of the parties involved, the methods used for resolution may, in fact, be inappropriate. It may well be that future patterns of conflict resolution in the public sector may call for hybrid forms of settlement. While there may sometimes be a desire for administrative tidiness and order, it is important to recognize that there are many forms of conflict resolution which are still emerging that will have to be tailored to the wishes of the parties, as well as the nature of the issues. When one looks to a democratic society, one expects a certain degree of openness and tolerance of diversity. These chapters have certainly examined the dispute resolution format within many different settings. Those who carry out the process, as well as those subjected to it, have also been described. It is hoped that this volume helps to shed light on the range and scope of dispute resolution in contemporary American society.

REFERENCES

Edwards, Harry T. 1986. "Alternative Dispute Resolution: Panacea or Anathema." *Harvard Law Review* 99:668–684.

Goldberg, Stephen B., Eric D. Green, and Frank Sander. 1986. "ADR Problems and Prospects: Looking to the Future." *Judicature* 69 (February–March):5

Kheel, Ted. 1985. "Where Will ADR Be in the Year 2000." *Dispute Resolution Forum.* National Institute for Dispute Resolution.

McKay, R. 1985. "The Many Uses of Alternative Dispute Resolution." *Arbitration Journal* 40(13).

Susskind, Lawrence. 1983. "Court Appointed Masters as Mediators." *Negotiation Journal* 1(4) (October).

Vargas, Gabe. 1985. "Alternative Dispute Resolution: An International Approach." Book Review. *Negotiation Journal* 1(4) (October).

PART ONE

Overview of Conflict
Resolution Approaches

PUBLIC ADMINISTRATORS AND CONFLICT RESOLUTION: DEMOCRATIC THEORY, ADMINISTRATIVE CAPACITY, AND THE CASE OF NEGOTIATED RULE-MAKING

Max O. Stephenson, Jr., *and* Gerald M. Pops

THE RECENT popularity of a wide range of conflict resolution theories and techniques has generated increased interest in an enhanced role for public administrators as negotiators in the policy process. Federal and foundation funding has led to experiments which have employed this growing technology. For example, the Federal government has encouraged the formation of area labor-management committees to train negotiators to engage in more problem-solving and employ less traditional position-based bargaining.

Yet, history suggests that optimism about new decision modes in public administration has invariably been followed by a set of cautionary judgments enunciated after some experimentation and reflection. Widespread use of conflict reduction and resolution strategies in administrative settings as diverse as international diplomacy, rulemaking, collective bargaining and community and dispute settlement, suggests that the time is now ripe to begin to assess the theoretical and practical limitations and implications of these initiatives.

The purpose of this chapter is to begin to analyze some of the limitations of the use of conflict resolution technology in public policy-making by applying two criteria commonly used to assess the effectiveness of methods to make public decisions: democracy and administrative capacity. Our argument consists of two basic parts. We first introduce each of our criteria and suggest their general relevance to evaluating conflict resolution. Next, we attempt to demonstrate the specific utility of our approach by applying each criterion to ongoing efforts to develop and employ negotiated rulemaking. We investigated negotiated rulemaking and employ it as an exemplar because it represents a sophisticated and logical extension of the use of negotiation in conflict resolution in the policy process. Moreover, proponents of negotiated rulemaking have heralded its advantages and utility in terms of the criteria in which we are most interested.

There are undoubtedly other ways by which conflict resolution methodology could be evaluated but the criteria of democracy and administrative capacity appear especially useful for two reasons. First, there is a well developed and rich intellectual tradition— multidisciplinary and involving some of America's most noted scholars—that is directed to the very questions upon which conflict resolution techniques rest, *viz.:* even if negotiated resolutions are empirically possible, how *ought* public decisions to be made? For any large scale advance in the use of conflict resolution technology to occur, students of government must be able to reconcile it with this intellectual tradition. Secondly, conflict resolution strategies confront a range of practical problems arising from how public policymakers—legislators, chief executives, administrative officers, and judges—go about their craft. Any technology, if it is to enjoy a genuine chance of acceptance, must be perceived by these critical players as consistent both with the pressures of their environment, including the federal Constitution and our multitiered system of government and laws and with their background and training, including their capacity for understanding, analyzing and applying the tools that conflict technology offers them.

Limits Imposed by Democratic Theory

To say that a decision technology must be judged via "democratic" principles is to enter immediately into a thicket of ambiguity and historical controversy. Not only is "democracy" incapable of precise definition, it is broad enough to encompass most prescriptions that have been advanced since the beginnings of the Republic as to how our political system should be fashioned. A full explication is not possible here. What can be done in this space is to sketch the range of views and then to indicate how concepts of democratic theory might influence and constrain changes in decision technology. We are particularly interested in depicting the import of these ideas upon efforts to develop negotiated rulemaking processes.

The spectrum of theories of democracy varies directly with the degree of participation which is allowed in the decision-making process and runs the gamut from mass participation by all affected citizens to participation only indirectly through designated constitutional instrumentalities. "Direct" or mass democracy most closely approximates the Athenian model in which free citizens participated directly in raising, debating and discussing issues in public and in making decisions. "Pluralist" democracy, a midpoint along the path, is a form of representative democracy in which players from multiple centers of power, representing diverse interests, bargain and compromise to produce decisions that are broadly acceptable to the affected groups. "Constitutional" democracy envisions a government which, although either directly or indirectly selected by the people, insulates decision processes from undue popular influence and insures action by a set of institutions which together act "for," rather than according to, the people (Mansfield, 1987).

Each of these conceptualizations implies a different set of methods for making decisions. Direct democracy requires full disclosure of information, open debate and majority decision through voting. Pluralist democracy involves wide participation of citizens and interests through organized groups, some official and some unofficial, which bargain with each other and with government officials concerning their specialized bailiwicks of interest—toward the end of achieving consensus or compromise outcomes. Constitutional democracy employs a complex network of institutions legitimized through a constitution, some of which are responsible to the people but only episodically.

These three basic methods of choice are conveniently contrasted on the point of the individual's access to the decision-maker. In the first, approach to decision-making is direct—the citizen as decision-maker. In the second, access is to a set of groups, both official (within government, i.e., a legislative committee) and unofficial (interest groups in which the citizen holds membership). In the third, public access is limited to a voice in the periodic election of legislators and executives, as contributors to the public debate and as litigants in the courts dealing with the meanings of institutional, statutory or judge-made law.

In practice, in the United States, there has been a clear drift over time away from the constitutional toward the pluralistic and mass models of democracy. The founders debated and clearly chose the constitutional framework of limited access and heightened responsibility of officials to work on behalf of the public interest. Both senators and the president were chosen indirectly by state legislatures and special electors, respectively. These institutions were to be peopled by individuals of property, education and community stature. The development of political parties, the advent of public education systems, the industrial age and mass immigration during the nineteenth century brought the extension of suffrage, the formation of powerful political interest groups, an economic industrial elite and the communication systems necessary for the articulation of both private and public power centers. These trends continued and strengthened well into the twentieth century.

The result has been the kind of decentralized, pluralistic, bargaining-dominated, political decision-making system observed favorably by such enthusiasts as Truman (1955) and Dahl (1956). In the middle and late twentieth century, the explosion of mass communications, the development of policy technology, and the rise in participation devices (constitutional and legislative initiative and referendum, judicial recall and political party primaries are examples) have put into place the elements essential for the rise of mass democracy which allow elected officials, politically appointed administrators and civil servants, judges, and interest group leaders to determine and to pattern their action on the preferences of their constituents, clienteles and members.

The drift from constitutional toward popular democracy has produced a significant dilemma for the individual public administrator. On one hand, the administrative official looks to perform a well-practiced traditional role as an implementer of the law and as an agent for the executive function. More recently, within the last twenty-five years, the courts have likewise imposed obligations upon public administrators—those of fealty to doctrines of due process and equal protection. Taken together, these forces find the administrator acting as a constitutional balance wheel attempting to provide simultaneous service to the three institutions of government (Rohr, 1986: 181–86).

On the other hand, administrative officials face palpable pressures to behave as a kind of handmaiden to public opinion and popular participation. These growing demands have been strengthened by the booming technology of opinion polling. Such a service role is not exactly what Carl Friedrich had in mind when, in his famous essay in 1940, he argued that "popular sentiment" should provide a touchstone for administrative action (Friedrich, 1940). Instead, first and foremost in his view was the obligation to act in pursuance of professional judgement acquired through a process of education and training. Indeed, Friedrich urged administrators to follow the dictates of their professional judgement when they believed that that course met the needs of the general public. He counseled the exercise of informed professional discretion and individual responsibility even when legal direction was wanting or incomplete. Implicit in Friedrich's prescription was the obligation of the public administrator to act *for* the public, on behalf of its best interest, not simply to react to popular clamor and the passions of the moment. Nonetheless, his arguments helped to lay the groundwork for independent administrative behavior that can help to justify discretionary use of conflict resolution technology.

The debate concerning the role and responsibility of the public administrator is thus a reflection of a broader conflict over the meaning of democracy. Conflict resolution technology must be examined in the context of this debate. To illustrate this point, we next examine critically the arguments for negotiated rule-making in the context of these broader concerns.

Democratic Theory and the Case of Negotiated Rule-Making

A growing literature in recent years has advanced a specific form of mediation, negotiated rule-making, as a more democratic, less costly, and more efficacious method of addressing policy controversies within the administrative framework (Susskind and McMahon, 1985; Perritt, 1986; Susskind and Cruikshank, 1987). Proponents of this form of conflict resolution suggest that it will produce "fairer and wiser" rules at lower cost. (Susskind and McMahon, 1985: 140). That stance is premised in turn upon a number of assumptions which may be traced to conceptions of democracy and to the role of the bureaucracy within it.

Advocates of negotiated rulemaking ("reg-neg") criticize traditional agency decision (rule-making) processes for failing to provide sufficient opportunity for dialogue among affected contending parties. These critics argue that the one-way communication process implicit in informal rule-making has encouraged groups to exaggerate their demands and unduly harden their positions. In this view, negotiated rule-making overcomes these difficulties precisely because it involves disputants directly in a process of face-to-face negotiation. Unlike traditional rule-making, advocates assert, negotiated rulemaking results in "win-win" decisions (Susskind and McMahon, 1985: 136–37). Thus, regulatory negotiation not only produces better outcomes but also increases the likelihood that the process itself will not be challenged later in the courts.[1] Such a participatory process, "reg-neg" proponents assert, represents an important form of direct democracy which legitimates the decisions which arise from it. These contentions deserve careful consideration.

Reaching the Stakeholders

While advocates clearly assume that all relevant stakeholders can be identified and should participate in any negotiation which occurs, it is by no means self-evident that negotiated rulemaking can be structured to reflect all plausibly significant forces in the public debate. The manifestly uneven and unequal resources of players on the pluralist chessboard suggest that the prudent observer should approach such assumptions with considerable caution, if not skepticism. Might not public officials, knowingly or not, be most likely to invite those stakeholders with the highest profile and visibility to any proposed rulemaking? Put differently, while the onus to reach all affected parties rests with the policy-maker, it is not clear that less well-organized parties will petition to negotiate (they may fail to do so out of ignorance or fear) or that decision-makers either will be inclined or sufficiently informed to insure that they do so (Amy, 1987: 129–35).

Implications of the Resources of Partisans

At another level of analysis, problems are posed by the resources which the players bring to the mediation process. In the area of environmental policy, for example, in which the largest share of experimentation with negotiated rulemaking has occurred, industry representatives often bring two attributes to the table which environmental groups are very often unable to match: ample fiscal resources and long and broad experience in negotiating (Amy, 1987: 204–208).

As with any art, negotiators tend to develop and hone skills and strategies only with experience. All other things equal, stakeholders with long familiarity with negotiation will be advantaged vis-a-vis claimants without such experience. As Amy (1987: 102) has observed,

> good negotiators often view the process as something akin to a long military campaign where the side with the most resources and the best strategies and tactics will come out the winner.

To the extent that the least organized claimants are also novices in negotiation and unlikely to possess significant resources (organizational and fiscal), negotiated rule-making emerges *not* as an innately fairer form of democratic consultation, but instead, as a form of cooptative power politics.

What is of particular practical significance here is the fact that mediation efforts are much less formal and far less structured than the processes which they replace. That fact, in turn, implies ample room for experienced unethical players to exploit any inadequacy of expertise among their counterparts. Importantly, there are few legal obstacles to such manipulation. More subtly, the very informality and lack of structure which is so characteristic of negotiation and which encourages the development of trust and familiarity among participants may raise new possibilities for exploitation and manipulation by advantaged players. Familiarity breeds "humanness" and trust—the chemical producer seated across the table from the environmental activist is no longer a faceless industrial automaton wantonly dumping toxins into waterways but, instead, an individual with specific interests and an identifiable personality. But the existence of trust may allow its misuse. Such an eventuality appears far more likely when the stakeholders arrive at the negotiating table with unequal financial resources, negotiation experience and technical expertise.

The significance of resources (both technical and economic) to negotiation outcomes points to an additional characteristic of negotiated rulemaking: the interests which are most likely to prove powerful within a specific negotiation are also the most apt to be able to pursue alternative paths to achieve their policy ends should negotiations falter. Weaker players may engage in the mediation effort precisely because they possess no other alternative. To the extent that such behavior occurs, such participants may fall prey to more advantaged stakeholders who *do* have recourse to alternatives but *choose* instead to press their claims through negotiation in order to secure the advantages that they perceive it may bring.

Process Legitimacy: Myth and Reality

One additional difficulty which arises from the use of negotiation as a method of conflict resolution results from the very decision by participants to adopt it. Proponents of negotiated rulemaking promote the process as a forum in which stakeholders may come to identify their interests rather than their positions in an atmosphere of mutuality, egalitarianism, and voluntarism (Perritt, 1986; Susskind and Cruikshank, 1987). To the degree, however, that players enter negotiations unequal in power, experience, and information resources, these frequently cited "advantages" of mediation may prove more myth than reality. Nevertheless, such arguments clothe negotiation with a powerful aura of legitimacy. In short, the mythology surrounding use of the tool may permit inequities which otherwise would be considered intolerable.

This unsettling possibility suggests an additional paradox: since proponents consider negotiation superior *per se* to traditional forms of conflict abatement and resolution, will stakeholders be persuaded to employ it even when it is not working? Will the pressures to reach agreement prove so strong as to structure outcomes against weaker players with otherwise plausible demands?

To be fair, it must be asked: Would the interests of the underorganized or unorganized be any better protected by having legislators or political executives act for them through other processes, than by and through negotiation within administrative settings? There is at least one argument to the effect that they would be. There is symbolic and therefore political significance in holding legislators, courts, and political executives responsible for decisions they make that do not serve the interests of the unorganized. If considered in the legislature or the courts these decisions would be more public in character and therefore more likely to evoke response from the underrepresented. Thus, in practical terms, the interests of the less organized may best be expressed and supported in terms of votes, demonstrations, civil disobedience, statements receiving media attention, or judicial challenges.

There is surprisingly little empirical data concerning how many legislators seek out the interests of all of their constituents and attempt to serve those and how many simply respond to the organized interests that press them. One might expect different results from the former model than negotiated decisions would produce. There is at least a reasonable expectation that legislators will count poorly represented groups in the calculus of building coalition support. There is little reason to suppose, however, that an individual stakeholder who believes that he is advantaged by negotiation will have any incentive to consider poorly represented groups.

Governmental Power, Democratic Theory and Negotiated Rulemaking

Also ripe for further investigation is the converse question of whether agency administrators are more or less inclined than legislators to include the interests of unorganized groups in their decision-making processes. This is in part a function of the public administrator's values and habits and in part (seemingly a greater part) a function of how administrative roles are structured by the interplay of the three branches of government.

What seems clear in the case of negotiated rulemaking is that the process itself is designed in a way which does not often encourage administrators to look to anything beyond securing agreement among the parties as a standard by which to judge the justness and efficacy of outcomes. "Good" rule-making efforts are those which result in agreements to which all of the involved parties can subscribe. Obviously, this evaluative standard arises from the negotiation process itself and not from any broader conception of the public interest. Indeed, the public interest is defined as the negotiated compromise among the various affected stakeholders. There is little need in such a perspective for the application of Friedrich's conception of informed discretion. The manager need look no further for legitimation than the process in which he has participated.

In certain kinds of disputes, it appears possible that the interests of all relevant publics could be encompassed by the stakeholders involved in the negotiation. The difficulty, of course, lies in *knowing* that all significant interests have been represented and that their claims, in combination, approximate those of the general public. It is worth noting that even when it can be said that the players represent the public adequately, it does not follow necessarily that the rulemaking *process* will be equitable or its *outcome* representative. Nor can it be said, proponents' arguments notwithstanding, that even at its best, negotiated rulemaking approaches a popular democratic decision-making method. Instead, at best, negotiated outcomes will approximate pluralist or constitutional conceptions of democracy.

Negotiation and Administrative Capacity

Are administrators prepared by education, training, and role to assume responsibility for negotiation in the policy process? At issue is the *capacity* of public administrators to perform the negotiation function.

Of course, the public administrator is scarcely a monolithic entity. There are a number of possible ways to group administrators. We have chosen two sets of categories: (1) type of appointment to the public service and (2) type of educational background. These are cross-cutting groupings as the matrix in figure 1.1 demonstrates. Two cases are identified for each category: appointments are either

Figure 1.1 Types of Public Administrators

Background and Education		Political Generalist	Career Generalist
	Administration	*Political Generalist*	*Career Generalist*
	Profession	*Political Professional*	*Career Professional*
		Political Appointment	Civil Service Appointment

Status of Entry into the Public Service

political or through the civil service system and education is either in a specialized profession or in a field of administration.

The characteristics of these types may be examined in relation to their suitability as negotiators in administrative settings. Those appointed to the political public service (they fill the top policy-making managerial posts in government) are prone to identify and articulate the broad range of interests affected by a dispute. This is to be expected. Such people are selected, by and large, for the purpose of aiding the chief executive in achieving political consensus on policy and in maintaining and expanding the chief's political base. To do this, they need to be sophisticated in the task of surveying the political map and in predicting who will be affected by various policy initiatives, how they will be affected and how they are apt to react. However, although political appointees may be expected broadly to address these and like questions, they are not likely to seek mutually accommodating, win-win results in policy-related disputes. Each political regime has its favored interests reflecting the support base which brought it to power. The most probable course is that it will instruct its legions, who are drawn from those interests, to reward its friends and punish its enemies, although motives may be hidden behind the fiction that wide agreement is being sought. Negotiation technology lends itself perfectly to creating the *image* of consensus development and for that reason should not be entrusted solely to political appointees, lest tenets of mass and pluralist democracy be violated.

This point suggests a number of implications for negotiated rulemaking. First, the claimants engaged in negotiation are involved in that process only through the sufferance of the executive authority. What can be given can as readily be taken away. It matters very much, therefore, *why* government officials employ negotiated rulemaking. If negotiation is employed to assure greater participation by affected publics, it is more readily legitimated than if it is adopted merely to increase governmental efficiency—understood as increasing the probability of compliance with the policies and reducing the likelihood of court action with its associated delays and costs. It is even possible that negotiated rulemaking could be employed so as to deviate purposefully from legislative intent.

Secondly, a successful negotiated rulemaking process will protect final agency decision-making authority. If that discretion is assured by careful agency specification of the particular boundaries within which a final decision must fall, the government has effectively predetermined the outcome of the process and thereby, by definition, undermined it.

If process participants are given *carte blanche*, however, and the agency merely rubber-stamps the results of their deliberations, a different form of manipulation, no less pernicious, will have resulted. Between these opposing unacceptable extremes in which government either manipulates the rule-making negotiation or is itself manipulated by it, must be found middle ground in which the technique may be useful. It is difficult indeed to pinpoint precisely where between these extremes any particular negotiation will fall or whether its official sponsors are employing the process for other political aims (as instrument) or for itself (as end). Yet, it is how this issue is resolved in practice that will prove critical both to the specific and general utility of negotiated rulemaking.

Professionalism, in the sense of formal education in and association with a specialized field such as law, medicine, engineering, or social work, introduces another kind of administrative incapacity. Professionals are found in both the ranks of the politically appointed and the various career services. They hold ninety percent or more of the public administrative roles in the United States (Schott, 1976). Despite their generalist functions and their consequent need for political acuity and strong communication skills, many thousands of those serving as program administrators and bureau chiefs arise from narrowly defined professional fields (Mosher, 1982: 110–142). As members of different professions, they have undergone unique kinds of education and training which condition them to approach and to analyze problems in distinctly different ways. Their beliefs about what constitute the critical elements in decision situations will vary and they will hold and employ different causal theories.

Many of these preparations may be incompatible with the qualities generally seen as necessary for negotiator behavior. Prime among the latter may be the ability to empathize in order to understand communication and exchange. These qualities may be entirely absent from the preparation of an engineer or an accountant or even a lawyer who has persevered in an agency and been promoted to a position of administrative responsibility. Professional norms limit perspective. It is difficult for an accountant, no matter how capable interpersonally, to analyze a policy with a financial dimension as anything other than an accounting system problem.

For these reasons, the Political Generalist, the Political Professional, and the Career Professional all have built-in incapacity relating to the negotiation role. Only the Career Generalist, that person who is educated broadly in government and administration and who rises through the ranks in a career progression, is a person who *may* have the educational and experiential background and the requisite political neutrality to be an effective negotiator.

Concluding Comments

This chapter has evaluated conflict resolution technology and particularly negotiated rule-making, from the vantage points of democratic values and administrative capacity. Each of these criteria implies certain limitations for the use of conflict reduction strategies. Each also helps to clarify the roles which managers may play when adopting such technology. Administrators doubtless face a difficult task—implementing policy in an increasingly contentious climate. But this analysis suggests strongly that negotiated rule-making and conflict resolution techniques generally should not be considered guarantors of a more democratic decision process. Neither, should negotiated rulemaking be considered an alternative to political bargaining. Clearly, it is not. Rather, those who would employ such techniques should understand that conflict resolution efforts will inevitably occur in intensely political environments and will themselves emerge as another form of politics. That fact suggests that power and not calls for cooperation will likely determine the future of negotiated rule-making efforts.

NOTES

1. Many proponents of negotiated rulemaking see the technique as a means to avoid litigation and its costs. In fact, for some, avoiding litigation emerges as a central criterion.

REFERENCES

Amy, Douglas, J. 1987. *The Politics of Environmental Mediation.* New York: Columbia University Press.

Anderson, Frederick, R. 1985. "Negotiation and Informal Agency Action: The Case of Superfund." *Duke Law Journal* (March/April):261–380.

Dahl, Robert A. 1956. *A Preface to Democratic Theory.* Chicago, IL: University of Chicago Press.

Fiorino, Daniel, J. 1988. "Regulatory Negotiation as a Policy Process." *Public Administration Review* 48 (July/August): 764–772.

Friedrich, Carl J. 1940. "Public Policy and the Nature of Administrative Responsibility." In Carl J. Friedrich and E. S. Mason (eds.), *Public Policy,* vol. 1. Cambridge, MA: Harvard University Press.

Mansfield, Harvey C., Jr. 1987. "Constitutional Government: The Soul of Modern Democracy." *The Public Interest* 86 (Winter): 53–64.

Mosher, Frederick C. 1982. *Democracy and the Public Service,* 2d ed. New York: Oxford University Press.

Perritt, Henry, H. 1986. "Negotiated Rulemaking and Administrative Law." *Administrative Law Review* (Fall): 471–506.

Rohr, John A. 1986. *To Run a Constitution: The Legitimacy of the Administrative State.* Lawrence: University Press of Kansas.

Schott, Richard L. 1976. "Public Administration as a Profession: Problems and Prospects." *Public Administration Review* 36 (May/June): 253–259.

Susskind, Lawrence, and Jeffrey Cruikshank. 1987. *Breaking the Impasse: Consensual Approaches to Resolving Public Disputes.* New York: Basic Books.

Susskind, Lawrence, and Gerard McMahon. 1985. "The Theory and Practice of Negotiated Rulemaking." *Yale Journal on Regulation* 3 (Fall): 133–165.

Truman, David. 1955. *The Governmental Process.* New York: Knopf.

PART TWO

Labor Relations and Conflict Resolution

CHAPTER TWO

ARBITRATING DISCRIMINATION GRIEVANCES

Vern E. Hauck *and* John C. South

NEARLY TWENTY-FIVE years have passed since the Civil Rights Act of 1964 became law, and yet the debate regarding the wisdom of having labor arbitrators decide discrimination complaints continues. Regardless of which position is taken, the fact remains that the number of discrimination complaints submitted to arbitration has been increasing over the last two and one-half decades and appears likely to continue increasing right on into the next century. Practically speaking, the task faced by labor arbitrators is how best to serve the parties when discrimination grievances arise.

Hence, the aim of this study is to point out the differences between decision making for labor arbitration in general and arbitration cases involving discrimination. This study begins with a discussion of the literature explaining decision making by arbitrators confronted with labor matters such as seniority, discharge and promotion. Focus then swings to the theory, the legal decision rules and the decision policies used by arbitrators to decide discrimination complaints. Thirty-seven recently published arbitration awards dealing with civil rights are compared and reviewed to identify the decision making criteria most often applied to discrimination grievances. A model with two interlocking figures is proposed. Figure 2.1 explains the general theory of labor arbitration for discrimination complaints. Figure 2.2 probes deeper into the nature of the arbitral decision policy suggested in figure 2.1. Several related topics, including hearing procedure, burden of proof, arbitral decision priorities, consistency, and compliance with the law, are considered.

Figure 2.1 General Model of Employment Discrimination Arbitration

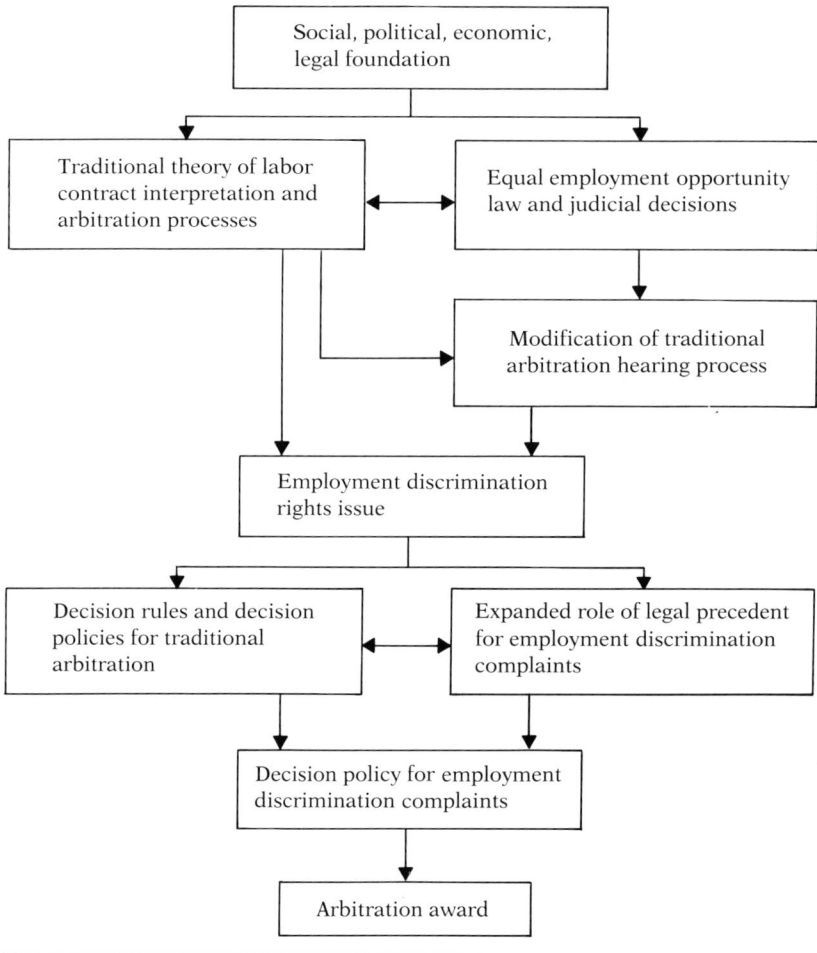

Background

The general theory of labor contract interpretation has been reviewed and analyzed in exhaustive detail since at least the end of World War II, an endeavor which continues because the field of labor arbitration must adjust to the changing needs of the parties (McKelvey, 1957; Zack and Bloch, 1983; Hill and Sinicropi, 1986). Probably the best known arbitral decision making studies suggest that arbitrators reach their awards by combining a multiplicity of decision rules that have evolved from the law. These legal decision rules predict, among other things, that arbitrators will follow specific rather than general contract language, that arbitrators will give meaning to the intent of the contract, and that arbitrators will make their decisions on the basis of the issue, the contract and the record.

Other research ties the legal decision rules to decision models that are activated by composites of cues (Prasow and Peters, 1983). One such model by Gullet and Goff (1980) argues that arbitrators have built a body of widely held belief systems which shape decision making in individual cases. Gullet and Goff formulated a Bayesian type flow chart (yes-no) decision model using fifteen decision rules common to arbitration. Their model depicts that arbitrators formulate judgments on the basis of contract language, past practice, precontract negotiations, past arbitral rulings, and the common law of arbitration.

A number of other studies illuminate a variety of aspects of arbitral decision making. For instance, Drews and Blanchard (1959) subjected 120 arbitration awards to factor analysis and identified five clusters of grievances that arbitrators normally face: central issues, job assignments and promotions, union rights and activities, supervision and working conditions, and coercion. Bass (1965) reports a study of demographic characteristics of 146 arbitrators judged by their peers as effective decision makers. Edwards (1976) and Coulson (1976) researched the experience of arbitrators with discrimination cases, outlining decision making difficulties and proper procedures.

Figure 2.2 Decision Policy for Employment Discrimination

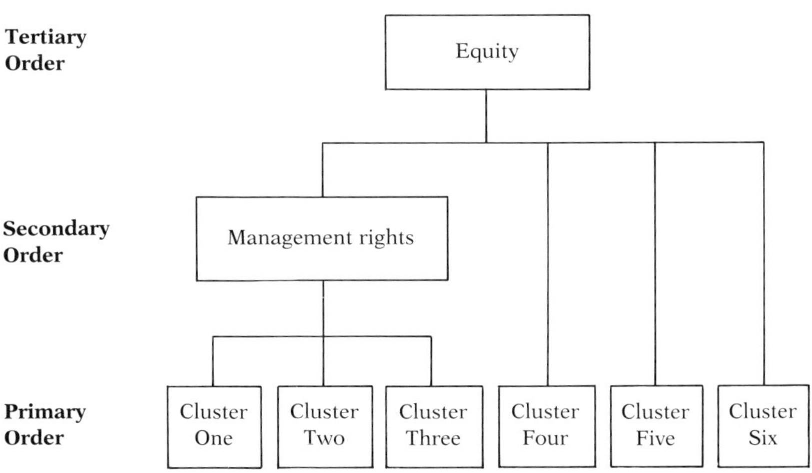

Oppenheimer and LaVan (1979) focused on case outputs by a group of arbitrators. They noted that grievants are more likely to gain a decision over a public sector employer when discrimination is judged by an arbitrator.

Cain and Stahl (1983) probed beyond the surface of legal reasoning and found that all arbitrators are probably quite consistent in the application of their respective decision policies. Cain and Stahl found that arbitrators decide most grievances on the basis of seven cues: management rights and efficiency, clear language of the contract, past practice, fairness, effect on the worker, negotiating history, and prior awards. When subjected to statistical analysis, these seven cues combine into a three-cue model indicating that arbitrators are actually guided, in order of priority, by considerations for:

1. Management Rights
2. Equity   = Fairness + Effect on Worker
3. Stability   = Contract Language + Past Practice + Negotiating History + Prior Awards

Methodology

Thirty legal decision rules commonly used by arbitrators (Elkouri and Elkouri, 1973; Prasow and Peters, 1970), as shown in table 2.1, were randomly placed in a structured questionnaire (Jauch, Osborn, and Martin, 1980). The questionnaire was pretested, refined, and an explanatory definition of each rule as well as procedural instructions for completion were included.

On four separate occasions three expert judges supplied assessment data. Initially, a single judge evaluated all thirty-seven cases to determine whether any of the thirty arbitral rules were used. The thirty-seven cases constitute about 10 percent of the total number of discrimination awards published in the Labor Arbitration Reports and Labor Arbitration Awards since 1974. Three months later, on occasion two, the same cases were re-evaluated by the same judge in a dissimilar order to minimize residual effects. On the third instance, using the thirty rules listed in the questionnaire, the second judge evaluated two randomly selected cases. The second judge's procedure was replicated by a third judge who evaluated two additional cases. The judges were instructed to answer "not used" in instances of doubt.

The study might have been improved and potential sample bias eliminated by the addition of more judges and a broader sample of cases, including some unpublished awards. Nonetheless, estimated intra- and inter-rater reliability was acceptable. Specifically, the median intra-judge rate/re-rate reliability coefficient was from .51 to 1.00. Agreement between the three judges ranged from 68 to 88 percent with a median of 81 percent.

Theory

The thirty-seven awards reviewed in this study suggest that arbitrators have changed emphasis and modified the general theory of labor contract interpretation in order to meet the needs of parties facing discrimination complaints. That is, the theory of labor arbitration in employment discrimination intertwines with and parallels the general theory of labor contract interpretation.

Figure 2.1 illustrates this juxtaposition. While the general theory of labor contract interpretation remains dominant, both theories emerge from the same, or nearly the same, social, political, economic, and legal foundations. The Commercial Arbitration Code, the Norris-La Guardia Act, the Wagner Act, the Taft-Hartley Act, the Landrum-Griffin Act, the Civil Rights Act of 1964, the *Steelworker's Trilogy* (1960), and *Alexander v. Gardner-Denver* (1974) can be located in the foundation of either theory, for example.

Continuing with figure 2.1, judicial interpretation of civil rights legislation has mandated that arbitrators revise longstanding arbitral hearing processes as a prerequisite to opening the employment discrimination hearing. Once the hearing is underway, the arbitrator must combine the pre-existing body of emerging arbitral decision rules and policy with legal precedent applicable to employment discrimination complaints. The last portion of figure 2.1 suggests the existence of an underlying arbitral decision policy which consistently governs employment discrimination awards, a matter detailed in figure 2.2.

Procedure and Proof

Several leading neutrals have taken great care to set out procedural guidelines for the proper handling of discrimination grievances. They suggest that arbitrators apply a greater degree of legality and procedural fairness during discrimination complaint hearings. Arbitrators considering civil rights grievances should normally plan to require a transcript; take greater care that the grievant's rights are properly represented; verify the ability of the advocates; insist on the production of essential legal documents; and relinquish arbitral jurisdiction over discrimination cases containing unusual points of law (Edwards, 1978; Siegel, 1977; Webster, 1978).

In assigning the burden of proof courts require a preponderance of evidence to establish a Title VII violation, except during one stage of the proceedings in disparate treatment complaints (*McDonnell Douglas*, 1973). Even in discharge cases the courts require the party making the discrimination challenge to retain the ultimate burden of persuasion at all times with the interim burden of proof shifting between the parties. Many arbitrators also hold the parties to a preponderance of evidence proof despite the fact that arbitration requires only the burden of going forward.

The danger exists, in arbitration involving both discrimination and discipline, that neutrals will act exactly opposite to courtroom procedural standards by requiring a preponderance of evidence in support of the employer's position and resolving doubt in favor of the union. Most arbitrators, however, have at least some legal training and all thirty-seven awards contained at least an obscure reference to proof. The cases reviewed here simply could not prove nor disprove the statement that arbitrators assigned either the interim burden of proof, the burden of going forward, or the ultimate burden of proof correctly.

Decision Rules

On the whole, the data validates statistically that arbitrators normally utilize a number of legal decision rules as well as civil rights law when they decide discrimination grievances. An important explanation of this phenomenon hinges on the law itself. *Gardner-Denver* establishes that a court may give great weight to an arbitral decision provided the arbitrator gives full consideration to the employee's Title VII rights. Footnote 21 in *Gardner-Denver* sets out the fundamental elements which should exist if the courts are to give an arbitral decision full consideration (*Stozier*, 1981). These four "relevant factors include the existence of provisions in the collective bargaining agreement that conform substantially with Title VII, the degree of procedural fairness in the arbitral forum, adequacy of the record with respect to the issue of discrimination, and the special competence of particular arbitrators" (*Gardner-Denver*, 1974).

In conformance with Footnote 21 in *Gardner-Denver*, neutrals follow any one of three approaches when interpreting discrimination grievances (Britton, 1982). One approach is exemplified in *Basic Vegetable Products* (1975). Arbitrator Gould assumed the authority equal to that of federal judges under Title VII. Using broad powers, he considered all aspects of applicable law, reinstated the grievant with 50 percent back pay, and granted reasonable attorney fees. A major advantage of Arbitrator Gould's approach is that every aspect of the civil rights law is openly considered and determined, making it a simple task for courts to give great weight to the arbitrators award under the guise of Footnote 21. The difficulty with Arbitrator Gould's method is that the courts may overturn the award because the arbitrator's decision hinges on the law rather than the labor agreement.

It is generally conceded that the authority of an arbitrator stems from the collective bargaining contract, and courts should not question arbitrators authorized to interpret the agreement (*Milwaukee Area Technical College* (1973), 40 AIS 8). However, when the agreement does not provide guidance or when Title VII conflicts with the agreement, the authority of the arbitrator is less certain and *Steelworkers* provides only limited guidance. The *Gardner-Denver* decision by the Supreme Court provides a partial answer to this dilemma. The arbitrator is required, as called for in *Steelworkers*, to follow the terms of the agreement and not civil rights law. Thus, if there is conflict between the contract and Title VII, the arbitrator, according to the Supreme Court, must follow the agreement. But, where the contract is silent or the contract requires following the law, the arbitrator can, and perhaps must as Arbitrator Gould did, turn to Title VII (*Hines*, 1976; *Bowen*, 1983).

The second approach differs only in that the arbitrator does not assume the same authority as a federal judge. Following this mode, Arbitrators Boals (*Southern Gage Company* (1977), 68 LA 755) and Koven (*County of Santa Clara* (1978), 71 LA 290) considered relevant law so that, if adjudication occurred, the courts could give their award great weight. But, after careful discussion of the law, Boals and Koven based their decisions squarely on interpretations of the collective bargaining agreement. This second approach has the advantage of signaling the court that the arbitrator has examined all law in accordance with Footnote 21, but keeps the award within the scope of traditional arbitral authority embodied in the labor contract.

The third general approach is followed by a vast majority of arbitrators. They do not openly consider civil rights law. Instead, as several bona fide experts agree, most neutrals decide discrimination cases by employing a multiplicity of traditional arbitral decision rules on a situation-by-situation basis (Edwards, 1978, and Elkouri and Elkouri, 1980). The advantage of this third approach is that the arbitrator's decision falls clearly within the bounds of the labor agreement. The disadvantage is that the court may not afford the arbitrator's decision great weight because no objective evidence exists in the arbitral award to show that the criteria of Footnote 21 has been satisfied.

The myriad of traditional rules available complicates the problem of identifying which set of these rules is actually used by arbitrators in discrimination grievances. Thirteen of the thirty evolving rules were found in more than 48 percent of the cases reviewed, see table 2.1. Two rules, intent of the parties and burden of proof, were judged present in every case, though often at an obscure level. Thus, in every case the arbitrator determined the mutual intent of the parties by examining the terms of the contract and deciding between the parties' opposing interpretations of disputed language.

Approximately 90 percent of the arbitrators followed the rule that "Specific contract language governs over general contract language." For example, Arbitrator Axon found no discrimination based on sex when the employee's attitude disqualified her from promotion and because a memorandum of agreement did not specifically require senior employees be promoted to supervisory positions (*Stayton*, 1980). In addition, 60 percent of the arbitrators made awards based upon the Language Which is Clear and Unambiguous rule. Heavy reliance on these two rules may be a consequence of professional efforts to avoid extra-contractual decisions and simultaneously not exceed arbitral authority as limited by the law.

Seventy-eight percent of the arbitrators based their decisions solely on the Issue, the Contract, and the Record; and arbitrators made Interpretations in Light of the Law in 73 percent of the cases. While both rules appeared in 45 percent of the cases, one or the other usually dominated. *Bristol Borough School District* (1978) was an exception. Arbitrator Belsky denied maternity sick leave because the denial was in line with applicable interpretations of Title VII and did not conflict with the collective bargaining agreement.

Title VII outlaws discrimination against an individual because of race, color, religion, sex or national origin, except when justified by business necessity. Arbitrators seldom judged employers according to the business necessity exemption concept, but favored instead the Reasonable and Prudent rule which is sometimes connected with business necessity. In *Olin Corporation* (1979), for example, Arbitrator Knudson found that the employer reasonably disqualified females of child-bearing age from some jobs since even OSHA admitted that removal of pregnant employees from lead exposure is advisable. It may be a necessity to disqualify most fertile women from jobs involving exposure to lead poisoning because of potential injury to an unconceived fetus. Arbitrator Knudson's decision included another

Table 2.1   Arbitral Decision Rules, Usage, and Clusters

Cluster Number		Percent of Use	
		Frequent	**Seldom**
1	Company manuals and handbooks		13.5
	Doctrine of implied obligations		13.5
	Major-minor test		8.1
	Parol evidence rule		2.7
2	Language is clear and unambiguous	59.5	
	Industry practice	48.6	
	Prior settlements as an aid to interpretation	75.7	
	Precontract negotiations		10.8
3	Interpretation in light of law	73.0	
	Specific versus general contract language	89.2	
	Normal and technical usage		16.2
	Doctrine of Ejusdem Generis		8.1
	Reason and equity		21.6
4	Construction in light of context	67.6	
	Custom and practice of parties	70.3	
	Arbiter refuses to substitute his judgment for management's	64.9	
	Reasonable and prudent	86.5	
5	Issue, contract, and record	78.4	
	Awarding back pay needs more justification		10.8
	No consideration to compromise offers		8.1
6	Agreement to be construed as a whole	56.8	
	Avoidance of harsh, absurd, or nonsensical results		10.8
	To express one thing is to exclude another		8.1
	Promissory estoppel doctrine		8.1
Nonclustering Decision Rules			
	Intent of the parties	100.00	
	Burden of proof	100.0	
	Avoidance of a forfeiture		2.7
	Experience and training of negotiations		2.7
	Interpretation against party seeking the language		10.8
	Past practice cannot be nullified by sweeping general provisions		10.8
			100.0

rule frequently appearing in the awards: he "Refused to substitute his judgment for management's."

Decision Policy

Whereas other decision policy studies have begun with defined cues, this study began with defined decision rules. The thirty rules were placed in a intercorrelation matrix (Hauck and South, 1988) and subjected to multiple cluster analysis using the Tyron-B coefficient procedure (Fruchter, 1954). Six clusters emerged. Each cluster is comprised of the rules arbitrators use to evaluate information and make judgments about discrimination complaints. When faced with similar discrimination problems arbitrators consistently applied similar decision clusters to resolve conflicts. The clusters which emerged from this procedure are defined as follows:

> *Cluster One:* Management's action is weighed in terms of equity to the worker and the language of the contract. Employee benefits are commonly assigned on the basis of the decision rules in this cluster when the contract is silent.
> *Cluster Two:* Management's action is examined on the basis of reasonableness and conformity with the parties' past practices. Decision rules in this cluster are often used to interpret parol evidence.
> *Cluster Three:* Management's action is examined on the basis of reasonableness and conformity with the contract and the law. Decision rules in this cluster often focus on the rendering of awards that do not give an unfair advantage to one party.
> *Cluster Four:* The arbitral award is justified in terms of the language of the contract, the impact on the parties, and the parties' past arbitral awards. Decision rules in this cluster are often used to interpret the law of the shop.
> *Cluster Five:* The arbitral award is justified in terms of the language of the contract and equity to the parties. Decision rules in this cluster commonly emphasize the assignment of the burden of proof and the elimination of unfair evidence.
> *Cluster Six:* The arbitral award is justified in terms of the parties' negotiating history and equity to the parties. Decision rules in this cluster focus on the contract as a whole.

Logic suggests that the six clusters operate as a result of arbitral policy which exists beyond the surface of legal reasoning. Testing this logic, the six clusters were compared by the judges to see if any of the seven cues proposed by Cain and Stahl could be found. Eight cues were found at the primary level, one more cue than Cain and Stahl identified: Management Rights, Reasonableness, Clear Language of the Contract, Past Practice, Fairness, Effect on the Worker, Negotiating History, and a new cue—the Law.

The probable existence of a unique set of decision policies consistently followed by labor arbitrators for discrimination complaints was first noted in figure 2.1. The findings pictured in figure 2.2, however, were obtained by subjecting the results displayed in table 2.2 to higher order statistical analysis. Table 2.2 verifies the unique nature of each cluster and its accompanying cues. While three cues were prioritized by Cain and Stahl's decision policy study, two cues emerged for discrimination cases. First, commonality was found at the secondary level among clusters one, two and three on the basis of Management Rights. Second, the Equity cue was verified statistically at the tertiary level, making it the common link between all clusters. Indeed, the hierarchical model in figure 2.2 illustrates that Management Rights is subservient to Equity. The two-cue model indicates that arbitrators prioritize and are consistently guided in discrimination cases by considerations for:

1. Equity   = Management Rights + Fairness + Negotiating History
2. Management Rights = Reasonableness + Effect on Worker + Contract Language + Past Practice + the Law

Table 2.2   Cluster Intercorrelation, Means, and Standard Deviations (n=37)

	1	2	3	4	5	6
Cluster One	1.00	−.30	.04	−.16	.18	.14
Cluster Two		1.00	−.30	.18	−.31	.01
Cluster Three			1.00	−.04	−.06	.13
Cluster Four				1.00	.10	−.04
Cluster Five					1.00	−.08
Cluster Six						1.00
Means	0.38	2.14	4.19	2.89	0.97	2.46
Standard deviation	0.89	0.98	1.37	1.20	0.64	0.87
Means as percent of maximum possible	9.5%	71.3%	69.8%	72.3%	3.2%	61.5%

Compliance

Evidence that arbitration awards normally comply with civil rights law was also found in the thirty-seven awards reviewed. This portion of the study focused only on the result of the award, the arbitrator's opinion aside. That is, was the result of the award, standing alone, in compliance with the law existing at the time the award was rendered? Twenty-seven of the awards (nearly 73 percent) were judged to be in compliance with the law regardless of the general approach chosen by the arbitrator for handling discrimination grievances. The remaining ten awards (27 percent) were potentially in compliance.

Like much of the legal process, civil rights law has been evolutionary and had not yet been determined by either the courts or the legislature when arbitrators rendered their awards in eight of the cases. To be specific, the law was not clear regarding unique questions associated with handicapped workers (*Masonite*, 1974), the Fair Labor Standards Act (*Evans Products*, 1978), affirmative action (*City of Detroit*, 1979), burden of proof (*Jacksonville*, 1977), racial harassment (*U.S. Steel*, 1977), maternity leave (*Bristol*, 1978), and lead poisoning (*Olin*, 1979).

In two instances the arbitrators' awards were arguably at odds with the law. Both cases concerned the promotion of black employees into jobs for which they were allegedly unqualified. In *Joy Manufacturing Company* (1977) the employer was potentially in violation of the law since the qualifying test given the grievant was not clearly shown to be job relevant (*Duke Power*, 1971). And in *Georgia Power Company* (1980), a court may have concluded that Title VII was violated since the foreman making the judgment against promotion gave testimony validating his own subjective bias against blacks (*Rowe*, 1972).

Other data relevant to compliance with the law was also found in the cases. First, discrimination was discussed in every award reviewed, often being contained in the position of the parties. Second, over 75 percent of the awards either quoted or referenced contractual antidiscrimination clauses. Research shows that 94 percent of the labor contracts in America contain antidiscrimination clauses (Staff, 1983). Third, the law has changed with time and several of the awards judged in compliance would violate today's civil rights law.

Conclusion

Concern for the wisdom of arbitrators deciding discrimination grievances pales beside the findings of this study. Almost all arbitration awards comply with the four relevant factors in *Gardner-Denver's* footnote 21. First, the majority of awards reviewed included references to antidiscrimination provisions in the applicable labor contract. Second, though shaky, the evidence in the awards suggests the existence of a more than adequate degree of procedural fairness. In fact, procedural adequacy may prove to be of secondary concern since justice under civil rights law is a normal by-product of arbitral conclusions. Third, discrimination was discussed in every award reviewed, usually in the parties' positions and less frequently in the arbitrator's opinion. Finally, the results of an overwhelming majority of awards reviewed in this study were judged in compliance with Title VII, documenting the competence of particular arbitrators to determine discrimination questions.

Statistical support exists for the models pictured in figures 2.1 and 2.2. Labor arbitrators reach conclusions about discrimination complaints based largely on interpretative decision rules traditionally used to decide questions such as seniority, discharge, and promotion. Furthermore, the decision policies posited by earlier studies of labor arbitrators are present in discrimination awards. For example, both kinds of cases require the arbitrator to make interpretations on the basis of the contract, the issue, and the record. Notably, arbitrators apply the same cues to both kinds of cases.

On the other hand, the demands of the parties and the law dictate that discrimination complaints be handled differently. Discrimination grievances involve procedural differences, careful attention to the allocation of proofs, the use of evidence outside the contract, and the law more directly than other types of labor arbitration cases. Beyond the surface, Management Rights is a significant connecting link for arbitrators confronted with discrimination grievances. But Stability is not a significant policy setting force. Unlike other arbitration, Equity dominates in discrimination cases.

ACKNOWLEDGMENTS

The authors thank the following persons for their helpful comments and contributions: the late Professor Irving Kovarsky, and Professor Anthony Sinicropi, University of Iowa; Professor James Craft, University of Pittsburgh; Professor Terry Leap, Clemson University; Professor Tom Pearce, Moorhead State University; and Mr. John D. Clemente, Esq., Brooks and Ewalt.

REFERENCES

Basic Patterns in Union Contracts, 10th ed. 1983. Washington, DC: Bureau of National Affairs Inc.

Bass, Bernard. 1965. *Organizational Psychology.* Boston: Allyn and Bacon.

Britton, Raymond L. 1982. *The Arbitration Guide.* Englewood Cliffs, NJ: Prentice Hall.

Cain, Joseph P., and Michael J. Stahl. 1983. "Modeling the Policies of Several Labor Arbitrators." *Academy of Management Journal* 26(1):140-147.

Coulson, Robert. 1976. "Title Seven Arbitration in Action." *Labor Law Journal* 27 (3):141-151.

Drews, D.W., and R.E. Blanchard. 1959. "A Factorial Study of Labor Arbitration Cases." *Personnel Psychology* 12:303-310.

Edwards, Harry T. 1976. "Arbitration of Employment Discrimination Cases: An Empirical Study." In *Proceedings of the 28th Annual Meeting of the National Academy of Arbitrators.* Washington, DC: Bureau of National Affairs, Inc.

Edwards, Harry T. 1978. "Arbitration as an Alternative in Equal Employment Disputes." *Arbitration Journal* 33(4):23-27.

Elkouri, Frank, and Edna A. Elkouri. 1973. *How Arbitration Works,* 3d ed. Washington, DC: Bureau of National Affairs, Inc.

_____.1980. *Legal Status of Federal-Sector Arbitration.* Washington, DC: Bureau of National Affairs, Inc.

Fruchter, Benjamin. 1954. *Introduction to Factor Analysis.* New York: Van Nostrand.

Gullett, C.R., and W.H. Goff. 1980. "The Arbitral Decision-Making Process: A Computerized Simulation." *Personnel Journal* 59(8):663-667.

Hauck, Vern E., and John C. South. 1988. "Arbitrating Discrimination Grievances: An Empirical Model for Decision Standards." *Policy Studies Journal,* 16(3):511-521.

Hill, Marvin F., Jr., and Anthony V. Sinicropi. 1986. *Evidence in Arbitration.* Washington, DC: Bureau of National Affairs, Inc.

Jauch, Lawrence R., Richard N. Osborn, and Thomas N. Martin. 1980. "Structured Content Analysis of Cases: A Contemporary Method for Organizational Research." *Academy of Management Review* 5(4):517-525.

Labor Arbitration Awards. Vols. 74-1 to 80-2 (1974-1980). Chicago, IL: Commerce Clearing House.

Labor Arbitration Reports. Vols. 62-75 (1974-1980). Washington, DC: Bureau of National Affairs, Inc.

McKelvey, Jean T. (ed.). 1957. "The Profession of Labor Arbitration." In *Papers from the First Seven Annual Meetings of the National Academy of Arbitrators.* Washington, DC: Bureau of National Affairs, Inc.

Oppenheimer, Margaret, and Helen LaVan. 1979. "Arbitration Awards in Discrimination Disputes: An Empirical Analysis." *Arbitration Journal* 34(1).

Prasow, Paul, and Edward Peters. 1970. *Arbitration and Collective Bargaining.* New York: McGraw-Hill.

Prasow, Paul, and Edward Peters. 1983. *Arbitration and Collective Bargaining: Conflict Resolution in Labor Relations,* 2d ed. New York: McGraw-Hill.

Siegel, Jay S. 1977. "An End to Multiple Litigation of Non-Meritorious Title VII Discrimination Claims." *Labor Law Journal* 28(4):195.

Webster, Carol. 1978. "Arbitrating Title VII Disputes: A Proposal." *Arbitration Journal* 33(1):25.

Zack, Arnold M., and Richard I. Bloch. 1983. *Labor Agreement in Negotiation and Arbitration.* Washington, DC: Bureau of National Affairs, Inc.

CASES CITED

Alexander v. Gardner-Denver, 415 US 36 (US SCt, 1974).

Basic Vegetable Products, 1975 ARB 8239 (1975).

Bowen v. U.S. Postal Service, 459 US 212 (US SCt, 1983).

Bristol Borough School District, 70 LA 143 (1978).

City of Detroit, 79-2 ARB 8597.

County of Santa Clara, 71 LA 290 (1978).

Evans Products Company, 70 LA 526 (1978).

Georgia Power Company, 75 LA 181 (1980).

Griggs v. Duke Power Company, 401 US 424 (US SCt, 1971).

Hines v. Anchor Motor Truck, 424 US 554 (US SCt, 1976).

Jacksonville Shipyard, Inc., 68 LA 1091 (1977).

Joy Manufacturing, 70 LA 4 (1977).

Masonite Corporation, 62 LA 558 (1974).

McDonnell Douglas v. Green, 411 US 792 (US SCt, 1973).

Olin Corporation, 79-2 ARB 8460 (1979).

Rowe v. General Motors Corporation, 457 F2d 348 (CA-5, 1972).

Southern Gage Company, 68 LA 755 (1977).

Stayton Canning Company, 75 LA 2 (1980).

Steelworkers v. American Manufacturing Company, 363 US 564 (US SCt. 1960).

Steelworkers v. Enterprise Wheel & Car Corporation, 363 US 593 (US SCt, 1960).

Steelworkers v. Warrior & Gulf Navigation Company, 363 US 574 (US SCt, 1960).

Stozier v. General Motors Corporation, 635 F2d 424 (CA-5, 1972).

United States Steel Corporation, 70 LA 146 (1977).

CHAPTER THREE

PUBLIC SECTOR BARGAINING IN THE SUNSHINE: EFFECTS OF PARTICIPATION ON COLLECTIVE BARGAINING

Richard C. Feiock *and* Jonathan P. West

SHOULD PUBLIC sector collective bargaining be open to the public and news media? The response to this question depends greatly on what effect citizen and media participation has on the process and output of collective bargaining. Extant writings on this question are based primarily on speculation and unverified claims, not empirical study. The research presented in this chapter attempts to provide a better answer to this question by examining citizen participation in public sector collective bargaining and presenting results of an empirical analysis of public participation in collective bargaining for the state of Florida.

Open meeting laws have become increasingly popular in recent years. In some instances public sector collective bargaining has been affected by this trend. While most states permit public sector negotiations to be conducted in secret, several states have sought to inject public representation into the process. The movement toward "public" negotiations under sunshine or open meeting laws opens certain parts of the bargaining process to the public and the news media. This approach is different from empowering public representatives to directly participate in a tripartite bargaining process.

Participation in bargaining is typically achieved by granting structural access to the bargaining process rather than direct participation in decision making. Structural access provides formalized citizen involvement by permitting public observation of negotiating sessions. Sunshine laws usually do not give third parties an active negotiating role in the bilateral bargaining process itself, other than to attend, observe and listen. Since these laws restrict the public and the media to the passive role of merely observing negotiating sessions, such parties may not attend on a regular or continuing basis. Nevertheless, in states where sunshine bargaining is authorized and where public and press representatives do attend negotiating sessions, the process and outcomes of bargaining may be substantially altered.

Florida and Kansas have both mandated more openness in public labor-management relations. Such actions are premised on the belief that bargaining participants will act more responsibly if they negotiate under the watchful eye of an attentive public. In Florida the law covers all public employees and mandates negotiations open to the public. Kansas law covers only teachers and provides that all bargaining sessions (except impasse resolution proceedings) be open to the public.

In sharp contrast, a number of states (e.g., Illinois, Michigan, Pennsylvania, Indiana, New York) have no legal requirements that bargaining sessions be accomplished in the "sunshine" at any point in the process. While only a few states have specifically exempted collective bargaining sessions from their sunshine laws, public employee relations commissions, courts, and attorneys general have frequently declared sunshine laws inapplicable to collective bargaining (Cassidy, 1979:4-6). Before describing the methodology of the study an overview of the Florida experience is presented.

The Florida Experience

The open meeting laws of Florida go further than any other state legislation in implementing the open-meeting approach to collective bargaining (Draznin, 1976:512; Suntrup, 1979:158; Levine, 1980: 712). Public employees in Florida have had the constitutional right to "bargain collectively" since 1968. Bargaining had occurred in many parts of the State for years before the passage of the Public Employees Relations Act (PERA) in 1974. A few years prior to enactment of this law, an injunction against the Dade County School Board was sought by a group of citizens who alleged that the board was not in compliance with the sunshine law when it conducted negotiations outside of open meetings. The Florida Supreme Court held in this case *(Basset v. Braddock)* that such negotiations could take place in private without violating the sunshine law and that the school board could legally consult with its negotiators in private. The court stated that "[to require open sessions] could well deny the employees' right to 'bargain collectively' as guaranteed" by the Florida Constitution. However, two years following this judicial precedent, the Florida Legislature implemented the constitutional right to bargain with the Public Employee Relations Act. By so doing, the legislature provided that all public sector collective bargaining sessions must be held in compliance with the Sunshine Law and Public Records Act. However, collective bargaining strategy sessions between the chief executive officer of the public employer (e.g., superintendent) and the legislative body (e.g., school board) are exempt from the open-meeting requirement.

Furthermore, all work products developed in preparation for negotiations are exempt from provisions of the Public Records Act. To the extent that the Basset decision conflicts with the PERA, the attorney general's office has held that "the statute must be considered as controlling." Since the 1974 law was implemented, there have been additional interpretations by the attorney general and the state courts, but none of these have fundamentally altered the "sunshine" requirement that whenever the representative for the public employer negotiates with the employee's bargaining agent, negotiation sessions must be open to the public and the press. This history makes Florida an ideal case in which to identify the impacts of participation on collective bargaining.

Bargaining in a Fishbowl

Although the question of whether public participation impairs the bargaining process or decisions is critical to the policy debate over the desirability of extending open meeting laws to cover public sector collective bargaining, rigorous studies analyzing the open-meeting approach to collective bargaining are lacking. What research does exist tends to be based upon either recitation of arguments for and/or against sunshine requirements in labor relations (e.g., Jones, 1975; Cheng, 1976; Suntrup, 1979; Barnum and Suntrup, 1985); a legal analysis of legislative, judicial and/or administrative developments pertaining to sunshine bargaining (e.g., McClintock, 1979; Wickham, 1973; Levine, 1980); or case studies of experience with sunshine bargaining in a specific setting at a particular point in time (e.g., Bowlby and Shriver, 1981; Casey, 1976; Slesnick, 1976; Sherman, 1979; 1980).

Nevertheless, empirical evidence on sunshine bargaining relevant to this study can be found in five studies. First, Nigro and Demarco (1980) examined the attitudes of a national sample of local government personnel managers toward selected issues in collective bargaining, one of which was sunshine bargaining. They found that only 36 percent of respondents agreed that "bargaining should be made public and anyone who wants to observe should be allowed to do so" (1980: 278). The authors conclude from such low levels of support that sunshine bargaining is not a "reasonable response to complaints that bilateral bargaining excludes the interests of many groups" (1980: 280). This finding was seen by the authors as an indication that public managers accepted the private sector tradition of closed-door negotiations. Nigro and Demarco predicted decreasing support for sunshine bargaining in public policy during the 1980s.

Schick and Couturier (1977) compiled case analyses of collective bargaining in Milwaukee, Philadelphia, and Berkeley. A small portion of this study dealt with sunshine bargaining. These authors found that while Wisconsin, Pennsylvania, and California all had open meeting laws, the government officials interviewed felt that such laws had not been applied to their labor negotiations. Despite their experience with bargaining which was essentially private, those surveyed were asked their opinion about open negotiations. Half the persons interviewed disagreed with the notion of sunshine bargaining. Strongest opposition was voiced by unions (88 percent) and elected officials (63 percent), while support was expressed by newspaper employees (83 percent), negotiators (66 percent), interest groups (55 percent) and other management officials (50 percent).

Previous research also includes three studies of collective bargaining in the state of Florida. The first of these was conducted by Magruder (1976) two years after PERA was passed. He focused on open bargaining in the educational sector of local government. His study found that a majority of superintendents (64 percent) and school board members (67 percent) preferred open bargaining to closed bargaining, while most management negotiators (62 percent) preferred to "bargain in the shade." Seventy percent of school board members and superintendents indicated they encountered no difficulties in open bargaining. A second poll of Florida general purpose governments was conducted by Dahl and Varney (1977) as a supplement to Magruder's survey. The general findings were similar to Magruder's with elected officials (mayors, county supervisors, and city council members) favoring open bargaining and reporting few difficulties with this approach; however, responses from city and county managers were less conclusive than those from Magruder's survey of school superintendents. While a slight majority of city/ county managers supported continuation of sunshine bargaining provisions in Florida law, a strong majority said "no" when asked their preference as to whether bargaining should be in public. A third survey of a random sample of thirty Florida school districts was conducted by Pisapia (1981). He found 73 percent of management negotiators judged Florida's experiment with sunshine bargaining to be a success. Sixty-seven percent of these negotiators thought open bargaining made it easier to expose "ridiculous positions" when bargaining. Nevertheless, two negative effects were noted; (1) it slows down the process and (2) it encourages side-bargaining.

The Impact of Participation on Process and Output

Previous study has focused in large part on case studies of the negative consequences that public participation is likely to have on collective bargaining. Implicit in many of the above cited studies is the assumption that public participation involves a number of potential negative effects. Negative impacts on the bargaining process include making the bargaining process more time consuming, making compromise more difficult, and at times restricting dialogue. While less than systematic, extant research has provided some support for the proposition that participation has negative consequences for the bargaining process (cf. Cassidy, 1979). Nevertheless, there has been no attempt to measure the extent of participation where it is permitted.

Public participation is asserted to have detrimental effects upon the outputs of the bargaining process: the decisions, agreements, or contracts between public employees and local governments (Suntrup, 1979; Barnum and Suntrup, 1985). It is also contended that public participation leads to a greater number of impasses where no agreement is reached and may encourage poorly developed decisions. As was the case with process, systematic empirical research is lacking with regard to output effects. This lack of attention to the negative consequences of public participation is especially unfortunate because resistance to opening up the bargaining process is typically based upon the assumption that these negative externalities indeed exist. The research presented here begins to fill this lacuna by examining the effects of citizen attendance levels and the extent of media coverage of bargaining sessions on perceptions of the bargaining process and outcomes.

The Sunshine Bargaining Survey

The population of 67 county school district superintendents, 349 school board members, 67 chief management negotiators, and 67 leaders of teacher union locals were surveyed regarding their experiences with open bargaining.[1] Responses were received from each of the state's 67 school districts. A total of 245 usable questionnaires were returned. The respondents included 33 (49 percent) superintendents, 96 (28 percent) school board members, 62 (92 percent) chief management negotiators, and 54 (81 percent) leaders of teacher/ association locals. The response rate for school board members was substantially lower than for other respondents. This was also the case in Magruder's sample. It is not surprising that schoolboard members would have a lower response rate than other respondents since they are unpaid elected officials and are only peripherally involved in the bargaining process. Nevertheless, the 96 responses include at least one response from each of the 67 school districts.

In the first stage of the analysis process and decision characteristics which may be affected by public and media participation are identified.[2] Perceptions of respondents regarding these characteristics are reported. Next, contingency analysis is used to examine the relationship between levels of participation and perceptions of process and outcomes. In addition the analysis provides statistical controls for the effects of school enrollment, urbanization, and the position of respondents.

Findings

Perceived Impacts

Based upon the literature reviewed, questions were constructed to identify perceptions of negative impacts of public participation on the bargaining process and bargaining outputs. Impacts on outputs were measured by asking respondents whether they agreed, disagreed, or were undecided with regard to the statements that, under open bargaining:

1. a higher proportion of impasses occur.
2. poorly developed decisions result from inhibitions on free give and take.

Perceived negative effects of public participation on the bargaining process were derived from responses to statements that under open bargaining in Florida:

1. compromise and change of position by the parties is difficult.
2. bargaining is more time consuming.
3. dialogue is restricted because negotiators can't take back statement reported by the media.

The responses to these questions are reported below in table 3.1. This table reports general disagreement with the hypothesized negative effects of public access on bargaining outputs. In response to the assertion that open bargaining results in a greater number of impasses only 26 percent of the respondents agreed, while 48 percent disagreed and 24 percent were undecided. With regard to the assertion that open bargaining results in poorly developed decisions, the refuting evidence is even more clear. While 36 percent agreed, well over half of the respondents (58 percent) disagreed.

Table 3.1 also reports responses to the statements expressing negative process effects resulting from participation. This analysis does find some support for negative impacts on the bargaining process. While a majority (51 percent) disagreed with the assertion that under sunshine bargaining compromise is difficult, a plurality agreed that participation tends to restrict dialogue and that it makes the process more time consuming. In the case of time there is strong support; over 70 percent think open bargaining is more time consuming.

Table 3.1   Perceptions of Open Bargaining Outputs and Processes

	Agree	Disagree	Undecided	N
Collective Bargaining Outputs:				
Results in greater number of impasses	63 (26%)	115 (48%)	55 (24%)	233
Results in poorly developed decisions	85 (36%)	139 (58%)	16 (7%)	240
Collective Bargaining Process:				
Tends to restrict dialogue	100 (42%)	87 (37%)	49 (20%)	236
Is more time consuming	169 (71%)	43 (18%)	29 (12%)	241
Makes compromise more difficult	101 (42%)	123 (51%)	19 (7%)	243

Level of Participation

The presence of sunshine bargaining is an indicator of structural access and not a direct measure of participation. This is important in that there can be great variance in the extent to which the public takes advantage of this access. West and Feiock (1989) found that in certain instances little change resulted from the institutionalization of open bargaining in that few citizens actually attend bargaining sessions.

There is significant variance in levels of public and media participation across districts under sunshine bargaining in Florida. In fact, in over half of the districts six or less observers are usually present at negotiation sessions, and in nearly 10 percent of the districts media representatives never attend.

In some jurisdictions the fact that open bargaining has not resulted in the predicted negative externalities may be due to lack of public participation in spite of formal access. While it would be interesting to compare the perceptions of the bargaining process of respondents in states with open negotiations and without open negotiations, such an analysis would not tell us the effect of participation. In order to identify the impact of participation on collective bargaining, it is necessaty to go beyond merely examining formal access to directly measure participation levels in jurisdictions where such participation is permitted. To test the proposition that participation has negative consequences for process and outcomes, direct measures of public participation were derived from the survey based upon the number of observers at bargaining sessions and whether the media was in regular attendance. Because of variance in participation among districts in Florida, the design used here is able to identify and measure the effect of various levels of participation on process and outcomes.

Effects of participation on bargaining are examined in two steps. The first step collapses the measures of the number of citizens and press representatives into dichotomous categories for contingency analysis of the effects of high or low participation on bargaining outputs and process. The second step examines these effects of citizen and media attendance for specific categories of school districts and respondents.

Table 3.2 examines perceptions of open bargaining for jurisdictions with high and low participation. The presence of numerous potentially vocal observers (e.g., union audience packing) and continuous scrutiny by the media (newspaper, radio television reporters) may lead to different consequences for sunshine bargaining than would be the case in a setting with few, if any, public and media observers. It is therefore hypothesized that open bargaining will be perceived as having more negative consequences for both outputs and process where levels of participation are higher. Low attendance districts are those in which zero to five citizens usually observe the bargaining sessions. High attendance districts average six or more observers. Media participation is defined as high when the news media is always in attendance and low when respondents report the media never or only occasionally attend bargaining sessions.

Table 3.2 provides no support for the hypothesized relationship between participation and poor decisions or impasses. The differences resulting from participation for these output measures were small and not statistically significant. On the other hand, there is support for a relationship between participation and negative process externalities. In particular, where the press regularly attend bargaining sessions the dialogue is more restricted. In districts where citizen attendance is high, the process is perceived as more time consuming and compromise is difficult.

The second stage of the analysis replicates the contingency analysis for cerain demographic and respondent groups which also might affect support for sunshine bargaining and its impact on bargaining. Three such factors will be controlled for. First is the "position" of bargaining participants. Some writers state that public managers oppose sunshine bargaining (Draznin, 1976; Nigro and Demarco, 1980); others find public employers favoring it (Levine, 1980; Magruder, 1976; Pisapia, 1981). Most authors indicate that

Table 3.2   Perception of Open Bargaining Outputs and Process by Level of Citizen and Media Participation

	More Impasses		Poorer Decisions		More Time Consuming		Compromise Difficult		Restricts Dialogue	
	Yes	No	Yes	No	Yes	No	Yes	No	Yes	No
Citizen Attendance										
Low	38%	62%	41%	59%	75%*	25%*	35%*	65%*	51%	49%
High	40%	60%	38%	62%	88%*	12%*	53%*	47%*	58%	42%
Media Attendance										
Low	38%	62%	36%	64%	77%	23%	43%	57%	58%*	42%*
High	34%	66%	40%	60%	82%	18%	42%	58%	69%*	31%*

*Chi square significant at .05

union leaders oppose bargaining (Draznin, 1976; Levine, 1980; Magruder, 1976; Schick and Couturier, 1977; Suntrup, 1979), but Pisapia's (1981) research in Florida hints that such opposition might be premature, since in initial sessions open bargaining "benefited unions more than management" (p.25).

In addition to the "position" variable, two environmental factors, extent of urbanization, and school district enrollments, are thought to affect support for sunshine bargaining. Heavily populated districts with large school enrollments are said to be more negatively affected by open bargaining requirements than sparsely populated areas with lower enrollments (Magruder, 1976; Bureau of National Affairs, 1979). For this analysis districts with elementary and secondary enrollments below 25,000 were classified "low enrollment" and those over 25,000 were classified "high enrollment." Districts in counties below the Florida average in percent urbanized in 1980 were classified "low urbanization" and those in counties above the Florida average were classified as "high urbanization." Finally, schoolboard members, superintendents, and management negotiators were classified as "management" and teacher negotiators as "union." Along with the measures of citizen attendance and the presence of news media, respondent position, urbanization, and district enrollment are included in the contingency analysis of sunshine bargaining.

The results are presented in table 3.3. This table reports the percent of respondents holding negative perceptions of bargaining outputs and processes. Levels of participation are cross-classified with the position of respondents, urbanization, and district enrollment. This allows us to examine the effects of participation within each category. In general, differences in the characteristics of respondents and districts do not result in great differences in assessments of processes and outputs under open bargaining. Moreover, while controlling for these factors the effects of participation on the bargaining process remain significant. As in table 3.2, this analysis provides little support for the hypothesized relationship between levels of participation and outcomes. Differences in perceptions of whether open bargaining leads to impasses and poor decisions, while generally in the predicted directions, are not large or statistically significant.

On the other hand, there is strong support for a relationship between participation levels and process externalities. Where media attendance is high, perceptions that dialogue is restricted exist across all categories of districts and respondents. Likewise, where citizen attendance is high, respondents in all categories believe that the

Table 3.3   Effects of Media and Citizen Participation Controlling for
Urbanization Enrollment and Respondent Position

	Urban		Enroll		Position	
	Low	High	Low	High	Management	Union
Impasses						
Low Media Attendance	35%	32%	39%	29%	36%	27%
High Media Attendance	46%	26%	48%	31%	39%	40%
Low Citizen Attendance	47%	29%	38%	38%	41%	21%*
High Citizen Attendance	42%	37%	41%	30%	40%	39%*
Poor Decisions						
Low Media Attendance	32%	47%	36%	39%	39%	30%
High Media Attendance	36%	40%	41%	34%	38%	33%
Low Citizen Attendance	37%	49%	41%	40%	45%	32%
High Citizen Attendance	34%	48%	39%	35%	43%	26%
More Time Consuming						
Low Media Attendance	77%	85%	68%	86%	83%	77%
High Media Attendance	82%	84%	80%	89%	80%	75%
Low Citizen Attendance	69%*	84%*	68%*	81%*	84%	55%*
High Citizen Attendance	85%*	95%*	85%*	96%*	89%	84%*
Restricts Dialogue						
Low Media Attendance	39%*	29%*	42%*	30%*	43%*	30%*
High Media Attendance	56%*	49%*	55%*	54%*	62%*	60%*
Low Citizen Attendance	49%*	30%*	54%	38%*	49%*	52%
High Citizen Attendance	59%*	69%*	57%	49%*	61%*	47%
Compromise Difficult						
Low Media Attendance	40%	35%	40%	43%	44%	23%
High Media Attendance	49%	46%	53%	52%	45%	39%
Low Citizen Attendance	37%*	33%*	27%*	36%*	38%*	24%
High Citizen Attendance	54%*	52%*	60%*	42%*	63%*	33%

Chi square significant at .05

bargaining process is more time consuming and compromise difficult.

Conclusion

Enhanced understanding of the effect of citizen and media participation on public sector collective bargaining has implications for both
the study and practice of open bargaining. For practitioners, the
evidence reported here does not confirm their worst fears about
providing the public and the media access to bargaining sessions. The

data demonstrate that there are some negative externalities associated with providing public access to public sector collective bargaining sessions. However, negative effects are not significant for outputs. The decisions and agreements resulting from open bargaining do not appear to be or substantially poorer quality than those resulting from closed bargaining. In general, the negative consequences are confined to process.

The constraints on the bargaining process which may result from open negotiations represent real costs to the participants. There is virtual consensus that public and media participation makes the process more time consuming. There is also evidence that participation can result in restricted dialogue and make compromise difficult. Nevertheless, where greater public participation is a positive goal, the benefits of providing structural access to negotiations may outweigh these costs.

The findings take a first step toward a systematic assessment of the consequences of citizen participation in public sector labor relations. The results are especially salient in that they do not support some of the negative consequences which in the past have provided rationales for excluding the public and the news media.

NOTES

1. Names and addresses of those surveyed were provided by the Florida School Labor Relations Service, the Florida School Board Association, the Florida Education Association/United (AFT), and the Florida Teachers Profession (NEA).
2. These questions which measure the negative externalities of citizen and media access to public sector labor negotiations were selected from a battery of questions on the survey instrument which asked about the positive as well as the negative affects of sunshine bargaining.

REFERENCES

Barnum, P.T., and E.L. Suntrup. 1985. "Multilateral Labor Relations in the Public Sector: Citizen Involvement." *Review of Public Personnel Administration* 5 (2) (Spring): 56-69.

Bowlby, R.L., and W.R. Schriver. 1981. "The Behavioral Interpretation of Bluffing: A Public Sector Case." *Labor Law Journal* 32 (August): 469-473.

Bureau of National Affairs. 1979a. "Bargaining in the Sunshine." *Government Employee Relations Report* 823 (August 13): 49-51.

Bureau of National Affairs. 1979b. "Basic Rights of News Media Affirmed by Conference, Best Quality of Coverage, Sunshine Laws Questioned." *BNA Special Report* 821 (July): 23-27.

Bureau of National Affairs. 1979c. "PSRC Panel on 'Sunshine Bargaining' Explores Aspects of Open Pact Talks." *Government Employee Relations Report* 832 (October 15): 14-17.

Casey, M.W. 1976. "What Is the Effect of a 'Sunshine Law' on Public Sector Collective Bargaining: A Management Perspective." *Journal of Law and Education* S (4) (October): 479-486.

Cassidy, G.W. 1979. "An Analysis of Pressure Group Activities in the Context of Open Meeting and Public Employee Relations Laws." *Journal of Collective Negotiations* 9 (1): 3-17.

Cheng, C.W. 1976. "Community Representation in Teacher Collective Bargaining: Problems and Prospects." *Harvard Educational Review* 46, 2 (May): 153-174.

Couturier, J.J. 1978. "Public Involvement in Government Labor Relations." *National Civic Review* (July): 312-316.

Dahl, R.E. 1980. "The Feasibility of Public Access in Governmental Collective Bargaining." In L. M. Miller (ed.), *The Impact of the Media on Collective Bargaining*. New York: American Arbitration Association.

Dahl, R.E., and M. Varney. 1977. "Bargaining in Public: Florida City and County Officials Reflect Mixed Views." *LMRS Newsletter* 8 : 2.

Draznin, J. 1976. "Letting the Sunshine into Collective Bargaining." *Personnel Journal* 55 (October): 511-512, 525.

Jones, P.G. 1975. "Should the Public Join You and Your Teachers at the Bargaining Table?" *American School Board Journal* 162 (September): 27-35.

Kearney, R.C. 1984. *Labor Relations in the Public Sector*. New York: Dekker.

Levine, M.J. 1980. "The Status of State 'Sunshine Bargaining' Laws." *Labor Law Journal* 31 (November): 709-713.

Lieberman, M. 1980. *Public Sector Bargaining*. Lexington, MA: Lexington Books.

Magruder, D.R. 1976. "Bargaining in Public: Help or Hindrance?" In National League of Cities, U.S. Conference of Mayors and National Association of Counties, *Special Report*. Washington, DC: Labor Management Relations Service.

McClintock, C. 1979. "Import of 'Sunshine' or 'Open Meeting' Laws: In Washington and Other States, Are Public Sector Negotiation Sessions Open or Closed to the Public? *Gonzaga Law Review* 15: 65-93.

Nigro, L.G., and J.J. DeMarco. 1980. "Collective Bargaining and the Attitudes of Local Government Personnel Managers." *Public Personnel Management* 9 (3): 160-168.

Pisapia, J.R. 1981. "Sunshine Bargaining: A Controversy Examined." *Compact* 14 (Winter): 25-27.

Schick, R.P., and J.J. Couturier. 1977. *The Public's Interest in Government Labor Relations*. Cambridge, MA: Ballinger.

Sherman, J.J. 1980. "Government in the Sunshine: How Has It Affected Collective Bargaining in Florida?" In L.M. Miller (ed.), *The Impact of the Media on Collective Bargaining*. New York: American Arbitration Association.

Sherman, J.J. 1979. "The Role of the Public in the Bargaining Process." In M.K. Gibbons, R.D. Helsby, J. Lefkowitz, and B.Z. Tener (eds.), *Portrait of a Process: Collective Negotiations in Public Employment*. Port Washington, PA: Labor Relations Press.

Slesnick, D.D. 1976. "What Is the Effect of a 'Sunshine Law' on Public Sector Collective Bargaining: A Union Perspective." *Journal of Law and Education* 5 (4) (October): 48.

Summers, C.W. 1979. "Public Employee Bargaining: A Political Perspective." *Yale Law Journal* 83: 1156-1200.

Suntrup, E.L. 1979. "New Dimensions in Sunshine Bargaining." *Personnel Journal* 58 (March): 157-159, 177.

West, J.P., and R.C. Feiock. 1989. "Support for Sunshine Bargaining in Florida." *Review of Public Personnel Administration*. 9(2)(Spring).

Wickham, D.Q. 1973. "Let the Sun In: Open Meeting Legislation Can Be Our Key to Closed Door in State and Local Government." *Northwestern University Law Review* 68: 481-501.

CHAPTER FOUR

DUE PROCESS IN THE WORKPLACE: UNION MEMBER ATTITUDES TOWARD THE GRIEVANCE PROCEDURE

Paul F. Clark, Daniel G. Gallagher, *and* Thomas J. Pavlak

UNION-MANAGEMENT RELATIONS can be classified into three broad phases: the organization and election of the bargaining representative, the negotiation (and renegotiation) of the collective agreement, and the administration or interpretation of the agreement. Although the organization and negotiation phases of the process are likely to generate high drama and attention, they are either one time or periodic activities associated with the on-going union-management relationship. In contrast, administration of the collective agreement occurs on a continuous basis as the parties deal with day-to-day concerns that arise in the workplace (Briggs, 1984).

An almost universal mechanism associated with the contract administration process is the grievance procedure. As it has evolved, the grievance procedure has come to represent an internal forum of jurisprudence consisting of a systematic and orderly process for the settlement of employee (and union) disputes over the interpretation and application of the negotiated agreement. The centrality of the grievance procedure mechanism in labor relations is evidenced by its frequent inclusion in labor-management agreements.

Despite common academic and practitioner claims associated with the value and importance of the grievance procedure in an employment relationship, research on the topic has been rather narrow in focus. Much of what has been written concerning the grievance procedure is either descriptive, prescriptive, or both (see Gordon and Miller, 1984; Lewin, 1983; Begin, 1971). Somewhat predictably, the empirical and analytical work that has been done has focused on largely objective measures of grievance procedure effectiveness (Briggs, 1984; Gordon and Miller, 1984; Lewin, 1983). Little attention has previously been given in the literature to the perceptions union members hold of the grievance resolution procedure.

The research described in this chapter addresses this void by first presenting a scale developed specifically to measure union member attitudes toward the grievance procedure. The results of a national survey of union members employing this scale are then detailed in an effort to provide insight into how union members view due process in the workplace. In addition, the relationship of member attitudes toward the grievance procedure to a number of other organizational and demographic variables is analyzed in an effort to shed light on how these attitudes are shaped and influenced.

The Role of the Grievance Procedure

The existence of a contractual grievance procedure has been frequently cited in the academic and practitioner literature as serving a number of functions. Employees, unions, and management in both the private and the public sectors benefit from the numerous roles the grievance procedure plays in the workplace.

One of the functions commonly cited in the literature is the grievance procedure's role in "policing" or applying the provisions of the contract. If either side fails to comply with the terms of the collective agreement, the grievance procedure can be invoked as a mechanism to force compliance (Thomson, 1974; Golden and Ruttenberg, 1942). A second function usually included in any discussion of the grievance procedure is the mechanism's role in the day-to-day interpretation of the contract. One observer of the contract administration process suggests that "every labor agreement contains a certain amount of unintentional ambiguity which may give rise to questions of interpretation" (Briggs, 1984:11). Honest disagreements over the intent of a particular provision as it was agreed to in the heat of negotiations are inevitable. Grievance procedures serve as a mechanism for the fair and efficient resolution of these disputes.

A third, and related, function involves the adaption and extension of the agreement to meet changing circumstances and unforeseen situations (Chamberlain and Kuhn, 1965:141). A contract cannot address, in specific fashion, all of the various situations that might arise while it is in effect; contracts often are, therefore, couched in general language. In serving to resolve the "intentional" ambiguity present in most contracts, the grievance procedure serves as a forum for the continuous bargaining over grievance issues, giving the bargaining and grievance processes a dynamic aspect.

A fourth function performed by the grievance procedure involves the management of conflict. Grievance procedures serve "to channel conflict into an institutional mechanism for peaceful resolution, thus preventing minor misunderstandings from being blown into major problems" (Thomson, 1974:1). In this regard, the grievance procedure also acts as an alternative to the strike as a means of resolving disputes. The grievance procedure plays a fifth role that is important to both parties. As a means of communication within the organization, it "provides a vehicle for individual employees to express themselves" (Briggs, 1984:12). This chance to "complain with dignity" gives the employee a voice in the workplace.

A sixth function of the grievance procedure often cited by observers of the process is the enhancement of institutional strength. Evidence exists to suggest that the grievance procedure builds loyalty to the union among the membership because of its visibility as a service the union provides on a day-to-day basis (Briggs, 1984).

Perhaps the "most widely heralded function" of the grievance procedure is as a system of due process and adjudication (Briggs, 1984:14). The formalized nature of the process, specifically the opportunity it provides to appeal decisions to authorities with progressively greater authority, provides the individual with due process rights not present in the workplace absent a grievance procedure. Coupled with an arbitration provision that removes management's right to make unilateral decisions in a wide range of areas, the grievance procedure assumes a quasi-judicial role in the workplace.

Past Research

Given the multiple functions it performs, and the important role it plays in the labor-management relationship, one would expect the grievance procedure to be a central focus of labor-management relations research. The grievance procedure, however, has received relatively little research attention, particularly in the contemporary period (Lewin, 1983:128). As suggested earlier, the research that has been done in recent years has tended to focus on grievance procedure effectiveness. Effectiveness, in this context, has commonly been defined in terms of such operational criteria as the grievance filing rate, the speed and level of grievance settlement, the extent of arbitration usage, the percentage of settlements favorable to the grieving parties, and the costs to the parties of resolving the grievance (Briggs, 1984; Gordon and Miller, 1984; Lewin, 1983).

While contributing to our understanding of the workings of grievance systems, these studies, and the approach they take, have a number of shortcomings. The effectiveness measures themselves have been criticized as having serious reliability and validity problems (Gordon and Miller, 1984; Landy and Farr; 1983). In addition, the findings have been difficult to replicate, resulting in a cumulative body of literature with little empirical or theoretical coherence (Kissler, 1977). And, as noted earlier, the existing empirical research has failed to recognize the importance of union member views in assessing grievance procedure effectiveness.

Developing a New Framework

A central focus of this research is the development of a scale to measure member attitudes toward the grievance procedure. The conceptual framework on which this scale is based draws on two streams of research. Its primary debt is to the literature on administrative due process which has developed in the field of administrative law (e.g., Mashaw, 1983; 1974) and the procedural justice research in social psychology (e.g., Lind and Tyler, 1988). The second source is the modest, but growing, body of industrial relations research exploring worker perceptions of the grievance procedure. While, as suggested earlier, this has not been the primary focus of work in this area, there are a limited number of studies that do contribute to our understanding of how union members view the process.

The central dimensions of the scale developed in the course of this study are derived from analytical and empirical work that has been done in the emerging cross-disciplinary field of "administrative justice." Recent work in this area has been greatly stimulated by the "due process explosion" of the 1970s and the landmark experimental work by Thibaut and Walker (1975).

It is difficult to define "due process of law" with any degree of precision, given that due process concerns a fundamental principle of justice rather than a specific set of rules. Most theoretical and empirical research on organizational justice has adopted the broad distinction generally made between distributive and procedural justice. The study of distributive justice focuses on the fairness of rewards and punishments (i.e., outcomes), while the study of procedural justice is concerned with the fairness of the procedures used in allocating rewards and punishments (i.e., process).

While much of the existing research on justice-equity-fairness has focused on distributive justice, in recent years a strong interest in procedural justice in organizational settings has developed. This increasing interest is based on the growing recognition that perceptions of fairness have as much to do with how individuals are treated as with objective outcomes (Lane, 1986).

Procedures are important because they serve both instrumental and value-expressive purposes (Tyler, 1986). Fair procedures are instrumental in that they are believed to contribute to fairer outcomes. However, some elements of procedure are valued for their own sake, for example, because they enhance human dignity or afford participants a voice in decisions that affect them.

A measure of employees' perceptions of the grievance procedure as a due process mechanism ought to capture its procedural as well as distributive dimensions, and both its instrumental and value-expressive purposes. In essence, the attitude measure should be based on the core elements of procedural and distributive justice as they are manifested in the grievance procedure.

The scale items utilized in this study were constructed, partly, by drawing on the due process research outlined above. A study by Buss, Kiriloff, and Pavlak (1981) identified, in a non-workplace setting, a number of factors individuals consider in evaluating due process systems. These factors focus on both procedure and outcome and include such considerations as the enhancement of equity, dignity, fairness, the accuracy of fact-finding, protection from arbitrary action, and satisfaction with outcomes. The work of Thibaut and Walker (1975) suggested an additional procedural concern, the quality of representation received from advocates, that plays an important role in shaping participant attitudes.

Research focused specifically on grievance procedures in the workplace also provides some insight into what factors influence the way union members perceive the grievance process. Studies by Slichter, Healy, and Livernash (1960), Peach (1972), and Anderson (1979) offer additional evidence that the kind and quality of representation members receive in the grievance procedure from their union will influence the perception those members have of the process itself. In addition, such diverse observers as Golden and Ruttenberg (1942) and Freeman and Medoff (1984) have cited the value union members place on voice. The grievance procedure is, in fact, the main mechanism providing members the opportunity to participate in workplace decisions. Clearly, any effort to measure union member attitudes toward the grievance procedure should include the degree to which the process provides members with a sense of voice in the workplace.

Development of the Scale

On the basis of insights provided by existing studies on due process and grievance procedures, a series of evaluative questions assessing member views toward the value and impact of grievance procedures were developed. As initially formulated, the study sought to measure member attitudes from two frames of reference: (1) member attitudes toward the value and importance of grievance procedures "in general" and (2) member assessment of the specific grievance procedure operating in their workplace. Such a measurement dichotomy was proposed in order to assess the extent to which members' perceptions distinguish between grievance systems in principle and the grievance procedure in their workplace, as well as to determine what effect, if any, such a difference has upon satisfaction with the operation of their own grievance system.

Drawing upon existing grievance and due process literature, a set of thirty questions was developed to assess member perceptions of grievance procedures "in general." These items focused principally on major elements of procedural and distributive justice, including employee voice, protection from arbitrary action, equity, employee dignity, the accuracy of fact finding, and the timely resolution of disputes. A second set of thirty-five questions was developed in an effort to measure perceptions of the grievance procedure in the member's own workplace. The vast majority of these "specific" items parallelled the first set of questions addressing the grievance procedure "in general." Additional questions were also added to the set of workplace-specific items in order to measure member opinions concerning the "quality" of representation they received from their union. Responses to the sixty-five items were measured on a five (5) point Likert-type scale which asked respondents to specify the degree to which each statement was consistent with their opinions of grievance mechanisms.

In order to test the clarity and reliability of the items comprising each of the two scales, the instrument was administered to a sample of 375 members of a single local branch of the National Association of Letter Carriers (NALC). Briefly stated, the analysis of this pilot study produced two central findings which were of significance to the scale development. First, the results of the pre-test indicated a very high correlation between parallel items presented in the survey sections dealing with perceptions of grievance procedures "in general" and the grievance procedure in the immediate workplace. This finding is particularly relevant as it suggests that overall member attitudes toward grievance systems are strongly influenced by the immediate workplace experience, making it difficult to separate the two perspectives. A second methodological issue of importance was the finding that, due to high item correlations and apparent subscale structures, the number of questions included in the survey could be reduced without seriously affecting the reliabilities of the initially identified response factor structures.

On the basis of the pilot study findings and factor modification of the instrument, a total of twenty-three items were selected for the purpose of measuring member perceptions of the grievance procedure in their workplace. The retained items included in the survey instrument focused upon seven key dimensions associated with the workplace grievance system. Six of these items related to due process characteristics: (1) enhancement of equity, (2) increased employee dignity, (3) protection from arbitrary action, (4) timely resolution of disputes, (5) fairness of the procedure, and (6) quality of union representation. The final dimension related to: (7) overall importance which the member attached to the grievance procedure in the workplace. Due to the apparent level of overlap, items focusing on the perception of grievance procedures "in general" were not included in the final survey.

The 23-item Attitude Toward the Grievance Procedure (ATGP) scale was incorporated into a larger 116-item survey questionnaire that included sections focusing on the demographic characteristics of the respondents, as well as on their experience in the workplace, in the union, and in the grievance procedure. The questionnaire was distributed, by mail, to a random sample of 3,030 members of the NALC, a postal union of approximately 210,000 active members. The national survey yielded a total of 1,088 complete and useable responses. A comparative analysis suggested that the sample closely parallelled the NALC population with regard to respondent age and gender, however, respondents had slightly less tenure in the postal service (13.4) compared with the total membership (14.2 years).

Dimensionality of ATGP

On the basis of both the pre-test results and subsequent identification of items for the national survey, each of the 23 items was placed into one of the previously indicated dimensions or classifications (i.e., enhancement of equity, protection from arbitrary action, etc.). The fit of the seven conceptually developed dimensions (factors) was then empirically examined using the confirmatory factor analysis capabilities of LISREL VI (Joreskog and Sorbom, 1981). While the LISREL procedure provides a goodness of fit index by means of the chi-square value (representing the extent to which the models fit the data), these values seldom reach the desired statistical significance levels with large samples. For this reason the Parsimonious Fit Index (PFI), an index that takes into account the goal of model parsimony, was computed (James, Mullaiki, and Brett, 1982).

Variations in the combination of the seven a priori groupings (ranging from a seven factor to a one factor solution) were sequentially tested with respect to both the LISREL goodness of fit and PFI measures. The results of the statistical analysis obtained from the measurement of ATGP for the national sample tended to support the finding of a four dimensional (factor) solution associated with the entire set of ATGP items. The four underlying factors or scales are as follows:

> **Dimension I**—"Effect": consists of nine items derived from the a priori item groupings intended to measure the degree to which the presence of the grievance procedure in the workplace enhances equity, employee dignity, and protection from arbitrary action by the employer. This grouping also included items specifically addressing member views of the grievance procedure as a means of providing increased employee "voice" and inducing greater fact-finding effort by the employer [alpha = .87, scale mean (s.d.) = 3.09 (.81)].
>
> **Dimension II**—"Process": comprised of five items reflecting union member perceptions of the grievance procedure in terms of the process itself. Three of the items focused upon the degree to which the grievance procedure is viewed as a "fair" process for resolving disputes. Also included in this grouping were two items dealing with the extent to which the grievance procedure is perceived as a timely or speedy procedure for dispute resolution [alpha = .78, scale mean (s.d.) = 3.72 (.78)].
>
> **Dimension III**—"Representation": consists of all six items designed to measure member assessment of their union's performance in terms of representing employee interests, keeping members well informed of the progress of grievances, and the achievement of satisfactory results [alpha = .89, scale mean (s.d.) = 3.56 (.78)].
>
> **Dimension IV**—"Importance": a three item scale measuring the level of importance which a member attaches to the

Table 4.1   Overall Mean Scores—ATGP Dimensions

	ATGP–Effect	ATGP–Process	ATGP–Representation	ATGP–Importance
Mean Scores	3.09	3.72	3.58	3.91
Standard Deviations	(.81)	(.69)	(.78)	(.81)

Paired T-tests: Differences between all means significant (p<.001).
N = 1072

presence of a grievance procedure in the employment relationship. All three items appear to be representative of individual perceptions of the overall importance or value of the grievance procedure [alpha = .69, scale mean (s.d.) = 3.92 (.83)].

Upon close examination of the individual items comprising each of the four dimensions, there appears to be some fundamental differences in the orientation or focus of each dimension. For example, ATGP-Importance appears to reflect or capture a more general or overall value which the member has toward the presence of the grievance procedure in the workplace. In contrast, ATGP-Effect tends to be more specific to the perceived results associated with the operation of the grievance system while ATGP-Process focuses narrowly on procedural aspects of grievance mechanism. In retrospect, the six items comprising ATGP-Representation are less evaluative of the grievance procedure itself than they are of the performance and style of the union representatives responsible for administering the process. The differences across these dimensions suggest that distinctions were drawn, by the respondents, between grievance procedure value, results, process, and union performance.

An examination of the overall mean scores for the sample, given in table 4.1, bears out the distinction between the dimensions. An analysis of the means found a statistical difference between all four of the dimensions (p < .001). Respondents evaluated the general importance of the grievance procedure (ATGP-Importance) more highly than the other three dimensions. ATGP-Effect was evaluated least positively of the four dimensions.

In order to determine the degree to which member evaluations of the grievance procedure, and the dimensionality of the grievance procedure measure, may be affected by the interest and/or experience of the survey respondents, confirmatory factor analyses were conducted among four respondent subgroups: (1) individual respondents who have held, or currently hold, an elected or appointed leadership position at the local union level; (2) rank and file members who have not held a leadership position; (3) rank and file members who have actually filed grievances; and (4) rank and file members who have never filed a grievance.

The results of this subgroup analysis indicated a four dimensional (factor) solution to the ATGP construct and considerable consistency in the items comprising each dimension. Such a finding supports the conclusion that the dimensionality of the ATGP measure does not significantly vary across the administrative or grievance filing experience of the union member respondents. However, statistical analysis of the data did indicate that union member responses on the four ATGP dimensions differed in terms of the level of agreement (or disagreement) depending upon union administrative and grievance filing experience.

The Relationship of ATGP to Other Variables

The above results clearly suggest that employee perceptions of the grievance procedure are multi-dimensional in nature. The findings are also consistent with the distinction made in the literature between the procedural and distributive aspects of due process. A subsequent issue of interest is the degree to which member perceptions of the grievance procedure are related to other intra-organizational and inter-organizational factors found in the employment relationship.

In an effort to gather information concerning the relationship between each of the four identified dimensions of ATGP and a number of intra- and inter-organizational variables, a multiple regression model was developed. The model was specifically designed to test for possible relationships between the four dimensions of ATGP and each of three measures of organizational attitudes. The organizational attitudes included in the analysis were union commitment (UC), employer commitment (EC), both intra-organizational constructs, and employee perceptions of the quality of the union-management relationship (QUMR), an inter-organizational measure. In order to control for the possible impact of other variables on UC, EC, and QUMR, the regression model included a number of additional independent variables commonly associated with these factors.

Dependent Variables

UC was measured using a seven item scale measuring employee loyalty to the union organization (alpha=.90). This variable has been found in previous research to be the principle dimension of union commitment (e.g., Gordon et al., 1980).

A five item scale was employed to measure EC, the second dependent variable in the model (alpha=.81). This scale was adapted from the organizational commitment measure developed by Mowday, Porter, and Steers (1982).

QUMR was measured through an eight item scale (alpha=.96). This scale was developed by Rosen, Greenhalgh, and Anderson (1981) to measure respondent's evaluation of the quality of union-management relations in the workplace.

Independent Variables

The four dimensions of ATGP, described above, were the variables of primary interest to this study. The additional variables included in the regression model fall into three general categories: demographic variables, work experience variables, and union experience variables.

Demographic variables included in the study were member age (AGE), level of education (EDUC), years of employment with the Postal Service (TENURE), and GENDER (0=male, 1=female).

Three variables related to work experience were included in the study. Extrinsic job satisfaction (JSATEXT) was measured using a three scale focusing on member satisfaction with extrinsic aspects of the job (e.g., wages, benefits, job security, etc.) (alpha=.64). Intrinsic job satisfaction (JSATINT), a variable concerned with member satisfaction with the intrinsic aspects of the job (e.g., challenge, sense of accomplishment, etc.), was measured using a three item scale (alpha=.80). An eight item scale was employed to measure attitude toward the supervisor (SUPSAT), including the member's satisfaction with the style, perceived fairness, and management skills of their immediate Postal Service supervisor (alpha=.94).

The final category of independent variables included three variables focusing on union experience. Participation in union activities (ACTIVE) was measured using a three item scale examining meeting attendance, participation in union elections, and the reading of union publications (alpha=.60). An eight item scale measuring the member's evaluation of the skill, style, and availability of their union steward was employed to gauge a second union experience variable, attitude toward the steward (STEWSAT) (alpha=.95). Finally, member knowledge of the grievance procedure (INFORMED) was measured using a five item scale that assessed the respondent's self-reported knowledge of the collective bargaining agreement and the grievance procedure (alpha=.90).

Analysis and Results

The results of the regression analyses focusing on the relationship between the four dimensions of ATGP and the broader organizational constructs of UC, EC, and QUMR are reported in Table 4.2. Among the four dimensions of ATGP, ATGP-Representation and ATGP-Importance appear to be particularly significant in their association with UC. A third dimension, ATGP-Process, was also found to be significantly related to UC. Consistent with prior research on union commitment, the results of these analyses also clearly indicate that union-related experiences, specifically level of participation, level of knowledge, and attitude toward the steward, play a greater role in shaping commitment to the union than do individual-specific characteristics such as gender or job tenure.

In terms of the second intra-organizational variable included in the study, two ATGP variables—ATGP-Effect and ATGP-Process— were found to be significantly related to EC. The regression results also revealed a conceptually consistent finding that commitment to the employer is strongly related to everyday workplace experiences. The two most significant variables in this regard are intrinsic job satisfaction and attitude toward the supervisor.

Finally, the analysis of the relationship between ATGP and the inter-organizational variable QUMR indicates that the perceived effect the grievance procedure has on the workplace (ATGP-Effect) is the only dimension of ATGP closely associated with QUMR. Intrinsic job satisfaction and attitude toward the supervisor were the non-ATGP variables most strongly related to QUMR. Level of knowledge was also found to be significantly related to QUMR.

When considered as a group, the four ATGP dimensions were found to be significantly related to each of the intra- and inter-organizational variables under consideration. When considered individually, however, it is clear that the dimensions of ATGP tend to vary in their relationship to these dependent variables. For example, ATGP-Representation is a particularly important determinant of UC. Alternatively stated, member perceptions of how the union performs in terms of the grievance procedure is a more important determinate of UC than the effect the grievance procedure has on the work-

Table 4.2   OLS Regression Results—Relationship Between Attitude Toward the Grievance Procedure and Union Commitment (UC), Employer Commitment (EC), and Quality of Union-Management Relations (QUMR)

Independent Variables	OLS Regression Coefficients (Standard Errors)		
	Dependent Variables		
	UC	**EC**	**QUMR**
Intercept	.281	1.060***	.560*
	(.187)	(.234)	(.273)
AGE	−.003	−.007*	.031
	(.012)	(.014)	(.017)
EDUC	−.059**	−.020	−.054
	(.022)	(.027)	(.032)
GENDER	.029	.083	−.068
	(.056)	(.070)	(.082)
TENURE	.002	−.003	−.005
	(.003)	(.003)	(.004)
JSATEXT	−.001	.066*	.049
	(.025)	(.031)	(.036)
JSATINT	.055**	.439***	.145***
	(.021)	(.027)	(.031)
SUPSAT	−.042*	.105***	.346***
	(.019)	(.024)	(.028)
ACTIVE	.185***	.098***	−.056
	(.021)	(.026)	(.031)
INFORMED	.082***	.007	.073**
	(.019)	(.024)	(.029)
STEWSAT	.132***	.012	.081*
	(.027)	(.034)	(.039)
ATGP-Effect	.007	.104**	.218***
	(.031)	(.039)	(.046)
ATGP-Process	.102*	.092*	.018
	(.042)	(.052)	(.062)
ATGP-Representation	.307***	−.094	−.044
	(.041)	(.053)	(.061)
ATGP-Importance	.197***	−.013	−.028
	(.027)	(.033)	(.039)
R =	.792	.673	.639
R² =	.627	.452	.409
R̄² =	.621	.444	.399

Significance levels: *p<.05, **p<.01, ***p<.001
N=977

place (ATGP-Effect). In contrast, ATGP-Effect is more central to the development of EC than is ATGP-Process, ATGP-Representation, or ATGP-Importance. In essence, from the member's perspective, the degree to which the procedure affects the fair treatment of employees in the workplace, the more positively the member will feel toward the employer. These results highlight the distinction between the procedural and the distributive aspects of the grievance procedure.

The relationship between ATGP and QUMR, demonstrated by this analysis, centers around the effect the grievance procedure has in the workplace. This finding is notable in that it suggests that although ATGP-Process, ATGP-Representation, and ATGP-Importance are central dimensions of ATGP, the overall labor-management relationship is, to a significant extent, evaluated based on the kind of concerns represented by ATGP-Effect. Specifically, members apparently tend to see QUMR more positively where the grievance procedure effectively contributes to increasing employee voice, reducing arbitrary employer actions, and enhancing employee dignity and equity. This finding might reflect a feeling on the part of employees that the kind of fair treatment suggested by ATGP-Effect is a joint responsibility of union and management. Where this kind of treatment occurs, QUMR is likely to be judged positively.

Related Research Findings

Although the above noted findings suggest a relationship between various dimensions of ATGP and UC, EC, and QUMR, prior research concerning ATGP has suggested that these measures themselves are influenced by a number of organizational factors (Clark, 1986). In particular, member assessment of the grievance procedure appears to be sensitive to an individual's view of their union steward and their immediate supervisor. In a 1988 study, three ATGP dimensions, ATGP-Effect, ATGP-Process, and ATGP-Representation, were found to be strongly influenced by a member's attitude toward the steward in his or her workplace. Specifically, the extent to which the union steward was perceived as being both skillful and available greatly influenced these dimensions of ATGP (Clark and Gallagher, 1988). ATGP-Importance was also found to be related to member perceptions of their steward, although to a much lesser extent than the other dimensions of ATGP. This difference may suggest that ATGP-Importance represents a more general evaluation of the grievance procedure and is, therefore, less predicated on the performance of the steward.

A similar pattern was also identified in terms of the first line supervisor's impact on ATGP. The research findings indicate that members who expressed greater satisfaction with the treatment they received from their supervisors more positively evaluated all four dimensions of ATGP (Clark and Gallagher, 1988). The findings that member ATGP are strongly related to member perceptions of the key individuals involved in labor-management relations in the workplace and, specifically, in the administration of the grievance procedure itself, have numerous practical implications for both unions and employers.

In addition to the role of stewards and supervisors, research has found one other factor to be strongly related to ATGP. A previous study (Clark, 1986) found that the greater an individual's level of knowledge about the collective bargaining agreement and the grievance procedure, the more positive that individual's assessment of the grievance procedure is likely to be. This relationship was found to be particularly important in terms of ATGP-Process and ATGP-Representation. Such a finding suggests that increased knowledge of the mechanics of the grievance procedure is associated with a greater appreciation of, or satisfaction with, the process itself and the union's representation role within the process.

Discussion and Implications

The research findings described here indicate that the level of commitment a member feels toward the union (UC) and an employee feels toward the employing organization (EC) are shaped, at least in part, by the way that member/employee perceives the grievance procedure in his or her workplace (ATGP). The research also suggests that a member/employee's perception of the quality of union-management relations in the workplace is strongly influenced by ATGP. These findings address a void that has existed in the scholarly literature concerning the grievance procedure. To that end, this work provides a foundation for further research in this area. As there are very clear benefits to both unions and employers able to maximize the level of commitment held by member/employees to their respective organizations, these findings also have important practical implications for both parties. And, in an era when many unions and employers are exploring ways to make the labor-management relationship work more effectively, information shedding light on the factors influencing QUMR may also be of some relevance to practitioners on both sides of the table.

Union Commitment (UC)

In the course of this research two dimensions of ATGP—ATGP-Process and ATGP-Representation—were identified as having the most influence on UC. It is significant to note that these two dimensions primarily focus on procedural concerns, while the one dimension of ATGP not found to be related to UC—ATGP-Effect—principally focuses on outcomes. This finding is in line with work on other due process systems that have identified procedural concerns, such as the quality of representation and the structure of the process itself, as critically important in shaping user perceptions of the system (Folger and Greenberg, 1985; Cohen, 1985). It is also consistent with recent work by Gordon (1988) and Gordon and Bowlby (1988) which found that perceptions of procedural fairness were more important in understanding union satisfaction than were distributive effects.

Labor leaders are obviously interested in maximizing member commitment to the union and they have long heralded the importance of the grievance procedure in meeting the needs of their members. Yet, there appears to be some question as to whether union leaders themselves recognize the relationship between member perceptions of the grievance procedure and commitment to the union. In 1985, the AFL-CIO conducted a detailed self-study in an effort to map priorities for the future of the American labor movement. The report issued as a result of that study focuses primarily on the need for labor to employ more sophisticated strategies to counter corporate power, to utilize advanced technologies, and to develop new organizational structures. Underlying each of these strategies is the desire to build a more committed membership. The important role of the grievance procedure in shaping UC is not specifically addressed (AFL-CIO, 1985).

The results of this study suggest that the labor movement's efforts to build UC should include strategies for positively influencing member ATGP. In the case of ATGP-Process, unions might examine the structure and mechanics of the grievance procedure itself to determine if there are problems that reflect negatively on the fairness and integrity of the process. ATGP-Representation might be positively influenced by increasing the number of professional staff involved in grievance processing, increasing the amount and effectiveness of training programs for representatives at both the local and staff levels, and implementing improved systems for tracking and monitoring grievances. And ATGP-Importance, the member's perception of the general importance of the grievance process, might be influenced by better educating the member as to the benefits and protections that accrue as a result of the presence of a due process mechanism in the workplace. Given the results of related research concerning the close relationship of member attitudes toward the steward and all four dimensions of ATGP, particular attention should be given to improving the skills and availability of stewards (Clark, 1986).

While this research clearly suggests that an effectively functioning grievance procedure can pay significant dividends in terms of increased UC, union leaders should also be aware that when such voice mechanisms are not perceived positively, members may become frustrated with the sponsoring organization. Past research in the area of administrative justice suggests that frustration with a dispute resolution system may translate into decreased satisfaction or loyalty to the organizations involved (Cohen, 1985; Hirschman, 1970, 1974).

Employer Commitment (EC)

Two dimensions of ATGP—ATGP-Effect and ATGP-Process— were determined to be related to EC. Looking at this relationship in the context of administrative justice research, it is interesting to note that ATGP-Effect generally represents distributive concerns while ATGP-Process focuses on procedural issues. This dichotomy seems to suggest that both the outcomes of the grievance process, and the process itself, play a role in shaping the level of commitment an employee holds toward the employer. It would appear that the employer, as well as the union, is given at least some credit by member/employees, for an effective, well-functioning grievance procedure.

This finding is generally consistent with the considerable body of research that has developed around the issue of dual commitment. Much of this research concludes that EC and UC share a number of common determinants and that commitment is not a zero-sum commodity that diminishes relative to the employer as it increases toward the union (Sherer and Morishima, 1989; Angle and Perry, 1986; Fukami and Larson, 1984). The finding that improving the way employees see the grievance process has a positive impact on both EC and UC is consistent with this prior research.

There is a great deal of evidence indicating that employers are concerned with increasing EC among their employees. This study suggests that employers should consider improving the effectiveness and efficiency of the grievance mechanism as one of the approaches they employ to pursue this goal. As in the case of labor organizations, employers should probably first look at the role of their first-line representative—the supervisor—in this process. The supervisor personifies management in the workplace. In terms of the grievance procedure, the initial point of contact an employee has with the process is at the level involving the first-line supervisor. Often supervisors at this level are ill-prepared to function within the grievance process. Sometimes, they are simply not given the requisite authority to play a meaningful role. Granting such authority, and providing appropriate training, can go a long way toward making the grievance procedure function better and improving employee perceptions of the process. This conclusion is backed up by related research demonstrating the close relationship between ATGP and employee views of the supervisor (Clark and Gallagher, 1988). By influencing ATGP, the employer can simultaneously build greater commitment to the employing organization.

Quality of Union-Management Relations (QUMR)

Of the variables examined in the course of this research, those with the greatest influence on QUMR were member attitude toward the supervisor and member perception of the effect of the grievance procedure on the workplace (ATGP-Effect).

It is not surprising that the way a member views his supervisor has the greatest influence on how he perceives the relationship in general. Contact with management beyond the first level is rare for most employees. Most union members when asked to evaluate the quality of the union-management relationship where they work most probably gauge their answer on the relationship between themselves, their local union representative, and their immediate supervisor. As supervisors at the point of contact with employees are expected to embody the management philosophy endorsed at higher levels, a union member's evaluation of this relationship is actually quite meaningful.

Somewhat more surprising is the finding that the way a member perceives the grievance procedure, particularly the effect the grievance procedure has on management action in the workplace, is the second most important factor shaping the way the member perceives QUMR. On reflection, however, this relationship is readily interpretable. The grievance procedure is the primary, and often the sole, mechanism for resolving the day-to-day conflicts that arise between the negotiation of the collective agreement (Chamberlain and Kuhn, 1965). It is where differences between the parties, both mundane and fundamental, are played out. If the process is ineffective, the labor relations climate will be negatively affected. If the process functions effectively, the grievance procedure can have a positive effect on organizational performance and on the employees' working environment. This, in turn, will have an inevitable impact on employee perceptions of QUMR (Kochan, Katz, and McKersie, 1986:83-84).

Specifically, the grievance procedure can affect the relationship between the union and management in at least two ways. First, in what Kochan, Katz, and McKersie call the displacement effect, the considerable amount of time and resources devoted to an ineffectual grievance process draws resources away from other problem-solving, communications, and human resource development activities. This draining process can adversely affect the climate in which union and management must operate. Second, the grievance procedure is often the forum in which deep-rooted problems of trust and communications are acted out. If fundamental problems in these areas are present, and if the grievance procedure becomes closely associated with these problems, the process and the larger issue of QUMR can become associated in a negative way.

The results of this study have important implications for a recent development in the field of labor-management relations—the initiation of workplace change programs. These change efforts, while varying greatly in terms of design and implementation, often share a common logic—improve the work environment and the quality of labor-management relations and a resultant change in organizational effectiveness will occur. This study points out two principle areas in which efforts to improve QUMR, at least from the union member's perspective, could fruitfully be directed.

The findings outlined here suggest that one of the primary focuses of workplace change programs should be on the first-line supervisor and his relationship to the employees he has responsibility for. Much of the literature on workplace change programs suggests that this is, in fact, an area that receives significant attention in the planning and carrying out of such programs.

Given much less attention, however, by both practitioners and scholars in this area is the role of the grievance procedure in influencing QUMR and, consequently, in achieving the goals of workplace change efforts. This study found that the grievance procedure can make a significant contribution to the goals shared by most workplace change programs. This finding suggests that practitioners can advance the goals implicit in these programs by focusing on the performance and the perception of the grievance procedure, as well as by focusing their efforts in the directions more commonly associated with workplace change programs.

The literature on workplace change programs provides clear explanations as to why the grievance procedure should be included in such efforts. Cohen-Rosenthal and Burton in describing the foundations of programs designed to improve the labor relations climate suggest that the goal of such programs is not to eliminate conflict, an unrealistic goal, but rather to better manage conflict (Cohen-Rosenthal and Burton, 1987:3). Kochan, Katz, and McKersie state that "The success of QWL programs and other workplace reform efforts over time depends on the ability of the organization to reinforce and sustain high levels of trust (Kochan, Katz, and McKersie, 1986:175)." Clearly, the grievance procedure plays a central role in managing conflict and in developing and sustaining the level of trust between the parties. To devote large amounts of time, effort, and resources to programs aimed at improving the quality of the union-management relationship, while ignoring the performance of an existing mechanism that plays such a fundamental role in shaping the relationship, would appear to be unsound and incongruous.

REFERENCES

American Federation of Labor–Congress of Industrial Organizations (AFL–CIO). 1985. *The Changing Situation of Workers and Their Unions.* Washington, DC: AFL–CIO.

Anderson, John. 1979. "The Grievance Process in Canadian Municipal Labor Relations." Paper presented at the Annual Meeting of the Academy of Management, Atlanta, GA.

Angle, H.L., and J.L. Perry. 1986. "Dual Commitment and Labor-Management Relationship Climates." *Academy of Management Journal* 29(1):31–50.

Begin, James. 1984. "The Private Sector Grievance Model in the Public Sector." *Industrial Relations* 10(1):21–35.

Briggs, Steven. 1984. *The Municipal Grievance Procedure.* Los Angeles, CA: Institute of Industrial Relations, U.C.L.A.

Buss, William G., Peter J. Kuriloff, and Thomas J. Pavlak. 1981. *Disciplinary Due Process: An Empirical Feasibility Study of Procedural Due Process, School Discipline, and Educational Environment.* Project No. 7–015. Washington, DC: National Center for Administrative Justice.

Chamberlain, Neil W., and James W. Kuhn. 1965. *Collective Bargaining.* New York: McGraw-Hill.

Clark, Paul F. 1986. "Union Member Attitudes Toward the Grievance Procedure: Measurement, Correlates, and Relationship to Union Commitment." PhD dissertation, University of Pittsburgh.

Clark, Paul F., and Daniel G. Gallagher. 1988. "Membership Perceptions of the Value and Effect of Grievance Procedures." *Proceedings of the 40th Annual Meeting of the Industrial Relations Research Association.* Madison, WI: I.R.R.A.

Cohen, R.L. 1985. "Procedural Justice and Participation." *Human Relations* 38 (7):643–663.

Cohen-Rosenthal, E., and C. Burton. 1987. *Mutual Gains: A Guide to Union-Management Cooperation.* New York: Praeger.

Folger, R., and J. Greenberg. 1985. "Procedural Justice: An Interpretive Analysis of Personnel Systems." In K. Rowland and G. Ferris (eds.), *Research in Personnel and Human Resource Management,* vol. 3. Greenwich, CT: JAI Press.

Freeman, Richard B., and James L. Medoff. 1984. *What Do Unions Do?* New York: Basic Books.

Fukami, C.V., and E.W. Larson. 1984. "Commitment to Company and Union: Parallel Models." *Journal of Applied Psychology* 69(3):367–371.

Golden, Clinton S., and Harold J. Ruttenberg. 1942. *The Dynamics of Industrial Democracy.* New York: Harper.

Gordon, M.E. 1988. "Grievance Systems and Workplace Justice: Tests of Behaviorial Propositions about Procedural and Distributive Justice." *Proceedings of the Fortieth Annual Meeting of the Industrial Relations Research Association.* Madison, WI: I.R.R.A.

Gordon, M.E., and R.L. Bowlby. 1988. "Propositions about Grievance Settlements: Finally, Consultation with Grievants." *Personnel Psychology* 41(3):107–123.

Gordon, M.E., J.W. Philpot, R.E. Burt, C.A. Thompson, and W.E. Spiller. 1980. "Commitment to the Union: Development of a Measure and an Examination of Its Correlates." *Journal of Applied Psychology* 65(4):479–499.

Gordon, Michael E., and Sandra J. Miller. 1984. "Grievances: A Review of Research and Practice." *Personnel Psychology* 37(Spring):117–146.

Hirschman, A.O. 1970. *Exit, Voice, and Loyalty: Responses to Declines in Firms, Organizations, and States.* Cambridge, MA: Harvard University Press.

Hirschman, A.O. 1974. "Exit, Voice, and Loyalty: Further Reflections and a Survey of Recent Contributions." *Social Science Information* 13:7–26.

James, L.R., S.A. Mullaiki, and J.M. Brett. 1982. *Causal Analysis.* Beverly Hills, CA: Sage.

Joreskog, K.G., and D. Sorbom. 1981. *LISREL Analysis of Linear Structural Relationships by the Method of Maximum Likelihood.* Chicago, IL: National Educational Resources.

Kissler, Gary D. 1977. "Grievance Activity and Union Membership: A Study of Government Employees." *Journal of Applied Psychology* 62 (August): 459–462.

Kochan, Thomas A., Harry C. Katz, and Robert B. McKersie. 1986. *The Transformation of American Industrial Relations.* New York: Basic Books.

Landy, Frank J., and James L. Farr. 1983. *The Measurement of Work Performance: Methods, Theory, and Applications.* Orlando, FL: Academic Press.

Lane, Robert E. 1986. "Procedural Justice: How One Is Treated Versus What One Gets." Paper presented at the Annual Meeting of the International Society of Political Psychology, July.

Lewin, David. 1983. "Theoretical Perspectives on the Grievance Procedure." In *Research in Labor Economics*, Supplement 2, vol. 6. Greenwich, CT: JAI Press.

Lind, E. Allan, and Tom R. Tyler. 1988. *The Social Psychology of Procedural Justice.* New York: Plenum Press.

Mashaw, Jerry L. 1974. "The Management Side of Due Process: Some Theoretical and Litigation Notes on the Assurance of Accuracy, Fairness, and Timeliness in the Adjudication of Social Welfare Claims." *Cornell Law Review* 59:772–824.

Mashaw, Jerry L. 1983. *Bureaucratic Justice.* New Haven, CT: Yale University Press.

Mowday, R.T., L.W. Porter, and R.M. Steers. 1982. *Employee-Organization Linkages: The Psychology of Commitment, Absenteeism, and Turnover.* New York: Academic Press.

Peach, David. 1972. "Union and Management Decision-Making in the Grievance Procedure." *Relations Industrielles* 27(4):757–767.

Rosen, N., L. Greenhalgh, and J.C. Anderson. 1981. "The Cognitive Structure of Industrial/Labor Relationships." *International Review of Applied Psychology* 30(2):217–233.

Sherer, P.D., and M. Morishima. 1989. "Roads and Roadblocks to Dual Commitment: Similar and Dissimilar Antecedents of Union and Company Commitment." *Journal of Labor Research* 10(3):311–330.

Slichter, Sumner H., James J. Healy, and Robert E. Livernash. 1960. *The Impact of Collective Bargaining on Management.* Washington, DC: Brookings Institution.

Thibaut, John, and Laurens Walker. 1975. *Procedural Justice: A Psychological Analysis.* Hillsdale, NJ: Erlbaum.

Thomson, A.W.J. 1974. *The Grievance Procedure in the Private Sector.* Ithaca, NY: Cornell ILR Press.

Tyler, T. R. 1986. "When Does Procedural Justice Matter in Organizational Settings?" In R.J. Lewicki, B.H. Shepard, and M.H. Bazerman (eds.), *Research on Negotiations in Organizations,* vol. 1. Greenwich, CT: JAI Press.

CHAPTER FIVE

THE FEDERAL SECTOR MEDIATION AND DISPUTE RESOLUTION PROCESS: THE FMCS MEDIATION EXPERIENCE IN THE PUBLIC SECTOR

Douglas M. McCabe

THE POLICY of the federal government regarding the concept of unionism has recently evolved from one of traditional opposition to tolerance, but short of enthusiastic acceptance. The present tolerant policy as officially promulgated is hampered to some extent by the reluctance of some individual federal officials to grant it more than lip service in their dealings with union officials. It is understandable that government officials should resist union contracts which restrict their authority. One of the features in the labor-management relationship in a unionized environment is the function of mediation, which the present policy of the federal government encourages but which is subject to severe "growing pains." Those "growing pains" are the subject of this chapter.

The scope of this chapter encompasses an examination and assessment of the symbiotic interrelationship between federal sector mediation by the Federal Mediation and Conciliation Service (FMCS) and federal sector labor-management relations under Executive Order 11491 ("Labor-Management Relations in the Federal Service"), and Title VII ("Federal Service Labor-Management Relations") of the Civil Service Reform Act of 1978, with particular attention to the most difficult dispute resolution issues in that area at the operating level of individual federal agencies: the procedural and institutional barriers which impact on the role of mediation and *alternative dispute resolution (ADR)* in federal sector disputes.

In this study approximately fifty interviewed mediators look at the federal sector's dispute resolution process and the sector's overall labor-management relations system in a critical manner, with the background of the interviewees experiences in private sector serving as a practical reference point for comparison, analysis, and appraisal.

The nature of the federal sector will be given close scrutiny, and emphasis will be placed upon its impact upon mediators as a determinant of what they can accomplish, how they should accomplish it, and the limitations which are imposed upon them.

For historical reasons, the mediators have had more experience in the private sector than in the federal one; this circumstance may be expected to color or bias their views of the relative conditions in the two sectors. On the other hand, their dual experience should enhance the quality of their critique of the federal sector and of their role in its dispute resolution process.

This writer interviewed the mediators individually, tape recorded their answers to his questions, and had the tapes transcribed; it was then his task to collate all their responses to each specific question, extracting the gist of their views. A statement is that of a single mediator except where otherwise indicated.

Public Policy Implications

The great desideratum of the citizenry in the area of labor-management relations in the federal sector of the economy is harmony based on the resolving of conflicting interests of employees and their government employers.

It has recently become a firm policy of the Federal government to accept the concept of unionism with one reservation, that federal employees shall not have the right to strike.

The experience of the private sector of the economy, supported by legislation in certain instances, is that when collective bargaining table negotiations reach a stalemate, the mediation function should become operative, and Federal law has recently confirmed this for negotiations in its own sector as official government policy.

Federal Sector Collective Bargaining: The Historical Perspective

The first question which the mediators were asked was what evolution they had seen in federal sector collective bargaining during the last decade. The mediators emphasized three basic facts: the federal sector started from scratch, having had very little prior bargaining experience; the sector is, as a mediator described it, "a different ball game" than the private sector; and the sector's labor relations, including its collective bargaining, has had growing pains which presently remain critical. The factor of evolution was seen in two aspects: first, the change in the sector's labor-management relations from control by the Presidential Executive Order No. 11491 to its control by law, namely, the Civil Service Reform Act of 1978; and second, some increase, varying from agency to agency and from union to union, in the sophistication of the parties. For some reason the word sophistication was a favorite one frequently used by the mediators and other interviewees to designate a desirable degree of quality on the part of labor and management in their mutual relations, including collective bargaining.

The unions were criticized for frequent personnel changes at the bargaining table, which prevents sophisticated negotiators from being developed. The staffs of national unions were seen as providing insufficient support to their local unions in the bargaining process.

Management was more severely criticized than were the unions. Its primary fault was seen as an unwillingness, particularly on the part of military agencies, to engage in collective bargaining, due to its disinclination to risk loss of its traditional authority.

Management was charged with at times engaging in the unethical delaying tactic of claiming falsely that various union proposals are non-negotiable because of their conflict with existing rules and regulations of the agency, its higher authority, which is the Federal Personnel Manual (FPM), or such regulatory agencies as the Office of Personnel Management (OPM). Delays ensued not only in arguments at the bargaining table but also during the referral of such arguments for decision by the Federal Labor Relations Authority (FLRA). Another criticism of management was its lack of decentralization of decision-making authority down to the negotiators' level, causing delays while proposals are cleared for approval through higher levels of authority.

The balance of power at the bargaining table was said to lie with management, which "holds all the aces," the two principal reasons being the illegality of federal sector strikes and the retention by Congress of authority over wages and fringe benefits; Congressional control of such "economic issues," which are the primary subject matter of private sector collective bargaining, leaves few areas which can be negotiated at the federal sector's bargaining table. Consequently, frivolous issues assume relative importance. At the same time, with no threat of a strike or lockout exerting pressure on its parties, negotiations drag on sometimes for months or longer.

Finally, because of the parties' inexperience in collective bargaining, some mediators found themselves giving instruction in bargaining procedures and even being looked to by the parties to provide solutions for deadlocked issues.

The point was stressed, as one mediator phrased it, "in the early years the parties really didn't know to a great extent what they were doing" when they faced each other across the bargaining table, with the mediators sitting between them being correspondingly frustrated.

The Federal Sector Collective Bargaining Environment

The mediators were reminded that economic issues (wages, etc.) are not negotiable in the federal sector and then asked how otherwise that sector differs from the private sector. The major difference was said to be illegality of strikes in the federal sector, with the second most important difference, due to the lack of economic issues, being the preponderance of relatively inconsequential issues on the bargaining table, such as union bulletin boards and parking privileges for union officials.

A tendency was seen on the part of federal unions to bargain for benefits for themselves as corporate entities, such as the above mentioned bulletin boards and parking decals and issues of special concern to a union's national headquarters, whereas in the private sector the bargaining emphasis is on benefits for individual union members at the local level. Federal unions were criticized because, unlike the private sector, they clutter the bargaining table with unfair labor practice disputes, which delays the handling of more proper negotiating issues. Federal unions were said to be substantially disadvantaged, in comparison with various private sector unions, not only financially but also in bargaining power to the degree, as is common, that their dues-paying membership is only a portion of the employees in the bargaining unit (the federal government is an "open shop"). Moreover, it was noted that the national headquarters of federal unions provide insufficient support and leadership in their locals' negotiations. The trend towards consolidation of bargaining units was expected to provide more sophisticated negotiations at a higher organizational level of unions, but with a caution about the possible loss of "grassroots unionism."

Federal management was deemed much more reluctant than private management to consummate agreements with unions, especially in the case of military agencies, an explanation being that federal government has not fully accepted the concept of unionism. Military officers, especially high ranking ones, serving as negotiators were said to adopt too authoritarian a stance at the bargaining table.

In the private sector labor and management have little outside interference while bargaining, while in the public (state and local) and federal sectors "silent partners" are at the bargaining table: in the public sector the city council, mayor, and citizens are pressuring for a dispute's settlement, and in the federal sector management negotiators have to clear proposals through the bureaucracy. Negotiators in the federal sector are impeded at the bargaining table by having to obtain approval from several layers of authority.

The most generalized contrast between the private and federal sectors was the inexperience and lack of know-how of federal labor and management in the collective bargaining process and lack of that mutual trust which private sector labor and management have built up during their much longer experience.

The establishing by mediators of "artificial deadlines" was suggested as a substitute for the pressure to settle which strike threats provide in the private sector, but a minority view was that such deadlines, precisely because they are not real deadlines, are mostly a bluff on the part of mediators.

Summary

The following are major differences, as seen by mediators, in federal sector collective bargaining in contrast with the private sector:

- Lack of negotiating experience by both parties.
- Lack of mutual trust between the parties.
- Excessive adherence by federal officials to the unsupported theory that any federal policy or practice written into Federal personnel regulations manuals is non-negotiable and therefore not debatable at the collective bargaining table.
- The tendency of management, for its own interest, to engage in unjustified delays at the bargaining table.
- Lack of the private sector's important economic issues (wages, benefits, etc.), causing relatively unimportant matters to monopolize the Federal bargaining table.
- Unions presently represent only some of the federal employees.
- Federal management personnel, especially military officers, are reluctant to accept limitations on their authority proposed by unions at the bargaining table.
- Voluminous printed federal personnel regulations clutter the bargaining table, with both labor and management personnel insufficiently familiar with them, causing confusion and delay.

(Only a specific regulation under discussion should be on the table.)
- The illegality of strikes in the federal sector. A pending strike develops a negotiating deadline, the absence of which sometimes induces a mediator to establish his own "artificial deadline," which is ineffective.
- Federal sector negotiating committees are too large, especially on the management side, developing their own internal problems.
- Lower management on the Federal side of the bargaining table must clear decisions up through layers of bureaucracy.

The Mediation Process in the Federal Sector

In this section, the mediators were asked about major influences over, and obstacles to, their efforts to perform the mediation function in the federal sector.

Problems Confronted by the Mediator

"Frustration" was a word used by a number of mediators to describe their situation in federal sector disputes, with various causes being assigned: the lack of sophistication (knowledge and skill) of labor and management negotiators with regard to the collective bargaining process; the absence of any pressure on the parties to arrive at an early settlement; the parties' ignoring of artificial deadlines established by mediators; ignorance of the parties regarding how they should use a mediator, with mediators being required to explain the role of mediation to negotiators; and the bringing in of mediators too early or too late, in the latter instance the position of one or both parties having become hardened.

Union staff personnel were said to be "peddling" not always correct interpretations of Title VII, making it difficult for mediators to keep union negotiators from improperly referring disputes to FSIP, while management negotiators are not always properly informed as to what the law is pertaining to labor-management relations and the treatment of employees.

Inexperienced negotiators on both sides of the table must be educated by mediators in the techniques of the collective bargaining process, such as how to make counterproposals. In general, it is difficult to get federal sector negotiators actually to negotiate because of the unfavorable environment for negotiations.

Management negotiators have limited authority, and some are fearful of asking higher authority to reconsider its previous decisions, while mediators have difficulty getting to higher authorities who hold decision-making authority regarding proposals on the bargaining table.

Title VII should more specifically spell out, for the information of negotiators, the authority of mediators and of FMCS, inasmuch as the Title gives FMCS only three lines, stating that it will proffer its services as it sees fit.

It was said the mediators coming from the private sector are inexperienced in federal issues and in the numerous organizations of the federal bureaucracy. Another mediator stated that mediators are "uncomfortable" in the federal sector and need training in that area.

Utilization of the Mediator by the Parties

The general opinion of the interviewed mediators was that labor and management in the federal sector do not properly understand the mediation function and what use they should make of it in their negotiations. It was noted that mediation is rather frequently used merely in its legal requirement as a prerequisite for the parties referring their dispute to FSIP.

Management was criticized for looking at mediation as a threat to its retention of management rights. Mediators were seen to be psychologically disadvantaged when they have a lower GS grade than the labor and management negotiators at the bargaining table, with accompanying lesser respect for the mediators.

Expectations of the Mediator

If the mediators had been asked to define negotiation, they would have said that it is not maneuvering at the bargaining table but rather only whatever maneuvering which ends in an agreement. This is seen in the importance, according to mediators, of negotiators being clothed with adequate decision-making authority, a situation which the mediators found lacking principally on the management side.

Unions were criticized for injecting employees' grievances into negotiations involving union contracts. Mediators want negotiators to understand the mediation function, listen earnestly when it is explained, and not give a false impression of their knowledgeability.

Mediators desire to be accepted in the federal sector, as they are in the private sector, as constructive contributors to the success of collective bargaining.

Expectations of the Parties Regarding Mediation

One mediator thought that some union negotiators identify mediators with the frustration and "bureaucratic mindlessness" which some unions experience in the federal sector, that is, mediation extends the fruitlessness sometimes present in negotiations.

Two mediators were contradictory in their observations of union attitudes towards mediators; one said that unions think that mediators come in carrying a message on behalf of management, while the other said that, because unions are "so damn weak," they welcome mediators as allies who help accomplish what the unions cannot do for themselves.

Regarding management's attitude toward mediators, it was stated that management dislikes them because they push to get something accomplished at the bargaining table which would benefit only the union. Another viewpoint with the same import was that management deems mediators to be unsympathetic towards its retention of its management prerogatives. A mediator observed that there is general acceptance of mediation by labor but a mistrust of it by management as "an arm of organized labor"; he complained that management will not confide in a mediator and allow him to perform his function, and that, because management is "status quo" while the union wants change, when a mediator presses for action by the parties he "winds up, from a management viewpoint, looking like a part of the union."

There was additional criticism of management's attitude toward mediation. It was stated that management wants a mediator to stay out of negotiations, will not level with him, will not tell him what is going on, and will not admit him to its caucuses. Agreeing with that, another mediator said that mediators have to "fight" to get into management caucuses whereas they are welcomed into union caucuses, the union wanting the mediator to help it get around the management attitude that management is "the only source of what's right and wrong."

The federal sector itself, rather than the parties, was criticized by a mediator who stated that the parties expect more from mediators than is expected in the private sector due to "the very frustration in the federal sector," which causes the invoking of mediation to be "grasping at a straw."

Federal versus Private Sector: Preference of the Mediators

The mediators were asked which sector they preferred to work in. The consensus was that the federal sector is more difficult and frustrating than the private sector, due to the absence of crisis deadlines that strikes provide. Then mediators stressed their frustration that their efforts do not often enough result in agreements. They have expressed the need as professionals for a stimulating and fulfilling sense of accomplishment. The private sector provided that sense to a substantially greater degree than does the federal sector.

A number of mediators expressed a preference for working in the private sector. One said that, in that sector, a mediator has the "tools" needed for maneuvering the parties into a settlement, and he added: "We all like to be successful." Another preferred the private sector if the case is an important one because it gives him the chance to "strut my stuff," and he liked federal sector disputes which end in a settlement "as otherwise there is no satisfaction." A different view was that the glamour is still in the private sector for a mediator, but with the federal sector providing a real challenge.

Role of the Federal Service Impasses Panel (FSIP)

It is evident from the extensive discussion which the mediators accorded to FSIP that that agency looms vividly in their consciousness, not only as a legal phase in the federal sector's collective bargaining process but also as something which has an important impact on their efforts to mediate deadlocked negotiations.

The fact that FSIP exists was seen as affecting mediation in two ways: beneficially, because sometimes a mediator can stimulate the parties to negotiate by warning them that FSIP is their next step, if the situation is one in which neither party wants FSIP's intervention in their dispute; and harmfully, because mediation is frustrated if a party desires FSIP to make the final decision in a dispute.

The mediators were asked what their understanding is of the role of FSIP in disputes which have become impasses. One view was the FSIP is the federal sector's substitute for the right to strike, another that it is a substitute for agreement, and a third that it is binding arbitration.

A mediator recommended that FSIP be abolished and be replaced by "Med/Arb;" that is, if mediation fails, the mediator would then serve as an arbitrator. His opinion was that FSIP's fact-finding and decision-making are basically arbitration and that, moreover, seasoned mediators could arbitrate more efficiently than can FSIP staff members with less broad experience in the area of collective bargaining, a situation which caused him to describe the process of the parties "going up" from mediation to FSIP as actually "going down," which he deemed "degrading" to career-type mediators. Finally, he saw no way to prevent federal employees from striking (despite its illegality) except by means of "Med/Arb" as a fast means for advancing not only justice but also compromise in collective bargaining.

That mediator stated that mediators would be more successful if they had the "clout" of FSIP fact-finders, and another, using similar phraseology, said that FSIP can succeed where a mediator fails because it has "more guns" in what resembles a "Med/Arb" situation; both of these mediators were referring to the psychological weapon with which an FSIP fact-finder stimulates the deadlocked parties to make one last energetic effort to arrive at an agreement by stunning them with the announcement that he has decided that D-day has arrived and that he is giving them only a few hours in which to avoid his sending their dispute to his agency's Panel for a decision.

The last mentioned mediator then brought up a subject which he and some of the other mediators found disturbing: the practice of FSIP personnel of engaging in the mediation of disputes after FMCS's mediators have failed and FSIP has assumed control; he deemed FSIP to be usurping the authority of FMCS instead of the two agencies' relationship being one of "total compatibility." On the other hand, he contrasted FSIP fact-finders with mediators, describing the former as "fantastic" and the latter as "good," his explanation being that the former work only in the federal sector whereas the latter are "generalists" working in the private, public (state and local), and federal sectors despite the fact that the federal sector has a very specialized collective bargaining process. He therefore recommended a "cadre" of mediators specially trained for the toughest 25 percent of federal disputes, with the alternative being to make FMCS just a "way station" on the parties' progress toward FSIP and with FSIP being given funds for the performance of the mediation function; he added, however, that that alternative would be the wrong way to go. He thought that the real deterrent to unions using FSIP more frequently than they do is the voluminous preparation and paper work required for making case presentations to FSIP.

Another mediator was critical of FSIP for entering disputes too soon, hinting in advance what its rulings might be, referring cases back to FMCS to avoid having to make written decisions, and issuing oral decisions.

In defense of FSIP's practice of performing mediation, a mediator pointed out that it is easier for an FSIP hearing officer to mediate than to hold a hearing, make a report, and get the report acted on by FSIP, and that, moreover, the primary consideration is that mediation by FSIP is "a natural adjunct" of cooperation between FMCS, FSIP, and FLRA in their joint task of promoting the process of federal sector collective bargaining. That mediator thought that a "cadre" of mediators specializing in federal sector disputes would be a disservice to the parties because the limited number of such specialists would render them unavailable promptly to parties desiring their assistance.

The two major points developed in this section are that FSIP is an important reality with which mediators must reckon and that there is concern among many of them regarding the practice (up to the time of this study) of FSIP personnel of endeavoring to mediate disputes after formal mediation by FMCS has ceased. It should be emphasized that these mediators did not know what opinion each was expressing regarding FSIP; it would have been interesting and informative, but impractical, to have assembled these busy mediators in a conference in which they could refine or revise their individual views in a joint analysis of the proper relationship between FMCS and FSIP.

Summary

The general picture developed in this section is the frustration of mediators serving the Federal sector, especially those with private sector experience, due to the following circumstances:

- Lack of negotiating ability of the parties.
- Absence of pressure on the parties to reach a settlement.
- Ignorance of the parties in how to utilize a mediator.
- Mediators often have to train the parties in how to negotiate.
- Management negotiators have limited authority, and mediators can't get to higher authority.
- Mediators coming from the private sector often lack necessary training in the Federal sector.
- Management personnel tend to look at mediators as a threat to their authority, deeming them favorable to labor, the party which wants change.

- Mediators are psychologically disadvantaged when they have lower GS grades than the union and management negotiators.
- Some negotiators want the mediators to do their work for them.
- Weak unions tend to use mediators as a "crutch."
- The parties often expect mediators to quote changes in Federal personnel laws.
- Mediators lack a fulfilling sense of accomplishment, due to lack of negotiating progress and no means for pressuring the parties.
- Military negotiators tend to act autocratically.
- The parties are often ignorant as to how to make counterproposals, and therefore a "No" by one party becomes a finality.
- The role of the Federal Services Impasses Panel, which is legally obligated to perform arbitration, is inefficient because its personnel prefer to perform the easier task of mediation, enter disputes too soon, and dislike the voluminous paper work in the presentations which the parties have to make to it.

Mediation Techniques in the Federal Sector

This section concerns the mediators' opinions regarding their preferred methods for accomplishing their jobs when sitting at deadlocked collective bargaining tables in the federal sector. The mediators' statements in this section can be expected to be a blend of objectivity and subjectivity. Subjectivity, to the extent that it may differ from objective fact is not a detriment in this section of this study; on the contrary, it is a definite contribution inasmuch as, in the sphere of human actions, what persons think may be more important that the facts in the case; the reason is the obvious one that men act according to their beliefs, and in this section the mediators will describe the details of how they perform their mediation and why.

In this section the mediators are presented with a score of questions with considerable relationship among them; mediation is not a jerky series of unrelated steps but rather a well-planned and coherent strategy. In this section each mediator's individual testimony will be presented in a single paragraph in order to preserve the flavor of personal temperament.

The mediators were presented with the following questions regarding their mediation techniques:

- What factors are essential for successful mediation in the federal sector?

- Should the mediator play a more active role at the federal sector collective bargaining table?
- How much guidance do you provide to the parties in negotiating?
- Should the mediator provide more guidance and suggestions than he normally would in the private sector?
- Should the mediator, after a series of meetings with little or no progress, use extended or prolonged bargaining sessions as a mediating tool as is done in the private sector?
- Should the mediator bring the parties to his headquarters or other neutral place?
- What specific mediation techniques that you have personally developed work in the federal sector?
- Have you created artificial deadlines, how, and with what success?
- Have you recommended settlement proposals to the parties?
- Have you made non-negotiable issues negotiable, if possible, by helping rewrite the language?
- Should the mediator educate the parties in the collective bargaining process, and how?
- What other techniques have you used to facilitate agreement?

The first mediator to be interviewed described his basic mediation technique as aggressiveness: "I normally push and shove." He keeps the time schedule for meetings under his own control, and he discourages negotiators from taking time out to consult higher authorities. He plunges deeply into a case the moment he receives a phone call asking him to mediate, digging out of the caller all the information he can obtain regarding the status of the dispute, including the opinion of the caller, whether he be a union or a management representative, as to how his side will fare if the dispute goes to FSIP. If pertinent decisions of FSIP are not known, he recommends that the matter be researched before he meets with the parties. He stated they save him considerable time later and, in addition, sometimes induce the parties to "soften up their position and save face." He acknowledged that the above described preliminary activities are not always practicable for mediators, but he has been able to use them extensively. He noted that the management of an agency is lax in informing its negotiators of previous FSIP decisions pertaining to the particular agency. He makes a strenuous effort to understand the position of the parties and, in fact, will not otherwise touch a dispute: "I have to understand it." He favored prolonged bargaining sessions as a mediating technique but saw no advantage in taking the parties to a neutral location, such as the FMCS offices. He never establishes artificial deadlines because they would be artificial and the parties would know it. He makes recommendations in a dispute, but only in a very special context: never in a joint session of the parties but only privately; moreover, before making a recommendation officially to one party, he ascertains informally whether it would be accepted by the other, as otherwise the result of the recommendation is too uncertain.

Another mediator stated that he does not bluff or establish deadlines, and, while avoiding making official recommendations, he makes suggestions. He occasionally cites case decisions in negotiability matters, but does so in separate caucuses, and he endeavors to rewrite language to make a proposal negotiable. He has found that his greatest available pressure to secure an agreement comes from continuing negotiations around the clock because negotiators do not feel any pressure during regular working hours. In his opinion mediators have to be more aggressive in the federal sector than in the private sector, and that they should, but do not, conduct separate meetings with the parties in order to learn their positions better. He prefers that mediation take place in the neutral environment of the FMCS offices. In his opinion, mediators should take the initiative to educate both sides of the bargaining table "because there is a lack of knowledge of what collective bargaining is all about in the federal sector," and he recommended, in addition, that government agencies provide extensive and frequent training. He explained that management causes delays in bargaining because the agencies "want no part of collective bargaining and are not prepared for it," with that being due to their lack of understanding of their legal responsibility to negotiate.

The next mediator considered the federal sector to require more patience on the part of a mediator than the private sector because of all the "nonsense" at the bargaining table. He was in favor of prolonging bargaining sessions into the night, but only as long as the mediator can detect opportunities to make progress. He objected to the "volumes" of written proposals in federal sector cases; his technique is to tell the parties to lay aside all their paper work and explain to him orally the "conceptual difference" separating them, and in the many instances in which they cannot do so, he tells them to rewrite one specific area at a time without referring to their previous written material and manuals of rules and regulations, and he instructs them: "We'll write it right here." He favored having mediators rewrite proposals to make non-negotiable issues negotiable, and

considered it a mediator's responsibility. He said that he stresses
the need for the parties to understand an agreement when they
reach it, particularly when the language was provided by higher authority.

Another mediator pointed out what he thought is the basic
difference between the private and public sectors' systems. In the
former, personnel matters are subject to collective bargaining,
whereas in the latter collective bargaining is merely a part of a vast
personnel system applying to a couple of million persons and
controlled by regulations, and "collective bargaining has to be
compatible with that personnel system." He thought it is a good
system, although saying that perhaps the details of the federal
personnel system should be subject to collective bargaining. He said
that some parties are so inexperienced that they do not know that
they may go to FSIP. He was in favor of mediators establishing
artificial deadlines but considered it difficult. He was in favor of
mediators helping rewrite the language of proposals to render them
negotiable, but preferred mediators inducing the parties to do it
themselves. He stressed the need for mediators to know more than
merely that their cases are in the federal sector, saying they need to
understand that sector's environment, the workings of its bureaucracy, and the varying structures of its agencies. He saw no value in
taking a federal sector dispute into a neutral location, such as FMCS'
offices, because federal personnel "see the American flag" every day
and are not impressed, whereas private sector negotiators find
federal offices inspiring.

Another mediator showed impatience at the idea of mediators
being knowledgeable in federal rules and regulations: "I've never
even looked at a federal personnel manual. I don't want to. I'm not
there to interpret it. I'm interested in settling issues." He explained
that, if a rule or regulation is quoted at the bargaining table, he looks
upon it as being just another issue. If management claims that a
union proposal is not negotiable because the government covers the
matter in a regulation, he says: "Let me see it," and "You mean to tell
me that can't be changed?" In that manner, he said, the regulation
can be handled like any other issue. He favored mediators being
aggressive; he cited a case which he was mediating in which the
management negotiator presented a fifteen-issue package deal, "all
or none," whereupon he established a three-day deadline and insisted
that the issues be considered individually. Further describing his
technique of aggressive mediation, he said that, in appropriate
situations, he brings the parties into the neutral locale of the FMCS
office and tells them: "Three more days for you." He finds it

preferable to set the number of days or sessions than to prescribe how late into each night the parties will meet; he tells them to come into the final meetings with their best feet forward, and says: "Frankly, we're not going to hold you if you want to go to the Federal Services Impasses Panel." He has only occasionally helped to rewrite the language of a union proposal to make it negotiable, principally where a union is abandoning an issue merely because management has said it is non-negotiable. As for mediators citing FSIP and FLRA case decisions to clarify bargainable issues, he did not think that mediators have to be legal experts; he has occasionally cited a decision with which he is familiar, but only in a separate meeting with one of the parties.

A different mediator saw a need for mediators to be well informed in the atmosphere of federal sector bargaining; he mentioned management's "very definite attempt to stall negotiations in the hope that the union will go away" and the problems of new unions in building up their strength and determining where they stand with their memberships before they go to the bargaining table. It was encouraging to him to observe that mediators, unlike their early days in the federal sector, "jump in" when parties are stalled in negotiations over ground rules, help them over that obstacle, and are no longer afraid at that point to pull out and permit the parties to negotiate alone until mediation is again necessary. He declared that, in the federal sector, "the mediator is as much an educator as he is a mediator" as he has to instruct the parties in what they can and should do prior to mediation. He recommended taking the parties to a neutral location, such as the FMCS offices; take them out of their own environment, he said, where they feel comfortable, and put them in a place where they are under the mediator's exclusive control and where "they can't be running out for advice and talking to other people." An additional advantage is that the parties are more likely to send negotiators who have more negotiating authority. He thought that mediators should create artificial deadlines but saw risks. While stating that mediators should be knowledgeable about FSIP and FLRA case decisions, he said the parties should not rely on mediators for case law but should look to their own legal experts for advice. He mentioned favorably the mediation technique in which a mediator who is having difficulty is joined by a more experienced one, which additionally enables them to "double-team" the parties.

One mediator stated that aggressiveness, in the limited sense of putting pressure on an individual negotiator who is stalling, is less effective in the federal than in the private sector because in the former sector the negotiators are very courteous and, when he "gets nasty" with them, they do not fight back but merely retreat into their positions. He has not found prolonged bargaining sessions to be successful because, once the parties have reached a point beyond which they cannot move, they just sit on their hands. He favored bringing the parties into the neutral setting of FMCS' offices. He asks the parties to state their positions on each of the issues; in each instance he then says, "that is not a change, so it is impasse"; the parties soon begin to realize that he is about to refer them to FSIP, whereupon they acknowledge they haven't made their final offers, and then do so. "I set them up. I haven't found one time that it hasn't worked." He only infrequently makes recommendations to the parties as he wants to keep the door open for additional mediation if FSIP rejects a dispute. He has only occasionally cited FSIP case decisions to clarify bargainable issues.

A different mediator had found that he can be more aggressive in the private sector, which accepts his attitude, whereas he has had instances in which FMCS has had calls from federal agencies asking it to "cool this guy down." He thought it would be an advantage for FMCS to have an authoritative desk on case law which mediators could phone, but preferred that mediators have a good grasp of it themselves. He makes recommendations but only when he has secured commitments from both sides which will assure him success. Regarding going over the heads of negotiators to higher authority, he has had instances in which management negotiators were happy to have their superiors carry the ball. "They'll even give you phone numbers."

One of the first steps in successful mediation, according to a mediator, in the federal sector is to ascertain whether both parties have adequate bargaining know-how; if not, the mediator should provide them with on-the-job training. It is not sufficient, he said, to wait to educate the parties until they are involved in negotiations; their need for education in the collective bargaining process should be a "red flag" for FMCS to work with them together or separately prior to the next negotiations so that they can effectively conduct negotiations.

The mediator should analyze the policy positions of the parties in order to sense whether various issues are amenable to collective bargaining or are inevitably going to FSIP. He saw advantage in an aggressive mediation style, particularly where the parties are prepared to move and merely require prodding. Regarding claims that proposals are non-negotiable, he pointed out that the same persons who are unskilled in bargaining are often making the determination without checking with higher and more competent authority; his recommendation was that the mediator take the position that FMCS has a responsibility to investigate non-negotiability claims and have them adjudicated by FLRA, the threat of such action beneficially discouraging negotiators from too liberally making such claims. He saw some value in bringing the parties to a neutral location in special cases, but said that generally federal employees are not impressed by the atmosphere in federal buildings. He also saw value in artificial deadlines established by mediators, but cautioned against situations where a deadline might relieve a party from responsibility to negotiate. He favored having mediators make both informal and formal recommendations for settling issues, the former being used to create some movement of the parties but not necessarily to a complete settlement; the formal recommendation, on the other hand, should be in writing, presented with as much formality as possible, and constitute a complete settlement, with the understanding that any issues not mentioned are to be dropped from the table. The mediator should impose a time limit for the parties' consideration of the recommendation, and without any indication of the action which he intends if it is rejected; the mediator will not permit the parties to debate the merits of his recommendation with him, although he will answer clarifying questions; finally, for the record, there should be a clear understanding as to how the recommendation was disposed of if it was rejected. He favored having mediators rewrite proposals to make them negotiable, as that "flows to the heart of the collective bargaining process, and any issue disposable by bargaining enhances the process." Further, on that subject, a party sometimes is willing to give up a really non-negotiable issue but first wants "its day in court" to express its views on the issue.

One mediator, when asked to discuss mediation techniques in the federal sector, begin by saying that "you have to start with a cadre or group of mediators who are committed to make the collective bargaining process in the federal sector work," adding that they will have to be supported, defended, and given the training and resources needed for their job, particularly motivation and incentive. He said a special type of person is required, one who is not only committed but also "excited" about the task, because the satisfaction of private sector work is absent namely, the satisfaction of one's name in the press, of preventing a strike and keeping a plant operating, and of preventing hardships in the community, as compared with the lack of satisfaction in mediating a small federal agency and a small and weak union. "You can't mediate unless you are excited about bringing about an agreement."

Another mediator stated that being aggressive does not match his personality. He said that if a mediator were to take the initiative in a high-level Teamster dispute he would get his head knocked off, whereas in the federal sector "no one is going to care." When asked whether mediators should provide federal sector parties with more guidance and suggestions than in the private sector, he replied that that has been one of his great problems over the years; he did not consider it a mediation function although, until very recently, more time was spent on educating the parties than on negotiating. "You're taking these people by the hand and leading them around the table." He mentioned the situation where a union negotiator does not recognize what management has said as being a counter-proposal requiring his understanding. He uses artificial deadlines, but only with the consent of the parties. One of his methods is to insist that an issue is not going to go to FSIP.

Analysis (Government Policy Obstructed by Implementing Problems)

The picture which unfolds in this section is one of an apparently simple policy, of recent origin, in the federal government, being rather seriously obstructed by implementing problems at the level of mediation at the collective bargaining table.

An analogy which comes to mind is the statement of a couple of decades ago by a president of General Motors that his most difficult task was to authorize a policy or practice and then get it adequately implemented at the various operating levels of the company.

The problem, as this section renders obvious, is in the idiosyncrasies of the human element, compounded by the conflicting interest of the interacting individuals, with very little interest on their part, as individuals, in complying with a formal policy of their government employer. A subsidiary problem, which is to be expected in any new policy or practice, is the education and training of the personnel at the operating levels, plus the need at the same time to instill in them the required motivation. (That problem faces every organization which initiates a new policy or practice. I gave it emphatic attention in another study, showing that if the policy or practice is developed by middle management, it should not be instituted until wholehearted support by top management has been obtained, and, following that, the implementation should be delayed until the affected operating personnel have been adequately trained and sufficiently motivated. Any less intensive preparatory action can be counter-productive.)

In this study, the evidence is that the federal government

instituted a new policy: acceptance of the concept of unionism, without adequately training and motivating its operating personnel at various management levels in the processes of collective bargaining, while at the same time the negotiating personnel of the newly formed unions similarly lacked negotiating training. The situation was further complicated by the fact that the government's mediators, who had previous experience only in the private sector, were thrown in the work of mediation in the federal sector without preparation for the radically different problems which they were to encounter.

Training of Mediators

This study consolidated ideas of various mediators regarding preparing them for service in federal sector negotiations. One such idea is "preventive mediation," in the same sense of preventive medicine, an early-bird system in which mediators endeavor to anticipate and forestall those labor-management crises at the collective bargaining table which trigger one or both parties into summoning a mediator as an act of desperation. There are probably practical difficulties in this idea, particularly in having mediators available for such work due to its vagueness. Furthermore, the turnover in mediators would impede their developing long-term good relations with the parties.

The principal idea is, of course, that mediators whose experience has been limited to the private sector be given intensive training in the very different environment of the federal sector, particularly regarding its voluminous and complex rules and regulations regarding personnel management, the special psychology of government managerial personnel, and the unique problems of federal unions in an environment in which wages and other economic issue are non-negotiable and strikes prohibited.

The mediators were divided on the advisability of their being furnished by their headquarters with on-going information, including developments in case law, in federal sector negotiations. The objection was to the volume of data, but one mediator proposed that summaries be provided, and another wanted to be informed only of landmark cases.

There were different opinions regarding the role of mediators with respect to the "ground rules" at collective bargaining tables, ranging from forcing the parties to use the mediators' rules to assisting the parties in writing their own rules. Negotiating "ground rules" is deemed important because they can be a bottleneck in arriving at a negotiated settlement.

Two negotiators recommended that a "cadre" of specially trained mediators be provided for service in the federal sector, instead of using mediators who work also in the private sector. The obvious merit in this proposal is diminished to the extent that it creates a budgetary problem in staffing the mediators' headquarters.

Conclusion

Mediators are neutrals when sitting between deadlocked parties at a collective bargaining table, and it is important to note that the ideas developed in this study are exclusively from their point-of-view as participants at that table.

Mediators are not clones of each other. Each has his or her individualistic style at the bargaining table, and to that extent mediation is an art rather than a science. One, for example, is a smiling Eisenhower while another is a scowling Patton. Each must use the mediating technique which conforms to his temperament, while adhering to the principles which may be called the scientific phase of mediation.

The basis for this study is the fact that the policy of the federal government recently changed from a traditional opposition to unionized federal employees to tolerance of them, with the study confined to the impact of that change on mediators employed by the Federal Mediation and Conciliation Service, who, unfortunately, had previously had experience only in the very different public sector. The lesson is the need, when a policy or practice is an organization is changed, for adequate training and motivation of the affected personnel.

Time will be required for federal managerial personnel to acquire the sophistication at the collective bargaining table which private employers developed during more than a century of dealings with organized labor. Similarly time is required for newly formed unions of federal employees to develop the bargaining sophistication of such unions as the Teamsters. The gradual development of negotiating skills on both sides of the bargaining table, although impeded by frequent changes in negotiating personnel, will make the lives of mediators a happier one, relieving them of the chore of training negotiators in the art of compromising conflicting interests in the pursuit of a negotiated settlement of a labor-management dispute.

Emphasis is directed to the "Analysis" at the end of the section titled "Mediation Techniques in the Federal Sector." That analysis demonstrates the necessity for an organization to exercise extreme

Table 5.1   Critical Differences of the Collective Bargaining
Environments of the Private and Federal Sectors

The purpose of this table is to provide a bird's-eye-view of a mediator's situation in the federal sector, especially for the benefit of those whose experience has been solely in the private sector. The two sectors differ so radically that a mediator should not move from the private to the federal sector without preparation for what has been called "an entirely different ballgame."

Private Sector	Federal Sector
Strikes legal	Strikes illegal, depriving mediator of his most effective negotiating deadline
Wages and fringe benefits negotiable	Wages and fringe benefits not negotiable, frustrating mediator because relatively unimportant issues clutter bargaining table
Labor-management relations accustomed to unionism	Unionism not fully established until Civil Service Reform Act of 1978
Management "rights" negotiable	Certain management "rights" not negotiable
Management usually desires to resolve negotiating impasse, with long experience conditioning it to compromise	Management usually not in hurry to achieve settlement, federal management being authorative and disinclined to compromise
Labor-management relations very flexible and usually free from outside influences (major exception: restrictive Railway Labor Act)	Bargaining table very restricted by laws and by complex rules and regulations of government agencies regarding labor-management relations
Negotiators usually very skilled and "sophisticated" on both sides of bargaining table	Negotiators lack the private sector's century of experience with unionism; require education in laws, rules, and regulations affecting labor-management relations; and are subject to only temporary assignment as negotiators. Sometimes a mediator must instruct them in how to negotiate and how to use his services
Arbitration voluntary (major exception: railroads)	Arbitration by Federal Service Impasses Panel obligatory if mediation fails
Mediators trusted due to management's and labor's long experience with them	Management may distrust mediator who advises compromise as it is usually the union that wants change; the union may distrust him because the Federal Mediation and Conciliation Service is a government agency

care when changing a policy or practice and developing its implementation. An indispensable feature is the enthusiastic support of top management, without which the motivating and training of affected personnel at all levels will be inadequate. At best, change has a disturbing effect on individuals, and this is notably the case with bureaucratized personnel. Consequently, the importance of the careful *planning of implementation* is secondary only to the importance of the change itself in a policy or practice.

CHAPTER SIX

DISPUTE RESOLUTION IN A MAXIMUM SECURITY PENITENTIARY: ALTERNATIVES TO VIOLENCE

Matthew Silberman

A NUMBER of outbreaks of prison violence have occurred over the last few years, increasing public awareness of growing problems in the prison system. In response to overcrowded conditions and other complaints, inmates at West Virginia's Moundsville Penitentiary rioted in 1986, taking hostages and killing three inmate "snitches" (Hodel, 1986). In addition, there have been several recent uprisings at other American prisons, including Lorton Federal Correctional Institution in Virginia and Western Penitentiary in Pittsburgh, Pennsylvania. Prison officials in Texas have resorted to "lockdowns" and anti-riot units (so-called "goon squads") to maintain order in a prison system bursting at the seams (Aric Press, 1986). Nor has it been very long since the 1980 New Mexico prison revolt in which thirty-three inmates were killed in one of the worst riots in American prison history.

The overriding factor that has created this turmoil in the contemporary American prison has been the abandonment of the rehabilitative ideal in favor of a more punitive approach to the treatment of criminal offenders. As a result, the prison population has more than doubled since the early 1970s and, in many cases, prison

This is adapted from a paper presented at the annual meetings of the Law and Society Association, June, 1988. The research was funded, in part, by the United States Bureau of Prisons and by a grant from Bucknell University. The analysis and interpretation of these data are solely the responsibility of the author and not those who provided the resources to conduct this research. I am grateful to the inmates and staff of the penitentiary for their advice and assistance.

officials have lost control over their institutions (Marquart and Crouch, 1985). In response to the outcry over prison conditions, public officials try to ease public fears by calling for more prisons and tougher sentencing policies. But this is counterproductive. The conditions in prisons today are the result, in part, of a poorly managed criminal justice system, one that is more likely to reflect the idiosyncrasies of judges and prosecutors than the seriousness of the crimes committed. Adding fuel to the fire has been a steady increase in the prison population at a rate of about ten percent per year for over a decade without a corresponding increase in either the crime rate or in prisoner facilities. The demand for punishment, more than doubling the prison population in a relatively short time, has loaded the powder keg we now see in American prisons. By creating institutional support for the mediation of disputes as an alternative to violence in the contemporary prison, it is possible to reduce the level of assaults and homicides in that environment. In other words, we must replace the "rehabilitation ideal" with the "mediation ideal" in the prison world (see Silberman, 1988).

In his study of the New Mexico prison riot in 1980, Useem (1985) attributes the disorder to the social disorganization of the prison during this period of transition to the new punitive regime. But the prisoners at Moundsville made the underlying problem clear when they demanded as one of the conditions for the release of their hostages that prison overcrowding be eased. From the inmates' perspective, overcrowding increases the probability that everyday disputes between inmates might erupt into more serious displays of violence leading to serious injury or death. Consequently, it is not clear whether change in prison management produces the disorganization that leads to violence or whether this change created conditions which make both the "management" of the inmate population and living conditions for inmates more difficult. It is clear, however, that policy change in prison management results in increased levels of violence in prison (Marquart and Crouch, 1985; McCleery, 1969).

Potentially explosive conditions exist everywhere in American prisons. In some prisons, however, conditions are better than in others. This chapter is a report of research conducted over a fourteen month period from mid-1984 to mid-1985 in a large maximum security penitentiary, one characterized by a relatively high degree of professionalism, less overcrowding than in most similar institutions, and relatively little gang activity. One way to represent the stance of the administration of this prison is to quote one of its key officials who, in a newspaper interview, described the primary goal of the prison as the "humane incapacitation" of inmates.

Although not as overcrowded as other prisons, this institution is typical of contemporary prisons in many ways. The old "tips" and "cliques" based on common experiences or interests are gone as in other contemporary prisons (Irwin, 1980: 58–60), replaced primarily by groups which form on the basis of shared ethnicity. The institution is also typical in terms of the seriousness of the offenses of those incarcerated, its isolation from the community, and the pains of imprisonment, that is, the long-term deprivation of taken-for-granted privileges of the free citizen (Sykes, 1958: 65–78). Nevertheless, this institution differs from others since many prisoners still try to "do their own time" in the traditional sense (Irwin 1980: 34). Unlike many prisoners in contemporary penitentiaries, these prisoners do not see themselves as doing "gang time" (see Irwin, 1980: 186–192; Jacobs, 1977: 157).

The purpose of this chapter is neither to analyze the historical origins of prison violence nor to suggest remedies for the problem; I do this elsewhere (see Silberman 1987). Instead, it focuses on contemporary conditions that exacerbate the problem. Employing a variety of research techniques, from interviews and questionnaires to the examination of institutional records, I have been able to identify some of the correlates of violence in prison. Four factors play an important role in explaining the level of violence in the institution. First, violence is a form of direct self-help in response to disputes among inmates and between inmates and staff. As such, it is not "deviant" but rather a "normal" response to expectations in the prison world. Second, staff morale affects the level of violence among inmates. Third, high levels of institutional alienation or "powerlessness" among inmates contributes to their assaultiveness. Finally, inmate violence can be reduced when alternatives such as access to attorneys and mediation are available when disputes arise among inmates or between inmates and staff.

Research Methods

I administered questionnaires to inmates, interviewed correctional staff and inmates, and analyzed official records of assaults and other inmate misconduct in a maximum security prison. The most useful and informative aspect of my research was the opportunity to walk freely throughout the institution (although not without some official and self-imposed restrictions) and to communicate with whomever I pleased. In this manner, I came to know a number of staff members and inmates, and to know intimately how they felt about the prison experience. With an office within the confines of the prison, I became a participant observer for a period of fourteen months. My field observations and interviews provide a rich supplement to otherwise sterile statistical data.

Official records of staff turnover and inmate conduct reports were available for a nine year period from 1974 through 1982 inclusive. There were some gaps in the data, however. Consequently, the present analyses of staff turnover rates, assault rates, and incident reports (rule violations by inmates) were based on the most recent sixty months for which data were available for all three variables, the five years up to and including 1982.

Questionnaires, which took on the average about ninety minutes to complete, were administered to a representative sample of ninety-six inmates. Inmates were selected according to their security classification and work assignment in order to assure that all segments of the population would be represented proportionately in the sample. A comparison of ethnic backgrounds and prison sentences in the sample and in the prison population as a whole reveals similar distributions, further validating the representativeness of the sample. The average sentence was fifteen years. More than half (56 percent) of the prisoners were black; about 12 percent were Hispanic.

Based on self-reports concerning actual assaults on inmates or staff, or threats to harm staff, by inmates, a general index of assaultiveness was constructed with a minimum score of "0" and a maximum score of "5." A score of "1" indicates that an inmate engaged in a given type of assault at some time during his stay at the present institution. Consequently, the scale does not measure the specific number of assaults or threatened assaults admitted to by inmates, but the *scope* of assaultiveness manifest by the inmate indicated by the number of different types of assault he has engaged in. Measuring the *scope* of criminality has elsewhere been found to be the most reliable indicator of the extent of criminality of respondents in surveys of self-reported criminal conduct (Silberman, 1976; Pasternoster et al., 1983: 463). A further strategy in eliciting responses was to seek indirect admissions by asking inmates if they were ever in a position where they felt it necessary to "defend" themselves against a threat by another inmate with a dangerous weapon, some other object, or with fists. Inmates were also asked if they were ever found guilty of an assault against an officer, assuming a one-to-one correlation between the event and the conviction; no officer would survive a minute in this institution if he did not bring immediate charges against any inmate who actually assaulted a staff member, including shoving, spitting, or other minor forms of contact. Threats directed at staff members, including verbal assaults, are included in the scale; these are chargeable offenses according to conduct rules of the institution as "threatening harm" and "insolence." (In one case, an inmate was convicted of calling a staff member a "fucking asshole.") The last is rarely used, but as we know from the law enforcement literature in general, police officers (and correctional officers) perceive such a situation as threatening to their future safety. (And the inmates know it, I should add.)

In order to validate the self-report Index of General Assaultiveness, I dichotomized the inmates according to whether they did or did not have an actual assault or threat to assault conviction *officially* on record. This provides a check on the truthfulness of the self-reports and the overall construct validity of the Index. Only 21.8 percent of the inmates have been convicted of assault while incarcerated at this institution (see table 6.1). None of the inmates who score 0 on the Assaultiveness Index were convicted of assault, whereas approximately half the inmates who score between 3 and 5 on the Index have been convicted of assault. It appears that there is a systematic increase in the percentage with assault convictions as a function of increasing assaultiveness indicated by self-reports. Furthermore, the more assaultive the inmate, the more likely it is that he has been charged and found guilty of an assault or threatened assault

Table 6.1 Official Assault Record by Index of General Assaultiveness (in Percentages)

	Score on General Assaultiveness Index						
	0	1	2	3	4	5	Total
Convicted of Assault	0.0	13.6	17.6	35.7	80.0	100.0	21.8
(N)	(18)	(22)	(17)	(14)	(5)	(2)	(78)
	0	1-2			3-5		
Convicted of Assault[a]	0.0	15.4			52.4		
Convicted of Assault and/or Insolence[b]	0.0	28.2			57.1		
(Number of Inmates)	(18)	(39)			(21)		

a. Chi-square = 17.48, p < .001 (d.f. = 2).
b. Chi-square = 15.28, p < .001 (d.f. = 2).

(as understood in the context of the prison environment); this finding is consistent with the notion that assaults that occur are not always detected and/or successfully prosecuted.

In order to test the significance of the association with self-reports and official conviction records, the assault index was grouped into three categories (see table 6.1). The significant correlation between these two measures of assaultiveness provides evidence for the construct validity of the self-report index of assaultiveness.

There were several inmates who were convicted of "insolence" for acts of verbal aggression directed at staff members. These acts are defined as assaultive within the prison world by both inmates and staff alike since they are perceived as direct threats to the authority of the staff members. Including these as "assault" convictions, we find that many of the inmates who measure between 1 and 2 on the Index have been convicted of "insolence" but not assault as such (see table 6.1). Consequently, it appears that high scorers on the Index are more likely to be physically aggressive and middle scorers are more likely to be verbally aggressive.

Violence as Self-Help

There are four possible responses to disputes between parties in the prison world: avoidance, direct self-help, informal mediation, or seeking a legal remedy. The first, dispute avoidance, is not feasible for most prisoners in a maximum security penitentiary. To fail to respond to a dispute with another inmate may be taken by others as a sign of weakness, endangering the future safety of the inmate. In his book on California prisons, Irwin (1980: 58–60) reports that, at one time, informal mediation of disputes among inmates was widespread, but in the contemporary prison this hardly ever occurs. In addition, legal remedies are rarely available for most disputes that occur in prison, and when they are, the barriers to effective legal counsel are often insurmountable. Court action is rare and only likely to occur when inmates have considerable resources and when a dispute reflects a fundamental conflict of interests between inmates and the administration of the prison. This explains, perhaps, why violence, as a form of self-help in the "settling" of disputes, has become the normative mode of dispute resolution in the prison world. The most common form of dispute "resolution" in the prison world is direct confrontation which, in this environment, is likely to erupt in violence.

It should be clear that violence should *not* be understood as an indication of the breakdown of social order, but rather a reflection of the existing code of conduct governing prison life today. Threats to honor, sexual harassment, and especially informing on fellow inmates ("snitching") are serious violations of the convict code of conduct. In the present study and elsewhere, it is evident that the penalty for "snitching" in the prison world is death. In the New Mexico and West Virginia riots, for example, many inmates who were killed were believed to be informants. In the present study, several inmates expressed support for the ultimate penalty for those who violate the norm prohibiting informing on other inmates. Paradoxically, no prison system would run effectively without a network of informants. Nor does it follow that those who express support for the use of violence to enforce the convict code would be the ones to carry it out.

The reduction of violence in prison, then, can be achieved by developing alternative dispute resolution mechanisms in a world in which direct self-help is immediately translated into acts of violence. Just as crime is a type of social control under certain circumstances in the wider community (see Black, 1983), a violent act in prison is often an act of social control in response to violations of the convict code.

The Effects of Staff Morale on Assaults by Inmates

Staff turnover, as an indicator of morale, varies over time as the policies and practices of the institution change. Periods of low staff morale can be expected to interfere with the effective management of the institution on a day-to-day basis, increasing the level of assaultiveness that occurs in the institution. There is a significant, positive correlation between the number of staff who leave the organization each month and the number of assaults committed by inmates during the same month over a five year period ($r = +.33$, $N = 60$, $p < .01$). In other words, a high incidence of turnover (i.e., low morale) is associated with a high incidence of assaults by inmates.

Little discretion is used in the writing of incident reports ("shots") for serious matters, such as assaults and homicides. Discretion in the writing of incident reports for relatively minor infractions varies over time and across staff and is affected by a variety of factors. Staff morale, indicated by the turnover rate, has a small, but statistically significant negative effect on the writing of incident reports ($r = -.24$, $N = 60$, $p < .05$). In other words, a high incidence of staff turnover (i.e., low morale) is associated with a low incidence of report writing (i.e., a high level of discretion).

More visible, forceful wardens generate the sort of respect among the staff that enhances both loyalty and group cohesion. Consequently, we can expect morale to be greater under some wardens than under others. Nevertheless, controlling for the administrative styles of the different wardens during this five-year period (wardens change frequently at this institution, itself a source of instability) has no appreciable effect on the correlation between the assault rate and the turnover rate. In other words, the process by which shifts in turnover rates affect the assaultiveness of inmates is not affected by external policy changes and the administrative styles of particular wardens who reflect these changes.

From the inmate's perspective, high staff turnover creates changing expectations on the cell block as new staff members become unknown quantities and new adjustments are required. Although such situations generate anger and hostility, these feelings are more likely to be directed at other inmates rather than at correctional officers who are perceived to be a more dangerous target for the expression of one's hostility.

The Effects of Institutional Alienation on Assaultiveness

In order to measure the effects of alienation on the willingness of inmates to resort to violence (see Etzioni, 1975: 3–16), I constructed two scales, one more general (the "little guy" feels overwhelmed by the powerful in society) and one that is institution-specific (the inmate feels that he must accommodate to powerful others, both staff and inmates). The latter is a much better predictor of assaultiveness than the former. It consists of four Likert-scale items adapted from general indices of alienation or powerlessness (see especially Neal and Rettig, 1967; Rotter, 1966; Thomas and Zingraff, 1976). Each item was scored 1 to 5 (reversed when appropriate), from strongly agree to strongly disagree; actual index scores ranged from 6 to 18, with 18 representing the highest degree of institutional alienation (powerlessness):

- I sometimes do things I don't like to do just to get along with other inmates.
- I often do things in prison I don't like to do just to get along with the staff.
- The staff run this institution and there is little the inmates can do about it.
- If they try hard, most inmates can make parole before mandatory release.

Table 6.2   Assaultiveness toward Staff and Inmates by Institutional
Alienation (in Percentages)

	Score on Alienation Index		
	Low (6-9)	**Middle** (10-13)	**High** (14-18)
Assaultiveness toward Staff and/or Inmates[a]	50.0	73.8	96.6
Assaultiveness toward Staff[b]	18.8	59.9	93.1
Assaultiveness toward Inmates[c]	37.5	54.8	65.5
(Number of Inmates)	(16)	(42)	(29)

a. Chi-square = 13.09, p < .001 (d.f. = 2).
b. Chi-square = 24.99, p < .001 (d.f. = 2).
c. Chi-square = 3.28, p < .10 (d.f. = 2).

Inmates who are highly alienated (i.e., feel powerless) are significantly more likely to be assaultive than those who feel that they have some control over their own fate (see table 6.2). Inmates who feel that they are in control of their own fate are more self-reliant, more likely to deal with problems themselves, and more likely to do so in a nonviolent manner. Empowering inmates, by whatever means, tends to reduce their alienation and, as a result, the likelihood of assaults against either inmates or staff members. Distinguishing inmates who are assaultive (i.e., score at least 1 on the General Assaultiveness Index) from those who are not, we find that those who score high on the Alienation Index are about twice as likely to be assaultive as those who score low on the Alienation Index (96.6 percent vs. 50.0 percent, p < .001; see table 6.2). In other words, institutional alienation has a considerable impact on the violent behavior of inmates in a maximum security prison.

Disaggregating assaultiveness in terms of whether the staff or inmates are the target of attack, we find that institutional alienation has a stronger impact on assaults directed at staff members than it does on inmates (table 6.2). Controlling statistically for the effects of powerlessness on assaults on staff, we find that the correlation between powerlessness and assaults on inmates is spurious. In other words, the effect of alienation on staff assaults completely accounts for the relationship between alienation and assaults on inmates. This suggests that disputes that erupt in violence among inmates are the indirect result of conflicts between inmates and staff that are structural in origin. Since staff members are riskier targets for the expression of hostile feelings, inmates often deflect their anger toward fellow inmates. In other words, many of the assaults on inmates by inmates are indirectly the result of hostility toward staff members.

Alternatives to Violence: Access to Lawyers

One might expect inmates who are more assertive, who do not feel pushed around by fellow inmates, and who feel they can make parole if they try hard would also be more likely to contact an attorney to assist them in disputes with others both within and outside of the correctional system. But this is not the case. Inmates who feel powerless are much more likely to contact an attorney for a variety of legal matters than those who feel that they are in control of their own fate (see table 6.3). These findings are consistent with the argument that access to law is an alternative form of social control (see Black, 1976: 107), that is, in prison, an alternative to the use of violence. Powerless inmates who might otherwise resort to violence are less likely to do so if they have access to lawyers.

Inmates who have access to attorneys are more likely to pursue their current legal case. Silberman (1985: 129–30) has shown elsewhere that access to attorneys increases the likelihood that civil disputes will be defined as legal matters. Here, too, we see that access to attorneys increases substantially the likelihood that inmates will actively pursue legal remedies in the criminal case for which they are currently incarcerated. Measuring access to attorneys in terms of contact with an attorney at some time during an inmate's incarceration, we find that inmates who have had such access are more than twice as likely (64 percent vs. 27 percent) to pursue their current case than those who have not had access to an attorney since their incarceration. Sometimes this is done with legal counsel; often

Table 6.3   Legal Contacts by Institutional Alienation (in Percentages)

	Score on Alienation Index		
	Low (6-9)	Middle (10-13)	High (14-18)
Inmate Contacts Attorney	31.3	66.7	82.1
(Number of Inmates)	(16)	(39)	(28)

Chi-square = 11.68, p < .01 (d.f. = 2).

this is done on one's own or with the assistance of a "jailhouse lawyer."

Inmates who pursue their current legal case with the assistance of counsel are less likely to be assaultive than inmates who pursue legal remedies on their own. In other words, the absence of access to the assistance of counsel in legal disputes increases the incidence of violence (also see Alpert, 1978: 46–47). As many as 94 percent of those who seek legal remedies without the assistance of counsel are assaultive (toward inmates and/or staff), whereas only 74 percent of those who have attorneys are assaultive. This is not to suggest that assaults are responses to specific instances of denial of access to legal assistance but rather, in the aggregate, less reliance on legal control leads to increased reliance on nonlegal forms of social control and in a correctional setting, this means violence.

On the other hand, inmates who have not contacted an attorney since their current incarceration are relatively unlikely to be assaultive, especially if they are not actively pursuing their current legal case. Only about half the inmates (56 percent) who have not had access to attorneys are assaultive as compared with 89 percent of those who have had such access. Again, only 52 percent of those who have not had access to attorneys and whose current legal case is inactive are assaultive, whereas 67 percent of those whose cases are active are assaultive. It appears that assaultiveness is the outcome of active disputes with legal authorities, but the degree of assaultiveness is mitigated when there is access to legal counsel.

To sum up, inmates who have never tried to appeal their case and have not relied on legal assistance for other matters while incarcerated are least assaultive. The most assaultive inmates are those who have had access to attorneys and now pursue legal remedies on their own. Access to legal counsel for those whose cases are still active reduces their assaultiveness.

Alternatives to Violence: Mediation

When staff morale is high, we find many correctional officers able to establish rapport even with some of the most aggressive inmates. In the present study, such officers are often assigned the special role of "correctional counselor." In situations where correctional counselors establish rapport with inmates, the incidence of assault appears to be greatly reduced. These correctional counselors act, in effect, as informal mediators when disputes arise among inmates and between inmates and staff members. Inmates know whom they can trust in sharing information essential to the successful resolution of disputes.

Mediation also empowers inmates in nonviolent ways by providing a mechanism for dispute resolution that does not require more formal or more violent means. Effective mediation identifies the mutual interests and shared orientations of the disputing parties, bringing them into the process rather than making them feel outside the process. Because mediation gives disputants some measure of control over the outcomes of disputes (Mills, 1988: 495), it reduces the institutional alienation that leads to violent forms of self-help in the prison world.

The existing formal system of written appeals, rather than increasing participation in a decision-making system, alienates inmates further by isolating them from the decision makers through several levels of bureaucracy. Although the availability of formal grievance procedures should not be diminished in any sense, the additional training of staff counselors in mediation skills should reduce the hostility associated with unresolved grievances before they erupt in violence. Moreover, resolving disputes rooted in conflict between staff and inmates can be expected to lower the overall level of violence in the institution, including inmate on inmate assaults.

During the past fifteen years, the "rehabilitation ideal" has disappeared from the American prison system without a suitable alternative emerging to take its place. This was, in part, a response to the reported "failure" of the rehabilitation efforts of the previous twenty years (see Martinson, 1974). There has emerged in its place a hostile environment in which the primary goal of corrections is the incapacitation of those who have committed acts of criminal violence (Gottfredson and Hirschi, 1988: 208). As a result, the forms of informal mediation that emerged during the earlier period (Irwin, 1980: 58–60) have virtually disappeared from prison life. I have proposed elsewhere (Silberman 1988) that the "mediation ideal" provides a framework for the reemergence of the sort of nonviolent dispute resolution processes which used to exist in American prisons. The evidence in the present study is that where the opportunity for the mediation of disputes exists, there is a lower incidence of violence.

A recent development in the management of prisons is the "Unit Management System" (see Smith and Fenton, 1978; Quay, 1984). Adapted for use in the prison studied here, the Unit Management System separates inmates according to the extent of their history of violence both on the street and in prison. Case managers and correctional counselors are then assigned to work with each group. This approach has the advantage of creating more intimate contacts between staff and inmates, the kind that can reduce the alienation that produces violence.

The counseling model still reflects the residue of the old rehabilitation ideal, without the full legitimation of the therapeutic model upon which it was based. In other words, neither staff nor inmates believe in the rhetoric of therapy underlying the counselor role. Moreover, the typical inmate is not in a position to reveal the sort of private information necessary in individual or group counseling in order to resolve inner conflicts. To do so would make one vulnerable to exploitation by fellow inmates. Survival in the contempory prison depends on not appearing "weak" and to seek to change oneself is frequently seen as a sign of weakness. In addition, counselors have a duty to report information which they have reason to believe might lead to acts of violence against others. Not only is this an ethical requirement in general for mental health professionals, but it is a necessary part of the effective maintenance of order in the prison. For this reason, mental health professionals who work in prison are perceived by inmates to be part of the "administration" and thus not to be fully trusted to maintain confidentiality. Training correctional counselors as mediators would be a more effective method for managing disputes.

Summary and Conclusions

The threat of violence is an everyday reality in the contemporary American prison. When disputes arise among inmates or between inmates and staff, in the absence of alternative mechanisms for dispute resolution, violence is often the only available response. Given the convict code with its emphasis on the display of strength and autonomy, to fail to respond aggressively may lead to sexual or other forms of exploitation by other inmates (Bowker, 1980: 10–13, 30–34, 41–49; Nacci and Kane, 1982: 142; Wooden and Parker, 1982: 13–24).

When disputes occur, there are several different possible responses, each of which constitutes a distinct form of social control; these are avoidance, direct self-help, mediation, and the pursuit of legal remedies. In prison, avoidance is an unlikely response since it will be taken as a sign of weakness and may lead to the further victimization of those who employ this strategy. Mediation may take place as inmates who are respected by other inmates or correctional counselors intervene before a dispute becomes more serious, and erupts in violence. In situations where counselors establish rapport with even the most aggressive inmates, the incidence of assault appears to be greatly reduced.

Nevertheless, the mediation of disputes among inmates is difficult and infrequent in the contemporary prison. The absence of effective mediation may then lead to self-help in the form of violence by one inmate or a group of inmates in response to a perceived grievance. Such behavior is itself a response to normative expectations in the prison world. On the other hand, disputes between staff and inmates may be handled by filing a formal complaint. This procedure, rather than mitigating the underlying conflicts that give rise to specific disputes helps to underscore the disagreements that occur concerning the daily routines of prisoners. Conditions that reduce the effectiveness of the informal mediation of disputes or the utility of formal grievance procedures increase the likelihood that disputants may respond by "taking the law into their own hands."

Effective dispute mediation depends on a correctional staff with high morale and rapport with inmates. Lower staff turnover and a more stable rate of change in turnover leads to a reduction in the level of violence among inmates because morale is higher and rapport with inmates can be maintained. The inability to control their daily routines, indicated by high levels of alienation or "powerlessness", contributes further to the level of assaultiveness among inmates. Since the effect of this alienation is more directly manifest as assaultiveness directed at staff, it appears that understanding the nature of the relationship between staff and inmates is essential to our understanding of the production of violence in prison. The sort of stable relationships that emerge due to reduced turnover increases the level of rapport between staff and inmates that makes dispute mediation possible. This, in effect, empowers inmates by making them feel that they have greater control over their safety and future, reducing their alienation and the sense of powerlessness that gives rise to violent responses to disputes.

Mechanisms of social control that empower prisoners in nonviolent ways tend to reduce the likelihood that they will engage in self-help in the form of assaulting another person. The existence of informal mediation is one such device. The existing formal system of written appeals, rather than increasing participation in a decision-making system, alienates inmates further by isolating them from the decision makers through several layers of bureaucracy. Access to attorneys, however, provides the inmate with a valuable resource that enhances his ability to control his own fate. This apparently reduces his alienation and the predisposition to respond violently to dispute situations.

Access to attorneys reduces the incidence of violence for those inmates who have grievances of one kind or another. On the other hand, increased access to attorneys increases the extent to which disputes are defined in legal terms, increasing the number of lawsuits and exacerbating conflict between inmates and the institution. Cain and Kulscar's (1982) distinction between conflict and dispute helps us to understand this apparent contradiction. Disputes are events between individuals which may or may not reflect underlying conflicts of interest between the groups that they represent. As Turk (1976) notes, law is a weapon that can be used by groups in the struggle for control (conflict) over scarce resources. In prison, this means control over the daily routines of prisoners. Consequently, the struggle over the legal rights of prisoners can create new disputes and thus the potential for violent confrontation. At the same time, once disputes occur, the availability of law as a type of social control (legal violence) provides an alternative to criminal violence. Increased access to the courts reduces the need for self-help—violence—in prison.

The findings reported in this chapter suggest three major conclusions. First, assaults by inmates are "normal" acts in the prison world; they are responses to normative expectations when alternative forms of social control such as mediation and access to legal remedies are limited. Second, the staff's morale and ability to mediate disputes play a major role in determining the level of violence that occurs in a prison. And third, high levels of institutional alienation or "powerlessness" among inmates contribute to their assaultiveness.

In a democratic society, access to law enhances the ability of the average citizen to mobilize the coercive power of the state to protect his or her interests. Disputants may avoid confrontation, engage in direct self-help, seek mediation, or resolve disputes through the courts. Since avoidance is not a realistic response to disputes in the prison world and mediation is not a widespread mechanism of dispute resolution in the contemporary prison, access to law is an important alternative to violence as a predominant form of self-help in prison. The evidence presented here and elsewhere (Alpert, 1978) is that access to lawyers reduces the level of violence in prison.

At the same time, there is evidence that, under certain conditions, correctional staff and inmate leaders mediate disputes that might otherwise erupt in violence. Staff members who have rapport with inmates both channel complaints and encourage their resolution on a daily basis. In order to lower the incidence of assaults in prison, correctional counselors should be trained to mediate disputes and to facilitate the growth of mediation as a strategy for dispute resolution among inmates.

REFERENCES

Alpert, Geoffrey P. 1978. *The Legal Rights of Prisoners*. Lexington, MA: Lexington Books.

Aric Press. 1986. "Inside America's Toughest Prison." *Newsweek* (October 6): 46–61.

Black, Donald. 1976. *The Behavior of Law*. New York: Academic Press.

———. 1983. "Crime as Social Control." *American Sociological Review* 48: 34–45.

Bowker, Lee H. 1980. *Prison Victimization*. New York: Elsevier.

Cain, Maureen, and Kalman Kulcsar. 1982. "Thinking Disputes: An Essay on the Origins of the Dispute Industry." *Law and Society Review* 16: 375–402.

Etzioni, Amitai. 1975. *A Comparative Analysis of Complex Organization*. New York: Free Press.

Gottfredson, Michael, and Travis Hirschi. 1988. "Career Criminals and Selective Incapacitation." In J.E. Scott and T. Hirschi (eds.), *Controversial Issues in Crime and Justice*. Beverly Hills, CA: Sage.

Hodel, Martha B. (Associated Press). 1986. "Finished: Inmates Slay 3 Before Yielding." *The Harrisburg (PA) Patriot*, January 4: A1–A2.

Irwin, John. 1980. *Prisons in Turmoil*. Boston: Little, Brown.

Jacobs, James B. 1977. *Stateville*. Chicago, IL: University of Chicago Press.

McCleery, Richard H. 1969. "Policy change in prison management." In A. Etzioni (ed.), *A Sociological Reader in Complex Organizations*, 2d ed. New York: Holt, Rinehart, and Winston.

Marquart, James W., and Ben M. Crouch. 1985. "Judicial Reform and Prisoner Control: The Impact of *Ruiz v. Estelle* on a Texas Penitentiary." *Law and Society Review* 19: 557–586.

Martinson, Robert. 1974. "What Works? Questions and Answers about Prison Reform." *The Public Interest* 35: 22–54.

Mills, Miriam K. 1988. "Overview and Implications of Alternative Dispute Resolution." *Policy Studies Journal* 16: 493–498.

Nacci, Peter L., and Thomas R. Kane. 1982. *Sexual Aggression in Prison*. Washington, DC: United States Prison System.

Neal, Arthur G., and Salomon Rettig. 1967. "On the Multidimentionality of Alienation." *American Sociological Review* 32: 54–64.

Pasternoster, R., L.E. Saltzman, G.P. Waldo, and T.G. Chiricos. 1983. "Perceived Risk and Social Control: Do Sanctions Really Work?" *Law and Society Review* 17: 457–479.

Quay, Herbert C. 1984. *Managing Adult Inmates.* College Park, MD: American Correctional Association.

Rotter, Julian. 1966. "Generalized Expectations for Internal versus External Control of Reinforcement." *Psychological Monographs: General and Applied* 60: 1–28.

Silberman, Matthew. 1976. "Toward a Theory of Criminal Deterrence." *American Sociological Review* 41: 442–461.

──────. 1985. *The Civil Justice Process.* New York: Academic Press.

──────. 1987. "Uneven Justice Erodes Deterrence, Jail Controls." *Pittsburgh Press*, March 4.

──────. 1988. "Dispute Mediation in the American Prison: A New Approach to the Reduction of Violence." *Policy Studies Journal* 16: 522–532.

Smith, W. Alan, and Charles E. Fenton. 1978. "Unit Management in a Penitentiary: A Practical Experience." *Federal Probation* 42: 40–46.

Sykes, Gresham M. 1958. *The Society of Captives: A Study of a Maximum Security Prison.* Princeton, NJ: Princeton University Press.

Thomas, Charles W., and Matthew T. Zingraff. 1976. "Organizational Structure as a Determination of Prisonization: An Analysis of the Consequences of Alienation." *Pacific Sociological Review* 19:98–116.

Turk, Austin T. 1976. "Law as a Weapon in Social Conflict." *Social Problems* 23: 276–291.

Useem, Bert. 1985. "Disorganization and the New Mexico Prison Riot of 1980." *American Sociological Review* 50: 677–688.

Wooden, Wayne S., and Jay Parker. 1982. *Men Behind Bars: Sexual Exploitation in Prison.* New York: Plenum Press.

PART THREE

Disputes Within the Environment

ENVIRONMENTAL MEDIATION AS AN ALTERNATIVE TO LITIGATION: THE EMERGING PRACTICE AND LIMITATIONS

J. Walton Blackburn

ENVIRONMENTAL MEDIATION is emerging as an alternative to litigation in the settlement of environmental disputes. While the theory and practice of environmental mediation are still developing, scholars are beginning to identify some of the characteristic practices and dynamics of this approach to dispute resolution. The field is beginning to develop an identity and fraternity of practitioners. Writers have identified a number of ways in which mediation is superior to litigation. As with any newly emerging, and apparently very promising, approach to solving difficult problems, however, the predominant emphasis is upon how it can be made to work better. Strong advocacy is needed to promote the use of environmental mediation so that the field can develop.

The application of mediation of environmental disputes has reached a point, however, that its weaknesses need to be examined carefully. Questions need to be raised about whether mediated settlements of disputes achieve the level of equity and justice which the well-established, long-tested use of the courts achieves. The practice needs to be evaluated as to whether the great benefits of flexibility and adaptibility to particular circumstances are not obtained at the cost of full consideration of all the potential interests which might be involved in a litigated settlement. Research is needed to determine whether the interests of particular parties are protected as well in mediation as they are in litigation. There is a need for a careful assessment of the strengths and weaknesses of mediation in comparison with litigation. This chapter describes the essential characteristics of environmental mediation practice as evaluated by practitioners and examines some of the strengths and weaknesses of environmental mediation in relation to litigation.

The Nature of Environmental Mediation

Environmental mediation is an approach which employs mediation to resolve environmental disputes. The Institute for Environmental Mediation uses the following definition when discussing the mediation process:

> Mediation is a process in which those involved in a dispute jointly explore and reconcile their differences. The mediator has no authority to impose a settlement. His or her strength lies in the ability to assist the parties in settling their own differences. The mediated dispute is settled when the parties themselves reach what they consider to be a workable solution. (Cormick, 1982: 16)

A number of important considerations are implicit in this definition: (1) Involvement of the parties in the mediation process and their acceptance of the mediator is voluntary. (2) The parties will jointly explore and debate the issues, both in joint sessions and in caucuses of one or more of the parties with the mediator. (3) The mediator facilitates the negotiation process by assisting the parties to reach a settlement acceptable to them. (4) An agreement requires the support of all parties. (5) The mediator shares with the parties the responsibility of ensuring that any agreement reached represents a viable solution that is technically, financially, and politically feasible to implement (Cormick, 1982: 16).

The Essential Model of Environmental Mediation

The theory and practice of environmental mediation are in a state of development. In an effort to establish a theoretical framework for environmental mediation, this writer developed an eclectic theory of environmental mediation based on an examination of the literature. The theory contained sixty-three propositions about the conditions, activities, and processes which are vital to successful outcomes of mediation. The propositions were tested by having thirty environmental mediation practitioners rate the contribution of each proposition to reaching a mediated agreement.

It was found that thirty-four of these propositions were rated as important in contributing to completed settlements. These propositions, then, encompass the major considerations and activities which favor the effective practice of environmental mediation, based on the literature available on the field and practitioner assessments of an eclectic theory. They provide a description of current environmental mediation practice, as seen by this author. The propositions, and the rationale for their inclusion, are presented here to provide a picture of how environmental mediation works in practice. They are called "The Essential Model of Environmental Mediation" because they constitute the key propositions which contributed substantially to effective mediation outcomes.

The Essential Model of Environmental Mediation is divided into ten stages. The propositions which describe mediation and the rationale for their inclusion in the Essential Model are presented as they occur within these stages.

Stage One. Identification of the Mediator

Once an environmental dispute emerges and the contending parties become aware that mediation is a possible means of settling the dispute, a mediator needs to be selected. One proposition is important to successful mediation in this first stage:

The mediator should not have an interest in the outcome of the dispute.

This condition is inherent in the concept of mediation. If the mediator stands to reap personal gain from the outcome of the dispute, the role of assisting the contending parties to reach a mutually satisfactory adjustment of interests in the mediated agreement would be compromised.

Stage Two. The Preconditions for Mediation

Once a mediator is selected, the dispute should be examined to determine whether it is suitable for mediation. A number of considerations may make an environmental dispute unsuitable for mediation. Mediation is a tool which is appropriate only under selected circumstances. The responses of environmental mediation practitioners indicated the importance of the following propositions:

The mediator should assess the suitability of the dispute for mediation.

Mediation is an alternative to the settlement of a dispute through the courts, or by determination of regulatory bodies. The mediator should determine whether the dispute fits these more traditional approaches, or possesses characteristics that make mediation a more suitable approach for resolving the dispute.

There should be real consequences to the parties if mediation is not attempted, and the consequences should be such that mediation appears to be the best alternative for settling the dispute.

Participation in a mediation effort may require a considerable amount of time and resources on the part of the contending parties. Unless there are real consequences of not participating in mediation, the disputants will not have sufficient incentive to maintain their involvement throughout the mediation process until a settlement is reached.

There should be uncertainty about possible outcomes of the dispute in a context other than mediation (i.e., in the courts, before a regulatory body, etc.).

If any of the contending parties to environmental mediation feels certain that it could obtain a favorable settlement through the courts or before a regulatory body, that party will be likely to pursue that route rather than face the uncertainty of outcome from a mediated settlement.

Stage Three. Recruitment of the Participants in Mediation

The resolution of disputes often involves actions which have widespread impacts upon the environment. The repercussions of decisions may have effects which touch the interests of a great diversity of parties. It is important, therefore, to choose participants in mediation carefully to be sure that the mediated settlement fairly represents the interests of those who will experience the impact of a mediated agreement.

Particular effort and attention should be devoted to the selection of participants.

Because participants in mediation often represent many other people with similar interests, they bear the responsibility for representing their perspective effectively. They need to be knowledgeable, articulate, energetic, and committed if they are to fulfill this responsibility. Careful selection is needed to choose those who will do the best job of representing the perspectives of the various parties whose interests may be affected by a mediated agreement.

All parties with a substantial interest in the dispute should be represented.

If all parties with a substantial interest in a dispute are not represented in mediation, there is potential for an unrepresented party to resort to a lawsuit, or other obstructive tactic, to block the achievement of a settlement or the implementation of an agreement.

The mediator should educate the contending parties on the mediation process.

Because mediation is a new and developing practice in settling environmental disputes, participants need to be educated in how the process works if they are to develop creative solutions which fairly represent the views and interests of all perspectives on the dispute.

Stage Four. Design of the Mediation Process

Because environmental mediation may involve a number of parties with strongly held positions on widely differing interests, strong emotions may surface during mediation. Careful attention should be given to designing a process in which positions may be clearly stated without leading to disruptive emotional displays. Although too much emphasis upon structure and procedure may impede the development of creative solutions, insufficient attention to these considerations may allow the process to become diverted into unproductive activities.

Contending parties should participate in designing the mediation process.

The participation of the contending parties in designing the mediation process gives them "ownership" in mediation, and assures a design which will give fair consideration to all perspectives. This ownership in mediation supports a strong commitment to the process so that participants continue to be active in working toward a settlement in spite of obstacles which develop.

The design of the mediation process should be done with the advice and consent of the mediator.

Because the mediator will manage the mediation process, it is important that the process be designed with his advice and consent. The approach of each mediator is different. The process should be designed to facilitate the use of the particular style of the mediator who will manage the mediation process.

The participants and the mediator should develop ground rules for the process.

Ground rules for mediation help to regulate and structure the interactions among participants, and between the participants and the mediator. Joint participation in developing ground rules assures that the participants share "ownership" in the process, that the procedures are suitable for the conflict being mediated, and that the activities are appropriate to the individuals who represent interests being mediated. Ownership in the process helps to assure that the participants will maintain participation until a settlement is reached, in spite of difficulties encountered and the time and resources which may be demanded of participants to make the process work.

Ground rules should be developed for dealing with the news media.

Because the mediation of environmental disputes often touches upon sensitive issues and particular trade-offs between contending parties which can easily be misinterpreted or misunderstood by the public, ground rules are needed to manage the release of information to the news media. Premature exposure of positions can lock participants into postures which may only represent initial bargaining postures, rather than vital perspectives that define ultimately desired concerns on which the outcome will be based. Flexibility is needed so that positions can be changed in response to concessions from opposing parties.

The ground rules for mediation should be approved by all participants.

The formal approval of the ground rules by all participants helps to strengthen the ownership of the mediation process. It helps to assure that ground rules are practical, fair and reasonable.

The mediator should obtain the trust of the contending parties.

Because the mediator needs to know more about the strengths and weaknesses of the positions of the contending parties than they know about each other, he has access to very sensitive information. The participants must trust the mediator to use this information without compromising the interests of the parties, or revealing more about particular positions than the parties wish. The development of trust in the mediator provides the basis for the contending parties to share this information with the mediator.

Stage Five. Identification of the Issues

Although the points of contention in an environmental dispute may appear to be simple and straightforward, different parties in the dispute may perceive the issues quite differently. An explicit effort may be needed to identify the issues clearly.

The issues in dispute should be clearly identified.

Because the different desires and needs of parties involved in an environmental dispute may lead them to perceive the issues from sharply different perspectives, an explicit effort is needed to identify clearly the issues at the center of the dispute.

Stage Six. Establishing the Information Base

Before the parties in mediation can make progress in settling a dispute, a base of data about the current state of the environment needs to be identified or developed.

Efforts should be made to be sure that all representatives of parties to mediation have an adequate understanding of the facts relevant to the dispute.

Misperceptions of points at issue in a dispute may be based upon an inadequate grasp of facts. An effort to be sure that all representatives have an adequate understanding of the facts helps to avoid confusion over issues.

The issues in dispute should be broken into logical pieces for consideration.

Environmental disputes often involve issues with many dimensions with great complexity. Breaking the issues into logical pieces for consideration facilitates a complete comprehension of each aspect separately in a manageable quantity.

Stage Seven. Development of the Preliminary Agreement

Once the mediation process has been designed, and an information base has been established, the participants can begin to develop a preliminary agreement. This statement spells out in a tentative way what actions will take place to modify the environment in a manner which is acceptable to all participants in mediation. The development of a preliminary agreement allows the representatives of parties to mediation to consult with their constituents on the suitability of this interim agreement before moving toward a final settlement. Several activities take place as the participants work toward producing a preliminary agreement.

A variety of alternative solutions should be generated by the participants.

It is important that a variety of alternative solutions be considered so that all perspectives in mediation can identify with an approach to settlement which incorporates their interests. The various alternatives bring out considerations which may be combined into an agreement which is satisfactory to all perspectives.

The contending parties and the mediator should hold informal meetings.

Because the mediator may need to obtain sensitive information about the positions of contending parties, he will need to meet informally with groups of participants representing different perspectives.

The contending parties should hold their own caucus sessions.

Representatives holding similar positions should have the opportunity to hold caucus sessions in order to reach agreement among themselves on the positions they will take in mediation. This enables them to present a united front and prevents confusion in the mediation process.

The mediator should spend time interacting with participants on a one-on-one basis.

The mediator needs to understand the orientation of each of the participants in mediation in order to determine whether proposed components of the preliminary agreement are satisfactory to these individuals. One-on-one interaction with these representatives in mediation facilitates the development of this understanding.

Communication should be maintained with those who will be responsible for implementing the agreement.

The implementation of a mediated agreement often requires a commitment to certain actions, and the commitment of resources, on the part of individuals and organizations which are not directly involved in mediation. Participants in mediation need to communicate with these parties as the preliminary agreement is being developed to be sure that actions proposed as a result of the agreement will be suitable and feasible for implementation.

Parties responsible for implementing the agreement should provide assurances that they will follow through.

As the preliminary agreement is being developed, it is important to obtain assurances from those responsible for implementation that they will follow through on their commitments.

Clear means should exist for binding the parties to the agreement.

As the process of developing the preliminary agreement moves forward, the participants should develop means by which the parties to the agreement will be formally committed to fulfilling their responsibilities in honoring and implementing the agreement.

A preliminary agreement should be reached.

A preliminary agreement should be reached so that constituents of representatives to mediation can react to something substantive and explicit before the mediation process moves toward a final agreement.

A preliminary agreement should be put into writing.

The act of putting a preliminary agreement into writing is

important to assure that all participants have a document in explicit tangible form which facilitates understanding. The preliminary agreement is a document which is communicated to constituents explicitly, assuring that the constituents of different parties to mediation receive the identical information.

Stage Eight. Consulting Constituents on the Appropriateness of the Preliminary Agreement

Once the preliminary agreement is developed, it needs to be submitted to the constituents of representatives to mediation for review. It should receive either their approval or suggestions for modifications.

Participants should maintain regular contact with their constituents.

The representatives in mediation may move substantially away from the positions they assumed at the initiation of mediation. Constituents need to be informed of the movements away from the original position, and the reasons for these movements, so that they will not be suddenly confronted with a substantial shift in position toward the end of the development of the preliminary agreement. Regular contact with constituents allows the representatives to bring along constituents in a gradual manner—which facilitates an understanding of the rationale for the changes needed.

The participants should consult with their constituents on the suitability of the preliminary agreement.

The consultation of the representatives in mediation with their constituents helps to assure that the terms of the preliminary agreement are in accord with the interests and concerns of the constituents.

The constituents consulted should approve the preliminary agreement.

Once the constituents of representatives of mediation have suggested modifications in the preliminary agreement, they should approve the agreement. This approval enhances the legitimacy of the position of the representatives to mediation and legitimizes the outcome of mediation.

No major group of constituents should oppose the preliminary agreement.

The preliminary agreement should reasonably accurately represent the interests of constituency groups represented in mediation. Consequently, no major group of constituents should oppose this agreement.

Stage Nine. Making the Agreement Final

Once the preliminary agreement has been modified to accommodate the concerns of the constituents of representatives to mediation, the stage is set to move toward the development of the final agreement.

Modifications recommended by constituents of representatives to mediation should be incorporated into the final agreement.

In order to satisfy the concerns of constituents of representatives to mediation, modifications which were suggested should be incorporated into the final agreement.

An agreement should be reached which is approved by all parties.

An agreement which is approved by all parties to mediation is the ultimate goal of environmental mediation. Approval by all parties assures that the agreement meets the needs of all participants, within the constraints of the competing demands.

Stage Ten. Assuring the Implementation of the Agreement

Once a mediated agreement is reached, measures need to be taken to be sure that it is implemented.

The agreement should be ratified or approved by the constituents of the representatives to mediation.

The final agreement should be ratified or approved by constituents of the representatives to mediation as a final, tangible endorsement to enhance the chances for implementation.

Means should be provided for monitoring the agreement.

Monitoring the implementation of the agreement is important to assure that the provisions of the agreement are being adhered to faithfully as they are put into effect.

Means should be provided to remake or redecide the agreement, if necessary.

Because conditions change, the implementation of the agreement may not be reasonable, practical or feasible in its original form. The agreement may need to be revised so as to adapt it to changing circumstances.

Virtues of Environmental Mediation

Writers on the subject of environmental mediation have made a number of claims about the benefits of the practice of environmental mediation. Three different writers extol the virtues of environmental mediation, as follows:

Mediation can provide conflict resolution for environmental disputes far less expensively, in terms of time and money, than can litigation. Moreover, it can provide all participants a greater sense of satisfaction because of their active role. It allows the participants to maintain a degree of control. It allows the consideration of more creative environmental options than does litigation. Most important, mediation promotes cooperation, which is the missing element in the solution of most environmental problems. It also allows consideration of a more comprehensive range of expertise and technical data affecting environmental decisions than does litigation. Environmental mediation is an attempt to manage resources and make decisions that incorporate as many relevant factors and consequences as possible. (Folberg and Taylor, 1984: 220)

The flexibility of mediation is probably one of its principal strengths. The mediators and parties to a dispute have had to design a process and ground rules to fit the specific circumstances of their particular case. (Bingham, 1986: 53)

[Mediation] is generally less expensive in time and money. . . . It deals more satisfactorily with the issues. In contrast to judicial review, which typically examines whether the administrative and procedural requirements have been adequately addressed, a mediated settlement deals directly with the "substance" of the dispute. It is this crucial aspect of the mediation process that should, over the long run, encourage greater use of the process. (McCarthy and Shorett, 1984: ix-x)

An evaluation of the success rate of environmental mediation efforts provides a favorable picture. Bingham (1986: ix) writes that by mid-1984, a decade after environmental mediation had first been attempted, mediators had been involved in at least 160 environmental disputes. Results of many of those efforts were successful, remarkable for the positive climate of public opinion they fostered and for the sense among the parties that they had won, each of them. In the cases in which the purpose was to achieve an explicit agreement, the success rate was 78 percent (Bingham, 1986: 73). Among the 103 cases in which an agreement was reached, approximately 70 percent had been fully implemented, 14 percent had been partially implemented, and 15 percent were unlikely ever to be implemented (Bingham, 1986: 77). The mediation process, however, is not without weaknesses.

Weaknesses of Environmental Mediation

The potential weaknesses of the practice of environmental mediation are particularly evident in the processes of recruiting mediation participants and in the management of the mediation process.

Recruitment of Participants

A critical and basic initial task in environmental mediation is the recruitment of participants. Obtaining an equitable selection of representatives in mediation is important and sometimes difficult. Practical considerations produce pressure to limit the number of participants in mediation because the difficulties of reaching consensus multiply with an increase in the size of the group involved. Lake (1980: 64–65) notes that if nonjudicial dispute settlement processes are to become viable alternatives to environmental litigation, it will become necessary to regularize equitable, feasible selection criteria so that the results of negotiations are not invalid because of arbitrary or capricious exclusion of parties. The task is challenging because the interests are often diffuse and there are multiple groups claiming to represent the same interest (e.g., hunters and wilderness preservationists). From this universe of parties and interests the mediator must select a small number of participants which will adequately represent all parties. Shorett (1980:59) notes that by excluding a critical party, the ultimate mediation result may be useless because litigation or other adversarial alternatives will continue to be pursued. It is not always easy to identify all the affected interests in a dispute or to determine how they can be represented most effectively (Bingham, 1986: 96).

Because environmental disputes vary greatly in the substance of the dispute, the geographical range of environmental impacts, the kind and number of interests potentially affected by a settlement, it is difficult to prescribe standard procedures for participant selection which are appropriate for all disputes. The mediator must exercise great initiative and discretion in selecting participants. The potential for misjudgment and bias in selection is great. Mistakes made at this stage have potential to distort the entire mediation process and subvert the eventual implementation of an agreement. Difficulties presented by this activity are a major potential shortcoming of environmental mediation.

Another problem in the recruitment of participants in mediation is that some interests may not have a group available to represent their interests. Cormick (1980: 28) argues that it is the responsibility of those promoting mediation to ensure that both the issues and the processes are sufficiently widely publicized that all who may reasonably wish to participate are aware of the opportunity to do so. Potentially contending parties may need to build a power base, establish a constituency, develop leadership, and gain sufficient public notice of the issues so that any eventual agreement will have sufficiently broad support that a recurring cycle of new issues and new parties appearing during actual implementation is forestalled.

This position, promulgated by one of the "founding fathers" of environmental mediation, is very idealistic. Mediators entering environmental disputes already face the challenge of selecting a representative set of participants from existing groups in order to keep the mediation process to a manageable size. They are unlikely to be willing to take the time and effort to foster the creation of additional groups. Once an environmental dispute has emerged, and a mediator has initiated involvement in the case, there is a need to maintain momentum in establishing a framework for the mediation process. The urgency of reaching a solution forestalls any inclination to slow the process while new groups develop. Thus, once a potential mediation process begins to move forward, it is extremely unlikely that initially unrepresented interests will have an opportunity to participate.

Mediation Management Activities

Environmental conflicts differ greatly in the subject of the dispute, the aspects of the environment which are affected, and in geographical scope. Each mediator approaches the development and design of the mediation process differently. This great variability in the characteristics of each mediation effort creates problems in the achievement of fair and just settlements to environmental disputes through mediation.

The methodology of environmental mediation is not standardized. Lake (1980:96) writes that a great concern is the development of a definable process called "mediation" in order that prospective users of the process have some reasonable expectation of what their involvement will entail and of what outcomes might be expected to result. The great variety in circumstances to be addressed in environmental mediation, and the diversity of parties and interests which may be involved in any one dispute, require flexibility and creativity in adapting the mediation effort to the case. The unpredictability of how each effort will be designed and managed creates uncertainty for potential participants.

The lack of an established methodology of environmental mediation means that potential participants must put their trust in the ability of the mediator to design and manage the process in a way which will advance and protect their interests. There are no guarantees of how well the process will work nor how fair the outcome will be for all perspectives. The lack of standard methodologies of environmental mediation precludes the development of standard requirements for the professional practice of environmental mediation. It appears that the mediator is more artist than scientist, for the three basic sources of mediator actions are:

1. The originality of ideas, the ability to understand issues, vigorous sales ability, and accumulated knowledge enhance a mediator's negotiating skills;
2. His or her ability to act unobtrusively, confidence-retaining abilities, thick hide, and demonstrated integrity and impartiality are qualities that support his or her communications activities; and
3. The authority of the mediator enables him or her to use the power of position to support agreements. (Sullivan, 1984: 155–156)

These qualities in a mediator are extremely difficult to evaluate.

Mediators are often recruited through informal channels. Bingham (1986: 150) notes that individual mediators and organizations with good reputations have cases referred to them by those who have worked with them in the past. Susskind (1981:41–42) writes that recent instances of environmental mediation have tended not to stress the formal credentials or the interventionist skills of the mediators involved.

The unpredictability of what skills mediators will bring to mediation efforts creates a source of uncertainty about what to expect from mediation on the part of prospective participants. The assurance that interests will receive fair treatment depends upon the ability of the mediator to manage the process to respect the needs of all perspectives.

The design and management of the environmental mediation process provides several points at which the mediator plays a key role in shaping decisions affecting the process and substance of the effort. The development of ground rules for mediation is a basic step in shaping how mediation will be carried out. Each mediator, however, will have a different approach based upon personal style and experience in mediation. Different environmental conflicts may require different sets of ground rules even when managed by the same mediator. The potential of different sets of ground rules to favor different considerations and interests in mediation creates potential for inequitable treatment of different parties in mediation. Whether a participant will receive a fair hearing and whether all sides of issues will receive equal consideration depends greatly upon what ground rules are established for the mediation effort.

The development of a mediation agenda and the definition of issues to be addressed in mediation provides an area in which the mediator may use substantial discretion. At some point, the issues may need to be limited or narrowed in order to be manageable. While the mediator may put these decisions primarily in the hands of participants, while acting in a more facilitative than directive role, there is still potential for the mediator to have a subtle, though indirect influence upon the choice of an agenda and the selection of issues. In addition, issues may arise which affect interests which are not represented in mediation. The desire of the mediator to maintain momentum toward a settlement may lead him or her to exert pressure to limit the scope of mediation. This creates the potential to leave important problems unexplored and significant perspectives unrepresented in mediation.

Mediation Compared with Litigation

Environmental mediation is gaining increasing acceptance as a means for settling environmental disputes. Questions must be raised, however, about the ability of mediation to protect the interests of less sophisticated parties and interests, and the concerns of those who do not participate directly in the mediation effort. Much of the responsibility to protect the interests of weaker or unrepresented parties, and the public interest, rests with the mediator. While the flexibility and adaptability of mediation to particular circumstances, and its informality, are strengths, the predictability of litigation is one of its major advantages. Concern for the protection of minority interests is a major strength of the court system. Questions need to be raised about the merits of environmental mediation relative to the benefits of the courts and litigation as means for resolving environmental disputes.

In regard to the recruitment of participants in a dispute resolution process, environmental mediation stands in strong contrast to litigation. In environmental mediation, the mediator often takes the lead in identifying the interests involved in a dispute. Who is involved may be a direct result of how energetic and thorough the mediator is in searching out potentially interested parties and affected interests. Once a mediator becomes interested in a dispute, there is the potential motivation to move rapidly toward developing and facilitating the negotiation process with as few delays as possible. The parties and interests initially identified may add their pressure to move the process forward. The logistical difficulties of engaging and organizing large numbers of parties in any coherent, manageable, and expeditious mediation process create the need to limit the number of participants. The pressures to move forward may simply not allow time for potentially affected, but unorganized parties, to organize, develop leadership, garner resources and publicity, and develop positions in regard to the dispute. A variety of pressures push toward the restriction of the perspectives and interests which will be represented in a mediation effort.

In cases in which litigation is the context of dispute settlement, a number of factors facilitate the identification of parties to litigation. The publicity garnered by the controversy which accompanies the filing of a lawsuit greatly aids the initial parties involved to gather support of constituents, and organizations, with similar interests. The delays which often accompany court proceedings may provide ample time for unorganized interests to develop and organize a campaign. The possibility of gaining national attention for the dispute may greatly facilitate the process of raising funds for litigation. The potential of a court case to set precedents for many other jurisdictions may make it worthwhile for interests from all over the country to contribute resources to the litigation effort. The availability of resources may make it possible for additional interests to become involved. Thus, varied dimensions may facilitate the identification of a great number of interests which were not in the limelight at the initiation of the litigation process.

The internal dynamics of environmental mediation are completely different than the courtroom context. Participants in mediation often develop bonds of trust, understanding, and even affection, toward their opponents. The climate of understanding and progress in working toward mutually satisfactory solutions creates subtle pressures to be reasonable and conciliatory. These dynamics may undermine the determination of unsophisticated parties to stand their ground on issues. Less sophisticated parties may be overwhelmed by technical information marshalled by opponents with superior resources and technical support. The typical low key atmosphere, and press exclusion, of the proceedings protects the parties from the scrutiny of their constituents, and shields them from the awareness that they might be sacrificing constituent concerns in the interests of achieving a settlement. The parties with less experience and sophistication may walk away with an agreement which favors their perspective much less than would have been possible in a more public, adversarial context.

The context of litigation is not conducive to intimacy and trust between contending parties. Adversarial relationships and the development of competing evidence heighten the differences between opponents. The use of expert witnesses leads to the development of elaborate information and contrasting interpretations of the same data to support different positions. The public nature of the courtroom spurs lawyers and experts to make their utmost efforts to enhance their reputations in light of future opportunities and helps to attract the resources to involve highly skilled professionals. The public context assures widespread awareness of the proceedings and protects litigants from the temptation to sacrifice the interests of their constituents in the desire to achieve a settlement. The dynamics of starkly competing perspectives, the context of legal precedent, and the emphasis upon proper procedure help to assure that each side ends up with the maximum benefit which is justified within the law. The internal dynamics of litigation protect the interests of weaker parties much better than environmental mediation.

The unstandardized nature of environmental mediation, and the lack of professional guidelines or standards for mediation practitioners, create substantial uncertainties for prospective participants in mediation. Parties which wish to enter into a mediation process will have little sense of how the procedure will work, how agreements will be guaranteed, how their interests will be protected, nor how the results will be implemented. They must rely upon the integrity and reliability of the prospective mediator to provide assurances that the process will be beneficial. They must rely upon the skills and experience of the mediator to facilitate interaction in which all substantial issues are confronted and in which all participants receive a fair hearing. They must rely on the mediator to keep the process focused upon the issues at hand without neglecting related concerns.

The courtroom context and legal traditions of litigation provide a predictable setting for dispute settlement. Prospective litigants have the precedent of court cases to draw upon. They can utilize the resources of highly trained and experienced lawyers and expert witnesses. The procedures of the courtroom are standardized and well known. Prospective participants in litigation know in advance how the process works and how their interests will be protected.

The necessity in environmental mediation to design the process itself and develop ground rules creates substantial room for discretion and puts a heavy responsibility upon the mediator. The ability of mediation to assure just and fair outcomes for all participants is rooted to an extent in how mediation is conducted. Prospective participants in mediation are heavily dependent upon the orientation, experience, and skills of the mediator to facilitate the development of ground rules which assure fair treatment of all perspectives.

In the context of litigation, the rules of procedure and interaction between opposing parties are well known. Long standing precedent and practice provide a predictable context in which to resolve the dispute. There is little uncertainty about the ground rules which structure litigation and assure fairness to litigants.

In environmental mediation, the identification of issues is often highly subjective. The selection of participants in mediation will also shape the choice of issues. The approach which is used to narrow the agenda and focus the issues in dispute is dependent upon the ground rules which structure mediation. These areas of unpredictability create substantial uncertainty for prospective participants in mediation. They must depend upon the mediator to assure that their concerns receive adequate treatment.

In litigation, a preliminary task is to identify the issues in conflict. The disputing parties must understand where their interests lie in the dispute in relation to the concerns of their opponents before they can initiate litigation. The definition of issues in conflict is established before the parties engage in legal combat. No structure of procedures needs to be developed to lay this foundation. The issues in dispute are clear at the initiation of ligitation.

The value of legal precedent in establishing conditions which must be considered in like circumstance in other jurisdictions is a major strength of litigation. Once a legal settlement has been reached, this precedent provides a model for settling environmental disputes in similar cases. An interest group or party will achieve widespread impact for its interests by concentrating all of its resources on the particular dispute in question. Environmental mediation, in contrast, only settles the dispute for the local conditions and circumstances of the mediation context. While the approach to mediation may be copied beneficially in similar circumstance, the lack of grounding in a litigated settlement limits the applicability of the solution to other jurisdictions.

Critics of environmental mediation suggest that mediated settlements may detract from the potential of court settlements to establish precedents for dispute settlements. Jaffe (1984: 3) argues that resolving cases in forums that are informal, without a record and a set of precedents, will have results inimical to future development of the law and may undermine the ability of law making institutions to establish and enforce specific norms.

The potential long-term effects of environmental dispute settlements raise questions of accountability. The effects of agreements may be irreversible (Bacow and Wheeler, 1984). While mediated settlements may stipulate responsibilities for implementation, and provide for revisions in an agreement over time as environmental conditions change, such settlements do not carry the force of law which court settlements provide.

Conclusions

The practice of environmental mediation is beginning to emerge as a distinct and definable entity. Mediation practitioners have mediated a number of environmental disputes with an impressive record of success. Research on the practice of environmental mediation is beginning to identify the practices and conditions which favor successful outcomes of conflict management efforts. A variety of claims have been made about the advantages of environmental mediation over litigation. Enough is known about environmental mediation to raise some questions about some of the potential weaknesses of mediation compared with litigation. The literature on environmental mediation, and the case studies of the practice available, however, are too sketchy to provide a basis for a comprehensive comparison with litigation. It is difficult to evaluate the extent to which the potential weaknesses of mediation actually lead to the neglect of interests in a dispute or unjust settlements. What is needed, therefore, is the development of research which systematically compares environmental mediation with litigation. This examination of the emerging practice of mediation suggests a number of different directions such research could take.

REFERENCES

Amy, Douglas J. 1987. *The Politics of Environmental Mediation.* New York: Columbia University Press.

Bacow, Lawrence S., and Michael Wheeler. 1984. *Environmental Dispute Resolution.* New York: Plenum Press.

Bingham, Gail. 1986. *Resolving Environmental Disputes.* Washington, DC: The Conservation Foundation.

Busterud, John. 1980. "Mediation: The State of the Art." *Environmental Professional* 2:34–39.

Cormick, Gerald W. 1982. "The Myth, the Reality, and the Future of Environmental Mediation." *Environment* 24(7) (September):15–17, 36–37.

———. 1980. "The 'Theory' and Practice of Environmental Mediation." *Environmental Professional* 2:24–33.

Creighton, James L. 1980. "A Tutorial: Acting as a Conflict Conciliator." *Environmental Professional* 2:119–127.

Folberg, Jay, and Alison Taylor. 1984. *Mediation—A Comprehensive Guide to Resolving Conflict Without Litigation*. San Francisco, CA: Jossey-Bass.

Jaffe, Sanford M. 1984. "The Courts and Dispute Resolution." *Resolve* (Winter): 2–3.

Lake, Laura M. 1980. *Environmental Mediation: The Search for Consensus*. Boulder, CO: Westview.

McCarthy, Jane E. 1976. "Resolving Environmental Conflicts." *Environmental Science and Technology* 10:40–43.

McCarthy, Jane, with Alice Shorett. 1984. *Negotiating Settlements—A Guide to Environmental Mediation*. New York: American Arbitration Association.

Sachs, Andy. 1982. "Nationwide Study Identifies Barriers to Environmental Negotiation." *Environmental Impact Assessment Review* 3:95–100.

Shorett, Alice J. 1980. "The Role of the Mediator in Environmental Disputes." *Environmental Professional* 2:58–61.

Sullivan, Timothy J. 1984. *Resolving Development Disputes Through Negotiations*. New York: Plenum Press.

Talbot, Allan R. 1983. *Settling Things—Six Case Studies in Environmental Mediation*. Washington, DC: Conservation Foundation.

CHAPTER EIGHT

IMPEDIMENTS TO ENVIRONMENTAL DISPUTE RESOLUTION IN THE AMERICAN POLITICAL CONTEXT

Barry G. Rabe

FEW SPHERES of American domestic policy are as riddled by conflict or as dependent upon the judiciary for direction as environmental policy. In fact, the frequency and intensity of conflict have created a policy-making void that the judiciary has, for better or worse, filled. Given the incapacity of executive and legislative branches of government to resolve such fundamental disputes, the courts have become a dominant force in American environmental policy.

Court-shaped policy, however, is suspect in terms of its capacity to protect human health, limit interference with economic growth, and stimulate the search for innovative methods to improve environmental quality. And it has attracted a host of critics in recent years, many of whom question the basic ability of courts to make competent decisions on science-oriented matters.

The growing unrest over our judicially dominated environmental policy system has led to the exploration of alternative approaches to resolving environmental conflicts. These approaches include mediation, regulatory negotiation, and policy dialogue. Many of these are intended to mitigate conflict through direct and systematic interaction among disputants. Rather than delegate dispute resolu-

Author's Note: I am grateful to the Hewlett Foundation and Program on Conflict Management Alternatives at the University of Michigan for funding that has supported my research on environmental dispute resolution and to Margaret Boone, Toby Citrin, Terry Davies, Lynn Deniston, Robert Katzmann, Philip Mundo, Pam Puntenney, and Kenneth Warner for helpful comments on earlier versions of this chapter.

tion to a judge, jury, or arbiter, these alternatives force varying parties to design their own solutions, with policy reflecting group consensus rather than judicial decree.

In theory, these approaches offer ways to forge a style of environmental policy that is more cooperative and effective. And in practice, there are considerable grounds for optimism on both counts. Other spheres of domestic policy, including labor and management relations and special education, have long relied on comparable approaches that have generally been deemed effective. Even in conflict-riddled environmental policy, a growing number of disputes have been at least partially resolved through utilization of such approaches.

These initial experiments have resulted in an outpouring of publications on "environmental dispute resolution" (EDR). Many of these chronicle one or more environmental conflicts that were resolved through mediation or a related approach. Most are extremely enthusiastic about the potential of EDR and few perceive any significant impediment to vast expansion in its use or any significant policy shortcoming if it were to be widely employed.

This chapter is intended to inject a sense of balance into the current search for alternatives to judicially dominated environmental policy. It recognizes the considerable potential of EDR but suggests that it is best viewed as a possible regulatory reform rather than a proven alternative that can and should transform environmental policy. The rationale for EDR in the current conflict-ridden climate and an assessment of its considerable promise will be explored in greater detail. However, most of this chapter will examine possible obstacles that any effort to expand EDR may face given the realities of American politics. It will also question the potential capabilities of EDR to deliver more effective environmental policy, even if these political hurdles can be cleared.

The Penchant for Conflict and the Pursuit of Alternatives

The American political system is poorly equipped to resolve conflicts when passions run deep and interests are well-entrenched on both sides. Such problems are rare in distributive or developmental policies, in which elected officials are only too happy to authorize revenues or services for designated constituencies. But they are common in redistributive or regulatory policies, where some constituencies are likely to be disadvantaged by any decision. This is particularly evident in the context of environmental policy, where the economic and social stakes are quite high and a compromise position is rarely apparent.

Elected officials are likely to balk at resolving conflicts in such situations. They may try to placate proregulation constituents with legislation that is symbolically impressive but not overly threatening to antiregulation constituents (such as the Toxic Substances Control Act). Or they may transform regulatory policies into distributive policies by directly funding most of a mandated cleanup activity (such as the Water Pollution Control Act). But they will enter fundamental conflicts with considerable trepidation and will be, in all likelihood, only too happy to defer to the judiciary on such matters.

Congress has in fact encouraged shifting of decisions that it might have made to the judicial realm with the expansive definitions of legal standing and broad citizen suit provisions included in many major pieces of environmental legislation. As a comparative analysis of environmental policy in American and other industrialized nations concluded, "U.S. law erects the lowest entry barriers against both associations and individuals wishing to challenge administrative decisions" (Brickman et al., 1985:109). The ever-growing body of pressure groups that have formed around environmental issues has seized this opportunity to challenge virtually every aspect of environmental policy. These groups represent both pro- and anti-industry forces and take advantage of the relatively lower costs of trying to shape policy through legal challenge instead of legislative lobbying. As a result, many of the major environmental policy conflicts—from interpretation of the Clean Air Act to siting a hazardous waste facility in a particular community—must ultimately be resolved by the judiciary. Federal environmental officials generally assume a tentativeness to any action that they might take since approximately 80 percent of the regulations issued annually by the agency are challenged by suits (Stanfield, 1988:2764).

This pattern is consistent with the historic American reliance on dispersal of power among branches of government and distrust of ceding European-style authority to the agencies responsible for carrying out regulatory legislation (Price, 1983; Heclo, 1977). It also follows a growing American tendency to resolve fundamental policy problems through litigation. As Jethro Lieberman has observed, America has become a "litigious society," and he uses litigation-laden environmental policy as a cornerstone in defending his thesis (Lieberman, 1981).

The Doubts Concerning Judicial Capacity

Judicial domination of spheres of domestic policy would probably not be very controversial if there were no doubts over the capacity of courts to make timely, informed, and balanced decisions. But once one dispenses with the aura of judicial mystique that long dominated social science accounts of judicial behavior, a very serious set of questions must be explored. In fact, a growing number of criticisms have been raised in recent years that pose basic challenges to the ability of courts to confine themselves to appropriate areas of intervention and effectively address complex issues.

At one extreme, critics assert that judges have aggressively sought to fill the political void in dealing with controversial issues. Full-blown theories of "judicial imperialism" are rare, but a charge of judicial overzealousness in various policy areas is rather widespread. This aggressiveness is seen as particularly dangerous in instances where courts move beyond resolution of a specific dispute and begin to engage in far-reaching policy analysis. In "mass toxic tort" cases, such as the Agent Orange case and of the sort increasingly likely in large toxic exposure incidents, Peter Schuck has observed that the court and jury "do not simply prescribe and apply familiar norms to discrete actions; they function as policy-oriented risk regulators, as self-conscious allocators of hard-to-measure benefits and risks, as social problem solvers" (Schuck, 1987:4). At their worst, courts are alleged to seize these multiple roles in order to become the dominant governmental force.

Courts have also become suspect in terms of their basic competence to deal with the kinds of highly technical issues that are so common in environmental cases. Not only are courts burdened with the host of cases requiring conversance with a wide range of policy issues, but few judges or clerks are trained in the scientific and related methodological skills needed to develop a basic understanding of many cases. Most judges are legal generalists and many were trained before environmental law became a fairly common elective in legal education.

Courts may also have unusual difficulty in dealing with environmental cases because they deviate from the bi-polar pattern that is common in many other dispute areas and for which they are best suited. Consistent with Lon Fuller's doctrine of "polycentrism," courts are poorly equipped to sort out the competing claims of more than two parties (Fuller, 1981:87–124). Environmental cases commonly involved three or more parties, consistent with the multiplicity of agencies and pressure groups active in environmental policy.

According to R. Shep Melnick, they adhere to the model "that legal scholars for years claimed was not appropriate for judicial resolution" (Melnick, 1983).

The absence of environmental policy expertise and the proliferation of participating parties further explains the rather inconsistent ad hoc way in which many environmental cases are decided. Melnick has detected considerable variation in cases concerning the Clean Air Act, finding that different U.S. Circuit Courts interpret the Act in very different ways (Melnick, 1983). Even within a single environmental case, a change in presiding judges in mid-case can result in a radically different interpretation of the proper role of the court and the outcome. (See, for example, Schuck, 1987:113.)

Uninformed, inconsistent decisions can obviously have serious policy consequences. But the basic process of a court-based approach to dispute resolution may have adverse policy ramifications regardless of the quality of the ultimate decisions. The reliance on adversarial procedures leads disputants to take extreme positions and may destroy any prospect of a reasonable central ground. And the penchant for extreme stands by litigants may only retard the capacity of governmental agencies, such as EPA, to devise sound regulatory approaches or bring contending parties together in search of consensual solutions. According to Gregory Daneke, "Court rulings have reinforced that adversarial relationship, and in some cases prevent any type of consultation between parties from taking place" (Daneke, 1984:145; Downing, 1983:577–586). This may contribute to the proliferation of "locally unwanted land uses" (LULUs) and "not in my backyard" (NIMBY) syndrome that seem to defy resolution by current regulatory and judicial systems. In fact, any regulatory innovation by government or industry may be thwarted under the judicially oriented system, because the letter of court decisions must be adhered to short of appeal to a higher court or new legislation from Congress.

Strong reliance on courts to shape environmental policy may thus prove extremely expensive, both in terms of implementation inefficiencies and the laborious process of resolving disputes. In the absence of an overarching political or social consensus, each challenge must be hammered out separately, involving all of the direct costs of operating courts as well as the far greater long-term costs of delay and indecision. These factors may help to explain why the costs of implementing environmental programs are significantly greater for government and industry in the United States than Western

European nations or Canada, although there is minimal discernible difference in the environmental and public health impacts of these regulatory programs (Brickman et al., 1985; Vogel, 1986).

The Search for Alternatives

These doubts surrounding judicial capacity to forge coherent, effective environmental policy have triggered a search for dispute resolution alternatives in recent years. Nonlitigative methods for dispute resolution are not new, but only in recent years have they been utilized with any frequency in American environmental issues. In theory, these various methods are linked by their emphasis on bringing contending parties together to explore possible settlements. This may involve mediation of a specific environmental controversy, such as the authorization of water quality permits at a single manufacturing plant. It may also address broader issues, as in a policy dialogue in which a neutral convener will help a large number of interested parties chart long-term strategies for environmental policy.

As recently as a decade ago these EDR approaches were clearly confined to the fringes of American environmental policy. Few EDR cases had been undertaken, much less resolved, and virtually no research had been conducted. This was in vivid contrast with several other areas of domestic policy in which dispute resolution alternatives were well established and the overall role of the judiciary more subdued. It was also in contrast with the practices of many other Western democracies, including Canada and most nations of Western Europe, in which the courts have far less influence in environmental and other areas of domestic policy and more consensual processes of dispute resolution are well established.

But EDR has clearly gained a foothold in American environmental policy since the mid-1970s and gives every indication of being utilized in more environmental conflicts in future decades. One of the major forms of EDR has been mediation, as the number of environmental disputes that have been mediated increased from nine in 1977 to 161 by mid-1984. These disputes have involved a wide array of environmental issues and 78 percent of them have reached some form of agreement (Bingham, 1986:7–8, 32–33, 73). Far-reaching policy dialogues have attained some degree of consensus in areas such as coal policy development and groundwater protection. And federal regulatory agencies, including EPA, the Occupational Safety and Health Administration, and the Federal Aviation Agency, have begun experimentation with "regulatory negotiation," a form of negotiated rulemaking that seeks to develop a consensus among contending parties in place of prolonged legal challenges to agency-proposed rules (Gusman and Harter, 1986:306–310; Susskind and McMahon, 1985:133–165; Fiorino, 1988:764–772).

EDR is also beginning to be used on more than an ad hoc basis. Six states have institutionalized some form of mediation in the siting of hazardous waste facilities before parties may pursue arbitration or litigation. These states include Massachusetts, Wisconsin, Connecticut, Rhode Island, Texas, and Virginia. Five states have established statewide mediation offices, funded in part by the National Institute for Dispute Resolution, that assist states in providing mediation services for environmental and other conflicts. These states include Hawaii, Massachusetts, Minnesota, New Jersey, and Wisconsin. (See Bingham, 1986:57–58.) A number of other states are considering additional measures that attempt not only to increase the frequency with which EDR is used but also to formally embrace it as a preferred alternative to court-resolved disputes.

The Possible Shortcomings of Environmental Dispute Resolution

Environmental dispute resolution has acquired a certain acceptability in environmental policy circles, having been embraced by such mainline environmental organizations as the Conservation Foundation and the National Wildlife Federation. Some of its strongest proponents have argued that the United States may be about to usher in a new era in which EDR use continues to expand at an exponential rate and becomes commonplace in resolving disputes. Jay Hair, president of the National Wildlife Federation, has predicted that more than half of all environmental disputes will be handled through EDR procedures by the year 2000 (Hair, 1984).

But before an era of EDR can or should be proclaimed, this alternative must be exposed to far more careful and critical scrutiny than it has been to date. American environmental policy has a history of lurching from panacea to panacea, in an ongoing search for a regulatory approach that will transform the regulatory system. Perhaps the most recent of these fads has been the variety of strategies designed to apply economic models to environmental policy, such as emissions trading. Oversold initially as an inherently superior form of regulation, these approaches have now come to be seen as far more complicated and suspect than anticipated (Kelman,

1982; Liroff, 1986). They warrant very careful examination before being used more extensively. It is entirely possible that EDR may be on the verge of becoming the next environmental policy panacea. While it may ultimately prove far superior to current methods of dispute resolution, we need to know a great deal more about the contexts in which it does and does not work effectively and the extent to which it advances fundamental objectives such as protection of the environment and human health.

Most prior efforts to analyze EDR have suffered from a variety of limitations. Only a relatively few cases have been completed until recent years, posing obvious research dilemmas. Moreover, very little effort has been made to place existing findings in the context of a politically oriented theoretical framework that would facilitate long-term analysis as the number of cases grows. Most efforts at theory construction have consisted of fairly general predictors of negotiation success; many rely primarily on highly descriptive case study accounts that lack a tightly structured comparative case perspective (Susskind et al., 1983; Talbot, 1983; Bacow and Wheeler, 1984). A new generation of research may be forthcoming, along the lines of Gail Bingham's *Resolving Environmental Disputes,* that establishes some systematic measure of mediation outcome and implementation success for dozens of cases. But we still have far too little evidence to make any other than very general claims about EDR.

The existing literature is also suspect in that many of the leading researchers in this area are also in the vanguard of activists promoting expanded EDR use. Much of what we know empirically about EDR and its effectiveness has been dominated by individuals with a strong normative commitment to EDR, many of whom are professional mediators. This poses enormous conflict of interest problems that call into question the rather upbeat arguments found in many of the leading publications on EDR. It is, in fact, tantamount to basing our understanding of regulatory behavior primarily on the self-analysis of leading regulators, such as former EPA Administrators, rather than on intensive and nonpartisan research completed by social scientists without a vested interest in demonstrating regulatory success.

There are also significant limits on the extent to which claims of EDR efficacy can be made on the basis of more extensive research conducted in other policy areas where dispute resolution alternatives are more easily established. Special education mediation, for example, often involves fairly straightforward issues and a common goal of devising the best educational service plan for each child; these are simplifying factors uncommon in environmental disputes (Singer and Naco, 1985). Resolution of claims disputes through mediation involves very specific conflicts between individuals, whereas environmental disputes tend to involve very broad conflicts between groups (McEwen and Haiman, 1984:41). Perhaps the most thoroughly institutionalized and studied area in which alternative dispute resolution has been employed, labor and management relations, may be of limited analogous value to environmental policy (Lentz, 1986:127–139). And in the one study that offers a framework for comparative analysis of alternative dispute resolution across policy areas, environmental policy was deemed an area in which the potential benefits to society were very high but the chances of success were very low (Marcus et al., 1984:236).

In the absence of a clear understanding of what EDR has accomplished and what can realistically be expected from it, subsequent sections of this chapter will outline a variety of potential pitfalls that need to be considered in further deliberations over EDR use and its continued expansion. They attempt to raise a number of issues that may pose major stumbling blocks for EDR, but have not yet been examined in any systematic way. These sections are drawn heavily from theoretical understandings of American politics and they caution that the American political context may prove incompatible in many respects with alternative methods of dispute resolution in environmental policy.

Potential Political Impediments

Any strategy to expand American reliance on alternative methods for resolving environmental disputes must recognize the realities of the American political system. These realities suggest a well-ingrained pattern of conflictual, highly adversarial institutions and procedures for resolving conflict and establishing policy. Consistent with this is a judicial branch of government that is intended to resolve fundamental conflicts and also serve as co-equal to legislative and executive branches. If not uniquely American features, they are far more firmly established in the United States than other Western democracies where more flexible and consensual, and less judicially oriented, patterns prevail.

The Absence of Unitary Democracy

Environmental dispute resolution would be most likely to flourish in a society in which interests were widely presumed to be common and basic patterns of governance were consensual. Such a society is reflected in many political philosophers, including Plato, Aristotle, Rousseau, and Hegel, and may be particularly compatible with certain contemporary non-Western societies. It may even be evident in certain Western democracies, such as those of Austria and the Netherlands, which use consociational (proportional, multi-party) as opposed to majoritarian (winner-take-all, often two-party) electoral methods.

Political philosopher Jane Mansbridge characterizes a society with consensual patterns of operation as a "unitary" democracy (Mansbridge, 1983). She acknowledges that unitary democracy can occasionally emerge in American politics, but that it is exceptional to a prevailing pattern of adversarialism. Under "adversarial" democracy, politics approximates a zero-sum game in which interests in both economy and polity are presumed to be in conflict. Through various forms of competition, whether in the marketplace or in a court room, conflicts are resolved and certain interests are elevated above others.

Applied to environmental policy, adversarial democracy would find an array of industrial, governmental, and anti-industry groups with very different interpretations of a society's responsibility for environmental protection. Rather than consensually arrive at environmental questions or conflicts, adversarial understandings and procedures would prevail, much as they do at present in the United States.

Mansbridge's emphasis on American adversarial democracy is consistent with interpretations by other leading social scientists. Robert Bellah and associates, for example, have characterized "utilitarian individualism" as an enduring characteristic of American political life (Bellah et al., 1985; Auerbach, 1983). With very little emphasis on communitarian responsibilities and little interest in consensual structures of governance, Americans are largely alien to approaches that Mansbridge could characterize as unitarian. These scholars emphasize that at certain times and in certain contexts, less adversarial approaches can emerge and even flourish, but that these are inconsistent with traditional American political behavior.

Research that compares environmental policy in the United States and various Western European nations highlights the enduring American penchant for adversarialism. Quite contrary to the more collaborative consensual pattern of interaction among major groups in the United Kingdom, David Vogel deems adversarialism a basic component of American policy. He notes, for example, that "the most important way in which environmental groups in American 'assist' regulatory agencies in policy implementation is by suing them" (Vogel, 1986:280). His findings are confirmed by additional comparative research that deems American environmental policy far more adversarial than that of France or West Germany. According to Ronald Brickman and associates, "The extensive use of adversarial proceedings, as well as the channelling of political conflict around fragmented points of decision in all three branches, encourage American groups to take unilateral, uncompromising stands . . . and to perceive each issue as a separate crusade that is unamenable to more comprehensive political compromises and trade-offs" (Brickman et al., 1985:270).

Groups that advocate environmental protection might find it particularly difficult to abandon adversarial- and litigation-oriented political strategies. Many such groups have taken full advantage of litigation opportunities to attain the maximum political impact with their limited resources. Moreover, some advocate such an adversarial posture as a good investment, as groups are often rewarded with settlement dollars that only bolster their treasuries and make possible future legal battles on other issues (Freudenberg, 1984:166–167).

The American penchant for adversarialism does not preclude the introduction of more unitarian methods for addressing environmental policy. The very emergence of EDR in dozens of specific cases suggests that, consistent with Mansbridge's thesis, unitarian approaches can exist in the same society alongside adversarial ones. Nonetheless, the adversarial culture of American politics and the related nature of its political institutions and processes impose a significant potential threat to any effort to expand EDR. Despite the encomia of EDR by its proponents, they have yet to demonstrate how American politics might be so transformed as to jettison—or significantly reduce its reliance upon—its prevailing adversarial patterns of operation and thereby be prepared to embrace some version of EDR writ large.

The Absence of Corporatism

Closely linked to the absence of unitary democracy in the United States is the absence of corporatist institutions and processes that facilitate flexible and informal approaches to policymaking. Once again, the United States appears in vivid contrast to many Western European nations in which such patterns are commonplace. Corporatist societies are far less rule-bound than more pluralistic societies such as America, and they sanction regular consultation between interest group and governmental leaders in the policy formation process (Katzenstein, 1984; Schmitter and Lehmbruch, 1977; Martin, 1983.86–102). It is assumed in such societies that most policies will be reflective of a broad social consensus and acceptable to groups with a direct interest, thereby obviating the need in most instances for adversarial proceedings to resolve conflict.

Corporatist societies tend to operate with much less tension between executive and legislative branches, consistent with their reliance on parliamentary democracy. They also tend to delegate far greater authority to program and agency administrators than do pluralistic societies such as the United States. As a result, the governmental role in policy making is dominated by specialized policy professionals who have the authority to interact regularly with leading pressure groups (particularly industrial groups) in shaping policy. These groups become quasi-public by virtue of their direct access and influence; government may even subsidize various organizations that represent the general public and thereby pull them directly into the collaborative process. Under such a regime, public administrators play far more of a mediation function than in pluralistic societies and operate in a system in which consensual conflict resolution is actively promoted. As a result, environmental and other areas of regulatory policy are quite stable and generally lacking the contentiousness so evident in American environmental policy.

Whereas nonadversarial approaches to environmental dispute resolution are entirely compatible with corporatist societies, they may prove foreign to pluralistic ones. Many analysts of comparative politics have noted the case of "American exceptionalism" from the corporatist structures of intermediation so prevalent elsewhere. There is, in fact, very little indication of an American shift toward corporatism. For example, Robert Salisbury has noted that in the United States, there has been "virtually no official incorporation of formal associations as participants in policy discussions" (Salisbury, 1977:221). Comparing the United States with the United Kingdom, David Vogel confirms that "Only in America are quasi-corporatist ties between interest groups and the state viewed as undermining rather than strengthening the legitimacy of public authority" (Vogel, 1986:92–93). As a result, regulatory negotiation and institutionalization of mediation in environmental disputes constitute steps toward corporatism that are quite far-reaching for the United States. But they are, by contrast, far more modest than existing and well-established patterns of consensual dispute resolution in corporatist societies.

The Disdain Toward Bargaining

The difficulty of introducing more consensual processes in American policy is compounded by the lack of public trust in the institutions with direct responsibility for protecting the environment and public health. The predominance of open, adversarial procedures of dispute resolution stems in part from an inherent mistrust of political bargaining that is confined to select elites. This is particularly evident in areas such as environmental policy, where potential environmental and health risks are so high and the track record of government and industry is so spotty. Environmental issues, in fact, are almost classic examples of the kinds of issues that can be characterized as having unusually high public salience and conflict and attract highly polarized pressure groups (Price, 1979). This saliency and conflict may be greater in health-related cases rather than those that focus solely on environmental and natural resource protection issues. The former may well be the kinds of matters that the American public is least likely to hand over to negotiation which seeks some form of middle ground. Instead, they may be issues that will be expected to be resolved in public, adversarial settings which seek, at least in theory, the most appropriate policy remedy.

Political bargaining has acquired an especially unsavory quality in the United States in recent decades, reflected in post-Watergate and post-Vietnam reforms that have opened up the American policymaking process to the public. These reforms have included greater citizen access to the courts, mandatory citizen participation in operation of federally-funded programs, greater reliance on public hearings in policy formation, and unprecedented disclosure of information, whether through campaign finance reforms or the Freedom of Information Act. This general trend reflects a growing disdain for any semblance of a closed process or political dealing. It differs dramatically from the severe restrictions on public information and access common to more consensual systems in Canada and Western Europe. As Wendy Emrich has observed, there is a danger that environmental mediation "may be seen as a reversion to backroom political dealing" (Emrich, 1984) by limiting the number of participants in dispute resolution and, in many instances, deliberating over public issues in a highly-private setting. This is particularly likely in environmental policy, given the unsavory quality of "voluntary compliance" and "negotiation" efforts undertaken by EPA in the Anne Gorsuch years.

The potential for conflict over restricting public access may well emerge in cases where states have attempted to institutionalize EDR.

In Virginia, notes from negotiation of land use planning disputes are exempt from the Freedom of Information Act. This is similar to negotiation-oriented legislation that has been proposed in other states, which also prohibits use of information that emerges from negotiations to be used in any future adjudicatory hearing. Both types of restrictions may be imperative to negotiation success, but run contrary to recent patterns toward openness in public policy.

Bargaining may also prove unpalatable to local citizen groups who view any likely outcome of negotiation as posing an adverse human health and economic threat. The mandatory nature of some negotiations may make local willingness to consider possible agreements even less likely. In Massachusetts, for example, the Hazardous Waste Facility Siting Act requires that a legally binding siting agreement must be reached through negotiation between a site developer and the local "host" community. The state role in the negotiation is confined to technical assessment of the proposal and assistance to the participants. This leaves virtually all aspects of the negotiation process, including safety provisions and compensation packages, to the site developer and community.

Touted as a mechanism to break the logjam that often paralyzes siting, it is doubtful that the mandatory negotiation legislation can overcome repeated local refusal to bargain with site developers. The six Massachusetts communities that have faced siting proposals have successfully responded with a variety of strategies—including formal protest and holding referenda—to thwart each proposal and defer any future developer from considering a return to the scene. In these cases, local citizen groups have developed rapidly and organized solely to deal with the perceived siting threat. Their common view has been that a rapidly terminated relationship with site developers and state officials is preferable to any continuing one.

Rather than overcome the local disdain toward bargaining by mandating negotiation in siting cases, recent Canadian experience indicates that other processes might prove more effective. These involve provincial governments more directly and extensively in the siting process in attempting to foster trust and consensus (Rabe, 1990). An element of negotiation between developer and community ultimately occurs, but only after a far more thorough series of interventions by government officials. However, the more corporatist nature of Canadian policy-making may serve to reduce any reluctance to engage in bargaining over siting details, contrary to the American case.

The Danger of Exclusivity

Environmental dispute resolution may also run the risk of attracting considerable political opposition in the United States because of its tendency to formally exclude certain groups from participating. By the late 1960s, American environmental legislation was under severe attack both for being too lenient on polluters and also for maintaining a highly cooperative and consensual relationship between government and industry. Among the leading goals of major environmental legislation enacted or amended in the 1970s was the establishment of highly specific standards and procedures that the new EPA would be required to impose upon industry. This growing reliance on highly exact pollution-reduction goals occurred alongside the general opening up of the environmental policy process that encouraged formation of a potpourri of pressure groups devoted to environmental and human health protection. Many such groups have made full use of participatory opportunities available in our highly adversarial system. They have greatly influenced policy and have become accustomed to fully participating in every stage of the policy formation process. New procedures designed to promote more consensual resolution of environmental disputes must operate in this context, and somehow find means to incorporate this substantial demand for participation with efforts to create a more stable and consensual process. It is by no means certain that such a blend is possible.

In fact, the consensual procedures so common to Western European corporatist societies rely in large part on the capacity to confine negotiation to a relatively small and stable number of well-established groups. The process of determining what groups do and do not get invited tends to reward moderate, compliant groups with participatory opportunities while excluding more strident ones. It also tends to favor industrial and other pollution sources rather than environmental protection advocates. This ensures the stability so envied by many observers of pluralistic societies, but runs all the risk of regulatory "capture" by vested industrial groups which has been so vigorously avoided in American environmental policy (Wilson, 1980). And it is particularly dangerous in technically complicated areas such as environmental policy in which industrial groups are likely to have the resources necessary to fund participation and research that opposing groups are likely to lack. It may lead to the potentially significant imbalance in negotiation strength that might be lessened in a more adversarial context. Moreover, opposition groups in a pluralistic society such as the United States are far less likely to receive direct governmental subsidies that curb adversarial tendencies and facilitate meaningful participation, contrary to the common pattern of their subsidization in Western Europe and Canada.

The Demand for Exactitude

Even if problems of exclusivity were overcome by providing broad and workable participatory opportunities, it is uncertain that pro-regulatory groups and the citizenry more generally would support the shift toward more consensual forms of dispute resolution. American environmental policy is complicated greatly by an extreme public aversion to health-related environmental risk. This aversion may greatly exceed justifiable fear, particularly in comparison to other public health dangers, such as smoking, which may pose a greater health hazard but which fail to trigger comparable alarm. But it is evident in the unusual specificity and stringency with which regulatory standards are set in this area, the extent to which absolutist health-protection goals are accepted in legislation, and the extensive use of science to measure health ramifications of pollution and guide policy. And in this climate, it might prove very difficult to gain acceptance for consensual procedures that could result in a bargained reduction of commitment to maximum health protection standards. By contrast, environmental disputes lacking a public health dimension might bypass this problem.

The American aversion to environmental health risk is linked to an unusually strong public belief that science can determine risk with precision and thereby mold policy remedies. Rather than trust governmental, industrial, and environmental group leaders to negotiate reasonable regulatory compromises, American environmental policy is uniquely deferential to prevailing scientific thought. Some analysts deem this deference to science excessive and suggest that it may not result in effective regulatory policy (Sapolsky, 1986; Price, 1983). Nonetheless, the political context in which EDR would have to be introduced might prove hostile to any process that emphasized negotiated compromise over science in guiding environmental policy.

The Burden of Proving Superior Outcomes

The ultimate litmus test of any effort to switch from adversarial, court-oriented methods of dispute resolution to more consensual ones in the United States will be the outcomes of that process. And yet there is virtually no analysis—and even very little explicit speculation—concerning the capacity of EDR to deliver more effective environmental policy in terms of protecting the environment and human health and doing so in a cost-effective manner. The vast majority of analysis has focused more generally on the process. It often asserts the inherent superiority of addressing the conflict in a consensual rather than adversarial manner, instead of providing a systematic basis for comparative analysis.

It remains by no means clear that consensual politics inherently leads to better environmental policy. Among political theorists who consider the efficacy of cooperative versus conflictual regimes, it is emphasized that cooperative systems have many attributes but are not without shortcomings. As Duncan Snidal has noted, "one must be somewhat wary of the presumption that stability—even stability of cooperative outcomes—is always a virtue" (Snidal, 1985). Conflict theorist James Schellenberg summarizes a general concern raised by many analysts in noting:

> The pressures toward unity . . . may have their casualties in decision-making effectiveness. One of the chief casualties is a biased scanning of alternatives for action, selecting only those for attention that are anticipated to have high acceptance by others in the group. The result may well be a group-induced tendency to omit consideration of unusual possibilities of action. (1982:196)

A leading analyst of comparative areas of planning and conflict resolution has emphasized that "conflict can be a very positive force in society (some argue that it is the one compelling force in true democracies). It should not be viewed only as something to be avoided" (Seley, 1983:15).

Such concerns are, of course, very general in nature and have yet to be demonstrated in environmental policy issues resolved through alternative dispute resolution. But they are the types of concerns that will need to be alleviated if EDR is to prove superior to adversarial procedures both in terms of providing a more consensual process and in attaining the fundamental goals of environmental policy. They also warrant attention in that other efforts to foster more consensual procedures have proven somewhat disappointing in terms of policy outcomes.

The system of environmental policy so well established in many Western European nations has clearly delivered a more consensual and less expensive process for dispute resolution and policy formation. But there is very little evidence to suggest that this system is more effective in protecting the environment and human health than the American adversarial system. Despite dramatically different systems, neither the United States, Western Europe, nor Canada has proven particularly effective in addressing serious environmental problems, including acid rain, hazardous and nuclear waste disposal, and toxic substances control. Comparative research is scarce but indicates fairly similar outcomes despite the fundamental systemic differences. And in certain nations, such as Germany and Canada, a more adversarial approach is emerging in response to growing public unrest over the reliability of their current regulatory systems.

Other areas of domestic policy in which prevailing adversarial approaches have been widely lamented further suggest that consensual alternatives do not necessarily offer better policy outcomes. Many analysts have targeted medical malpractice as an area that needs consensual methods of dispute resolution. Both state and federal governments have begun to explore alternatives to litigation such as screening panels, no-fault insurance, restrictions on contingency fees, mediation, arbitration, and expanded disability insurance. Some of these are explicitly designed to foster more consensual dispute resolution. But economists such as Patricia Danzon have cautioned that the current system may be far less flawed than realized. She argues not only that litigation costs tend to be exaggerated, especially given the large number of claims that are settled before trial, but that the threat of litigation may significantly deter malpractice (Danzon, 1985). Danzon acknowledges that methodological difficulties are inherent in any effort to compare alternative approaches, especially in estimating malpractice deterrence of various schemes. But she emphasizes that the current system may lead to policy outcomes that not only are better than is generally understood but may even be superior to certain consensual-oriented reforms. Similarly, environmental adversarialism may have certain desirable features that are difficult to quantify, including stimulation of technological innovation and broad public participation.

Conclusion

This chapter has cautioned against any embrace of environmental dispute resolution as a panacea that can be relied upon to cure much of what ails American environmental policy. It acknowledged the shortcomings of our current, adversarial approach to dispute resolution and policy formation in this area, but emphasized a number of fundamental qualities of American political life that may mitigate against any effort to employ EDR approaches on a broad scale. Nonetheless, EDR retains considerable promise as a component of environmental regulatory reform in the United States. If not an all-encompassing regulatory remedy that can be easily applied to all disputes, it still may be able to play a profoundly important role in facilitating more mature and effective environmental policy. EDR may best be thought of as one of a series of alternatives to current approaches, one that warrants continued experimentation and analysis that considers the conditions under which it is and is not likely to facilitate consensus and deliver superior policy outcomes.

REFERENCES

Auerbach, Jerold S. 1983. *Justice Without Law?* New York: Oxford University Press.

Bacow, Lawrence S., and Michael Wheeler. 1984. *Environmental Dispute Resolution.* New York: Plenum Press.

Bellah, Robert, et al. 1985. *Habits of the Heart.* Berkeley: University of California Press.

Bingham, Gail. 1986. *Resolving Environmental Disputes: A Decade of Experience.* Washington, DC: Conservation Foundation.

Brickman, Ronald, Sheila Jasanoff, and Thomas Ilgen. 1985. *Controlling Chemicals: The Politics of Regulation in Europe and the United States.* Ithaca, NY: Cornell University Press.

Daneke, Gregory A. 1984. "Whither Environmental Regulations?" *Journal of Public Policy* 4(2):145.

Emrich, Wendy. 1984. *Remarks to Second National Conference on Environmental Dispute Resolution.* Washington, DC: Conservation Foundation.

Fiorino, Daniel J. 1988. "Regulatory Negotiation as a Policy Process." *Public Administration Review* 48(4) (July/August): 764–772.

Freudenberg, Nicholas. 1984. *NOT in Our Backyards: Community Action for Health and the Environment.* New York: Monthly Review Press.

Fuller, Lon L. 1981. "The Forms and Limits of Adjudication." In Kenneth I. Winston (ed.), *The Principles of Social Order.* Durham: Duke University Press.

Gusman, Sam, and Philip J. Harter. 1986. "Mediating Solutions to Environmental Risks." *American Review of Public Health* 7:293–312.

Hair, Jay D. 1984. "Getting Ready to Win." Address to Second National Conference on Environmental Dispute Resolution, October 2. Washington, DC: Conservation Foundation.

Heclo, Hugh. 1977. *A Government of Strangers.* Washington, DC: Brookings Institution.

Katzenstein, Peter J. 1984. *Corporatism and Change.* Ithaca, NY: Cornell University Press.

Kelman, Steven. 1982. *What Price Incentives?* Boston, MA: Auburn House.

Lentz, Sydney. 1986. "The Labor Model for Mediation and Its Application to the Resolution of Environmental Disputes." *Journal of Applied Behavioral Science* 22(2):127–139.

Lieberman, Jethro. 1981. *The Litigious Society.* New York: Basic Books.

Liroff, Richard A. 1986. *Reforming Air Pollution Regulation: The Toil and Trouble of EPA's Bubble.* Washington, DC: Conservation Foundation.

Mansbridge, Jane J. 1983. *Beyond Adversarial Democracy,* 2d ed. Chicago, IL: University of Chicago Press.

Marcus, Alfred E., Mark V. Nadel, and Karen Merrikin. 1984. "The Applicability of Regulatory Negotiation in Disputes Involving the Nuclear Regulatory Commission." *Administrative Law Review* 36 (Summer):213–238.

Martin, Ross M. 1983. "Pluralism and the New Corporation." *Political Studies* 31:86–102.

McEwen, Craig A., and Richard J. Maiman. 1984. "Mediation in Small Claims Court: Achieving Compliance Through Consent." *Law & Society Review* 18(1):11–49.

Melnick, R. Shep. 1983. *Regulation and the Court: The Case of the Clean Air Act.* Washington, DC: Brookings Institution.

Price, David. 1979. *Policymaking in Congressional Committee: The Impact of "Environmental" Factors.* Tucson: University of Arizona Press.

Price, Donald K. 1983. *America's Unwritten Constitution: Science, Religion, and Political Responsibility.* Cambridge: Harvard University Press.

Rabe, Barry G. 1990. "Toward Cooperation in North American Hazardous Waste Facility Siting." *Canada-US Outlook* 1:87–106.

Salisbury, Robert. 1977. "Why No Corporatism in America?" In *Trends Toward Corporatist Intermediation,* eds. Phillippe C. Schmitter and Gerhard Lehmbruch. Beverly Hills, CA: Sage.

Sapolsky, Harvey (ed.). 1986. *Consuming Fears: The Politics of Consumer Risk.* New York: Basic Books.

Schellenberg, James A. 1982. *The Science of Conflict.* New York: Oxford University Press.

Schmitter, Phillippe C., and Gerhard Lehmbruch (eds.). 1977. *Trends Toward Corporatist Intermediation.* Beverly Hills, CA: Sage.

Schuck, Peter H. 1987. *Agent Orange on Trial.* New Haven, CT: Yale University Press.

Seley, John E. 1983. *The Politics of Public-Facility Planning.* New York: D.C. Heath.

Singer, Linda R., and Eleanor Nace. 1985. *Mediation in Special Education: Two States' Experiences.* Washington, DC: National Institute for Dispute Resolution.

Snidal, Duncan. 1985. "Coordination versus Prisoner's Dilemma: Implications for International Cooperation and Regimes." *American Political Science Review* 79:923-942.

Stanfield, Rochelle L. 1988. "Resolving Disputes." *National Journal* (November):2764.

Susskind, Lawrence, and Gerard McMahon. 1985. "The Theory and Practice of Negotiated Rulemaking." *Yale Journal on Regulation* 2:133–165.

Susskind, Lawrence, Lawrence Bacow, and Michael Wheeler (eds.) 1983. *Resolving Environmental Regulatory Disputes.* Cambridge, MA: Schenkman.

Talbot, Allan. 1983. *Settling Things.* Washington, DC: Conservation Foundation.

Vogel, David. 1986. *National Styles of Regulation: Environmental Policy in Great Britain and the United States.* Ithaca, NY: Cornell University Press.

CHAPTER NINE

ENVIRONMENTAL MEDIATION: REQUIREMENTS FOR SUCCESSFUL INSTITUTIONALIZATION

Michael S. Hamilton

DURING THE 1960s, several experiments were initiated applying third-party dispute settlement techniques developed in the field of labor-management relations to community conflicts (Lake, 1980:59-60). These efforts were extended to environmental disputes—social conflicts over issues of resource use and allocation—in 1973 when Gerald Cormick and Jan McCarthy mediated a dispute concerning construction of a flood control project on the middle fork of the Snoqualmie River near Seattle (Cormick and Patton, 1980:85-90).

Subsequently, a literature of environmental mediation has developed in environmental planning, sociology, and legal periodicals. Case studies are most numerous and several handbooks are available, but there are few attempts at broader conceptualization. Most of this literature was written by practitioners for practitioners (i.e., persons serving as mediators of environmental controversies) in either a how-it-was-done or how-to-do-it vein. Consequently, much of it has a distinctly promotional flavor, reflecting viewpoints of participant observers.

Environmental mediation has failed to settle some disputes (Lake, 1980:205–228), but there have been noteworthy successes with controversies over siting a flood control project and an interstate highway in Washington (Cormick and Patton, 1980), operation and reclamation of a uranium mine in Colorado (Watson and Danielson, 1983), interagency conflict over uses of the Columbia River (Gusman and Huser, 1984), and interjurisdictional land annexation controversies in Virginia (Richman, 1983). An eighteen year dispute over siting the Storm King pumped-storage electric power plant on the Hudson

River north of New York City, which had festered through four U.S. Court of Appeals decisions and numerous hearings before three federal agencies and the New York state courts, was settled through mediation in 1981 ("Calm after the Storm," 1981). By mid-1984, mediators had participated in attempts to settle at least 160 environmental disputes (Bingham, 1986).

What are the prospects for institutionalizing environmental mediation in regulatory processes for controversial public facilities? What conditions may be necessary and what difficulties may be encountered? What are the requirements for successful mediation of environmental disputes, and for institutionalization of environmental mediation?

This chapter reviews the uneven literature on environmental mediation to address the above questions. The thesis is advanced that institutionalization of environmental mediation in a state permitting processes on a contingency basis will establish a needed framework for negotiation of disputes and shape expectations of potential participants so as to increase the probability of successful implementation of settlement agreements.

Defining Environmental Mediation

Mediation is negotiation with the assistance of an independent intervener or third party (Simkin, 1971:25–26). Negotiation is a means of striking a bargain where the parties meet face-to-face to settle issues on which there is disagreement (Cormick, 1980:27).

When discussing mediation as applied to environmental controversies, one definition dominates the literature:

> Mediation is a voluntary process in which those involved in a dispute jointly explore and reconcile their differences. The mediator has no authority to impose a settlement. His or her strength lies in the ability to assist the parties in settling their own differences. The mediated dispute is settled when the parties themselves reach what they consider to be a workable solution. (Cormick, 1982a:16)

Several important practical considerations are implicit in this definition. They concern the necessity of conflict, the voluntary nature of negotiations, neutrality of the mediator, and mutuality of outcomes, each discussed below.

Necessity of Conflict

Until conflict emerges in a concrete dispute, there is no basis or need for negotiations. By conflict is meant a general disagreement over values or scarce resources. Conflict is distinguished from a dispute, or a specific disagreement involving an issue in which a more general value conflict is evident (Cormick, 1982b:3), such as controversy over the location of a new electric power plant or hazardous waste management facility.

Conflict is a necessary condition in a pluralistic democratic society, serving as an instrument of social integration and change.

> Conflict maintains, rather than disrupts, the well-balanced society by facilitating communication and defining relationships and group structures, so as to clarify for a participant his position and status relative to others. (Mernitz, 1980:51)

Civil rights activist Saul Alinsky has aptly characterized a free and open society as "an on-going conflict, interrupted periodically by compromises" (Alinsky, 1971:59).

Conflict may help cull weak ideas, spur innovation, and heighten awareness of our own self-interests (Cormick, 1984:6). It is through conflict that previously unorganized persons perceive shared interests and organize to represent them:

> It is a social reality that new social movements, such as that represented by the emergence of environmental concerns, require conflict to establish their credibility and influence. It is conflict and confrontation and the public notice they bring that develops the issues, mobilizes constituencies and develops leadership. (Cormick, 1980:25)

Constituencies which lack access to decision makers may utilize a variety of disruptive tactics to gain public notice and attract adherents to their cause (Lipsky, 1968). It is through conflict that changing needs, preferences, ambitions, and hopes of various constituencies can be clarified and made known to decision makers, generally without violence. A dialogue may be initiated that leads to negotiation and settlement of disputes (Coser, 1956:121–128).

Conflict, then, provides a basis for social change in a democratic society. Contrary to the common misperception that conflict is an undesirable aberration, it is a functional mechanism of adaptation and change, allowing shifts in the balance of power between value preferences over time, without destroying the political system in which it takes place. However, prolonged disputes may produce disruption and antisocial behavior. Accommodation and settlement of disputes are required for maintenance of the political system.

Conflicts and Disputes

Mediation can settle specific disputes, but it probably cannot resolve basic value differences that separate parties in conflict (Cormick, 1982a:36). The distinction between settling disputes and resolving value conflicts is significant because the former does not require basic changes in attitudes or preferences, and may therefore be less difficult to achieve than the latter.

Because mediation requires a dispute to settle, negotiations are necessarily somewhat adversarial in nature:

> Unless the parties remain mindful of their conflicting self-interests, they are unlikely to strike a bargain that is viable when faced with the difficult realities of implementation; both the parties and their agreements will be repudiated by their constituents. (Cormick, 1982a:37)

The purpose of mediation is to settle disputes, not to promote cooperation or improved personal relations between parties. To the extent cooperation occurs in mediation, it may be more of a liability than an asset. With mediation, adversarial behavior takes place in informal discussions which do not constrain negotiations as the more formal rules of court proceedings and administrative hearings often do (Lake, 1980:20–23, 58–70; Cormick, 1984:1). Scholars and practitioners who have conceived of mediation as a cooperative process have made a fundamental conceptual error.

Timing of Mediation

Mediation is appropriate only when an impasse or stalemate has been reached, and all parties to a dispute recognize their inability to achieve their goals unilaterally (Cormick, 1980:30). At the point of impasse, interested parties can be identified. Issues are defined, there is some sense of urgency, and there is at least a dawning recognition that no party can achieve its objectives unilaterally without high costs (Cormick and Patton, 1980:81–82). This view of mediation is generally shared by practitioners (Bellman, et al., 1981). Some writers maintain the increased complexity of contemporary environmental disputes requires intervention before an impasse develops (Strauss, 1980:124–125), but they describe approaches to intervention which cannot appropriately be labeled mediation.

Other approaches involving third party interveners available at earlier stages in development of disputes are sometimes confused with mediation. These have been described as "revisionist mediation" (Lentz, 1986) and include a number of consensus building techniques such as facilitation, conflict anticipation, conflict reduction, conciliation, and joint problem solving. In these techniques, an attempt is made—before positions become extremely polarized, and in some instances before parties or issues are well-defined—to identify potential disputes, define the issues, generate alternative courses of action, and (in some but not all cases) reach an agreement which will avoid or minimize conflict (Cormick, 1982a:16; 1982b:1; Bellman et al., 1981:4; Lake, 1980:60–61; Mernitz, 1980:73–76).

These consensus building techniques originated in the literature of planning and citizen participation and differ substantially from mediation in the concepts about conflict on which they are based, in the specific activities of interveners, and in anticipated outcomes (Lee, 1982:4). Discussion of these techniques as forms of mediation is an unfortunate source of conceptual confusion in the literature of environmental mediation, and perhaps in practice as well. An undesirable result has been the mistaken attribution to mediation of some shortcomings evident in cases which were inappropriately labeled as mediation. Two such cases are discussed below.

Efforts to institutionalize environmental mediation must be sensitive to the issue of timing mediation so as to occur after citizen participation efforts and stalemate have occurred, recognizing this form of intervention may not be appropriate at all times or for all disputes. Stalemate provides a convenient "trigger" point for assessment of whether mediation may be appropriate for a particular dispute.

Voluntary Negotiations

There is general agreement in the literature that participation of all parties in mediated negotiations must be voluntary. Requiring participation would disadvantage weaker inexperienced participants, decrease the likelihood of good faith negotiations, and increase the likelihood that an agreement would be repudiated by constituents. Participants must be able to withdraw or dismiss the mediator at any time.

Strong incentives favor voluntary participation in mediated negotiations where no party can achieve its objectives through unilateral action at acceptable cost:

The specific advantages to each party are likely to differ. For one, the process may reduce costly delays and uncertainty. For another, it may eliminate a "no-win" political dilemma. And for a third, it may help to temper a public perception of its unreasonableness. (Cormick, 1984:10)

The financial costs of stalemate, delays during regulatory proceedings and litigation—which may be avoided through mediation of disputes—have been amply described (Susskind and Weinstein, 1980:315; Lake, 1980:8, 17; Mernitz, 1980:47-48; O'Conner, 1980:250; Bellman, et al., 1981:6).

Other advantages of mediated negotiations which encourage voluntary participation include their informality and procedural flexibility, as compared to more formal court or administrative proceedings (Cormick, 1984:1-13; Lake, 1980:20-21, 70; Susskind and Weinstein, 1980:319-320; Stewart, 1975:1772-1773). Mediation may also reduce uncertainty in subsequent regulatory proceedings by bringing parties together in negotiations over concrete proposals and counterproposals. The settlement agreement—if one is reached —can increase predictability of outcomes in permit proceedings by specifying mitigation measures and other permit conditions acceptable to interested parties, which regulators may adopt with some expectation they will not be litigated.

There must be willingness to negotiate in good faith by all parties, with an intention of reaching a mutually satisfactory agreement, if possible. Negotiated settlement implies compromise. Parties are not likely to gain all they desire through negotiations. Further, where resource development proposals are concerned, compromise implies acceptance of at least some change away from the status quo. Some parties may prefer defeat or continued conflict to compromise. If *any* party is unwilling to accept change or to compromise, mediation is not an appropriate approach to settlement of the particular dispute. Similarly, if it appears participation of some parties in negotiations is simply part of a strategy of delay, the mediation effort should be terminated. This is a matter of judgment for the mediator and the parties involved (Lake, 1980:66).

Non-Negotiable Issues

Some issues are not negotiable in the eyes of one or more parties to a dispute, and mediation is inappropriate in these instances. A review of sixty environmental disputes over three years concluded that only 10 percent of them might be mediable (Baldwin, 1978:17). Other writers are more optimistic (Susskind and Weinstein, 1980), but do not support their conclusions with data.

Compromise is an inappropriate objective if it involves relaxation of a legal right or statutory standard (Lake, 1980:72). It may also be inappropriate in cases involving cherished principles or the desire to set a precedent for future decisions (Cormick, 1984:14). For example, a group opposed to construction of *all* nuclear power plants or hazardous waste management facilities is unlikely to compromise for a facility half as large as one originally proposed.

If a group can achieve its objectives through stalemate or other unilateral action at little cost, or if contending parties have nothing of value to trade, bargaining and mediation will not be effective (O'Conner, 1980; Susskind and Weinstein, 1980:354). Efforts to institutionalize environmental mediation should provide for an assessment at the time stalemate is reached to determine whether mediation is appropriate for a particular dispute. Evaluations of controversies by reputable consultants offering mediation services are not costly and could often be had in the mid-1980s for less than $2,000, including travel expenses (Cormick, 1984).

Neutrality of Mediator

To establish and facilitate negotiations between parties to a dispute, the mediator must be impartial as to the specific disposition of the issues (Cormick, 1982a:16; Stulberg, 1981:96).

> The perception of the mediator's neutrality is critical—it allows a bond of trust to develop between the mediator and the parties involved. This bond of trust enables the mediator to receive confidential messages from the stakeholders; these in turn, provide clues about the direction that bargaining must take in order to achieve a settlement. (Susskind and Weinstein, 1980:347)

It is this commitment to neutrality which ensures responsible, nonmanipulative, ethical actions on the part of the mediator and permits mediation to be an effective, principled dispute settlement procedure (Stulberg, 1981:86).

Independence

There are two essential characteristics of mediation neutrality. First, the mediator must be independent of all parties to the dispute (Cormick and Patton, 1980:79–80), including interested government agencies (McCrory, 1981:69). Persons employed by a party to organize citizen participation or encourage negotiations must be considered advocacy interveners, not mediators (Cormick, 1984:3). An example of advocacy intervention which has been mistakenly described as mediation was negotiation of an agreement by Malcolm Rivkin and Associates for Bloomingdales Stores settling a dispute with neighbors surrounding a proposed shopping center near Washington, D.C. (Rivkin, 1977).

Lack of Authority

Second, the mediator (unlike third party interveners in arbitration or fact-finding procedures) must have no authority to impose a settlement or a particular version of disputed facts on the parties (Cormick, 1980:27–28).

> The mediator operates without the benefit of any higher authority that can force the parties to keep meeting or that can impose sanctions on one of the parties if agreements are breached. (Susskind and Weinstein, 1980:347)

Thus, references in the literature to a "mediator with clout" (Susskind, 1981:35–36; Raiffa, 1982:205–211) actually describe a form of intervention more akin to arbitration or fact-finding than mediation. An example was intervention by then-Congressman Tim Wirth in a dispute over proposed construction of the Foothills Water Treatment Project near Denver, Colorado. In this dispute, the Congressman—who publicly favored construction of the project— used political pressure "to force concessions from parties who had insisted on winning it all" (Susskind, 1981:30–37), exercising "influence which approached the power of compulsion" (McCrory, 1981:60). Most mediators would not consider this to be mediation (Stulberg, 1981:108).

None of this implies the mediator is entirely without influence. Information and confidences shared by the parties convey increasing influence to the mediator as negotiation proceeds (Cormick, 1982b:5) and there are ample opportunities for use of persuasion by a person in such a privileged position. However, the ability of parties to disassociate themselves from mediation efforts and to repudiate agreements they feel have been forced upon them serves to inhibit advocacy by mediators. A perception on the part of any of the parties that the mediator is partial to another party, or able to impose sanctions, undermines the credibility of the mediator and creates distrust in the legitimacy and fairness of the process. If this occurs, litigation may become a more attractive course of action for some parties.

Confidentiality

There is disagreement as to whether information shared with mediators by parties to a dispute should be confidential. A related question concerns whether negotiations should be conducted in public or private meetings. The motives and neutrality of the mediator may be called into question and communication between parties inhibited if proposals for compromise are reported publicly before agreement on all issues is reached. Many practitioners experienced in labor-management negotiations maintain it is essential for the mediator to have a confidential relationship with parties to a dispute (McCrory, 1981:54), and commit themselves in advance to refrain from making public statements on areas of agreement or disagreement in the event a settlement is *not* reached (Cormick and Patton, 1980:78). Confidentiality of conversations between a mediator and parties in an environmental mediation effort was protected by a U.S. District Court in Washington when the mediator moved to quash a subpoena in 1979 (*Adler v. Adams*, 1979; Liepmann, 1986).

Wendy Emrich suggests disadvantages of open meetings may be overstated, but notes that "closed meetings have been justified on the basis of increasing candor, ensuring confidentiality, and maintaining the momentum of negotiations" (Carpenter, 1982:390). Susskind maintains that "at least some scheduled sessions should be open to the public," but that closed meetings are acceptable as long as negotiated agreements are subject to public scrutiny in subsequent regulatory proceedings (Susskind, 1981:44–45).

This issue is particularly sensitive in situations where it may be desirable for public officials to take part in mediation efforts, but where state or federal sunshine laws require open meetings in which they participate. Citizens may believe the spirit of the law calls for open meetings even if it is unclear whether they are mandated (Carpenter, 1982:390).

Government officials have for several years conducted negotiations with public employee unions behind closed doors, with resulting contracts subject to public scrutiny during consideration of appropriations to implement their provisions. Representation of interested parties in mediated negotiations, coupled with public scrutiny of settlement agreements during regulatory proceedings should be adequate to serve the purpose of most state sunshine laws. State legislation may be required in some cases to clarify this intent.

If open meeting laws provide a barrier to direct participation of public officials in closed meetings, an alternative involves coordination of split sessions. Open, joint meetings where public officials participate and separate, closed caucuses of nongovernmental parties may be held, with the mediator practicing shuttle diplomacy between them. Or, a negotiating group comprised of interested nongovernmental parties may be formed separate from a nonnegotiating technical advisory group which includes government officials and technical experts, the latter group providing advice on the technical, legal and financial feasibility of potential agreements in open meetings, or through consultation with a mediator. Government officials will be unable to commit themselves to specific terms, but will be able to identify proposals which will likely be unacceptable on the foregoing grounds.

Expertise and Neutrality

Disagreement exists about whether a mediator should have special expertise in the substantive area of the dispute to be mediated. Susskind maintains the mediator needs technical knowledge about environmental and regulatory issues at stake in a controversy (Susskind, 1981:42). Cormick (1981:42) argues persuasively that technical experts are less effective mediators, for four reasons:

> First, "experts" have a tendency to rely on their own assumptions and values, rather than allowing the parties to "teach" them about the dispute. Second, there is an inclination to filter information and communication based on their independent assessment of the facts. Third, the discussions tend to move away from the underlying sets of values and perceptions which led to the dispute, and end up focusing on technical concerns. This can result in solutions that are technically appropriate yet do not represent a real accommodation of the more basic value differences.
>
> Finally, the greater the technical expertise of the mediator in the subject area, the more the agreement is likely to be a result of the mediator's "leading" the parties and the less committed the parties will be to the difficult task of implementing the agreement. (Cormick, 1982a:38)

The danger of expertise is that the mediator will—perhaps unknowingly—introduce bias into the process, thereby undermining the mediation effort.

The concept of neutrality does not require ignorance of technical matters, but in practice it is questionable whether technical expertise is ever neutral. Engineers, economists, and attorneys, to cite only a few examples, reflect the values and norms of their professions. For these reasons, the mediator's focus and expertise should relate to the process of mediation rather than to scientific or technical knowledge (Cormick, 1982a:16, 38).

Mutuality of Outcomes

To minimize opportunities for utilization of the mediation process for grandstanding or waging war through the media, and to even up the distribution of power between parties to a dispute, any settlement agreement must be mutually acceptable to all parties. This requirement for consensus decision making gives each party— even the weakest politically and financially—an effective veto over the content of any agreement, and over the process itself.

Often one of the procedural ground rules established at the outset is that there will be no minority or majority reports issued and no support from the parties for less than the entire package of compromises contained in any agreement reached. These provisions help shape expectations of participants in ways that provide incentives for honest efforts at negotiation and improve prospects for successful implementation by increasing the sense of commitment and ownership of participants for settlement agreements. Some participants may retain superior persuasive abilities in group situations due to personal skills, but will be unable to use superior financial or political resources to forge coalitions capable of completely freezing out concerns of weaker parties. Efforts to institutionalize environmental mediation should explicitly embrace a requirement for consensus decision making during formulation of settlement agreements.

Environmental Mediation is Different

The foregoing features of mediation describe a relationship between the mediator and disputing parties. Many of the practices applied in environmental mediation originated in labor-management relations, but there has been little theoretical development distinctively related to environmental issues. It is as yet a new, and therefore somewhat unsettled area of negotiation practice and scholarship.

Situational Characteristics

Although the essential definition of mediation may remain consistent whether applied in international diplomacy, labor-management relations, or environmental disputes, situational characteristics which influence its effectiveness vary substantially from one area to another (Cormick and Patton, 1980:77). Significant characteristics of environmental mediation include multipolarity, unequal power resources of participants, lack of agreement on areas of

disagreement, unmitigatable effects, discontinuous relationships between parties, and lack of an accepted framework for mediated
negotiations, all discussed below.

Multipolarity
In contrast with the familiar bilateral model of labor-
management negotiations, environmental disputes usually involve
multiple parties with different interests, varying status, power, negotiating experience, and sophistication (Baldwin, 1978:2; Cormick and
Patton, 1980:77). Multilateral negotiations can be expected to be
more complex and agreement more difficult to achieve than in
bilateral negotiations.

Unequal Power Resources
Helen Ingram has observed that "people who have more power
tend to be more willing to address trade-offs" (Lake, 1980:72), and
Laura Lake has noted a corresponding hesitancy on the part of small
ad hoc environmental groups to participate in negotiations (Lake,
1980:71). However, participation by ad hoc local groups is evident in
many case studies of environmental mediation (Talbot, 1983; Folk-
Williams, 1982), bolstered perhaps by promotion of such efforts by
the Conservation Foundation, and participation by organizations
such as the Sierra Club, National Audobon Society, National Wildlife
Federation, and the Wilderness Society ("Update," 1982:7). Douglas
Amy has argued that mediation often obscures inequalities in financial, organizational, and political resources of participants which
may enable more powerful groups to coopt inexperienced parties
(Amy, 1987).

This appears to be a variation on the familiar critique of interest
group competition as a means for making public decisions. Like Amy,
J. Walton Blackburn (1988) believes that differences between participants in skill at negotiating, and in the ability to understand and
assess technical information may put less sophisticated parties at a
substantial disadvantage in mediation. Blackburn favors litigation
over mediation, in part because parties to litigation can utilize the
expertise of experienced attorneys.

Neither Amy nor Blackburn explain why parties who would hire
experts if they did engage in litigation would not seek to redress the
presumed imbalance in expertise in mediation efforts by retaining
attorneys or consultants experienced in negotiation or relevant
technical matters. An appropriate mechanism for funding expenses
of intervenors might be part of a preliminary negotiated protocol for
the mediation effort, or established by statute along lines commonly

used today in many states to fund intervenors in rate cases before state public utility commissions.

Mediation requires a relative balance of power between parties. A mediator may enhance the power of weaker parties by conveying legitimacy to their concerns through the act of intervention (Cormick, 1982b:6), but unless the parties have some ability to exercise sanctions or inflict unacceptable costs on one another, it is not likely all will negotiate in good faith (Cormick and Patton, 1980:81). The threat of increased costs due to stalemate, opposition in administrative proceedings, litigation, or an initiative campaign are therefore important sources of power for project opponents. Use of consensus decisionmaking in formulating settlement agreements was discussed above as a tool to help even-up the distribution of power between parties. Participation in mediated negotiations by government officials charged with searching for the public interest, and subsequent scrutiny of settlement agreements by them in regulatory proceedings help mitigate inequalities in the distribution of power between participants in mediation.

Disagreement on Areas of Disagreement

In environmental disputes, there is often little agreement on areas of disagreement, selection, or definition of issues requiring negotiation (Baldwin, 1978:2–3). Definition and clarification of non-negotiable and negotiable issues are often major initial tasks requiring a skilled mediator.

The mediator may function as an educator and interpreter by explaining implications of technical and legal matters to ensure understanding by all parties of their own positions and the concerns of others (Susskind, 1981:23, 29; Stulberg, 1981:92). This may involve translation of technical information into language understandable to the lay public (Stulberg, 1981:92–93), and assistance to inexperienced negotiators (with the concurrence of other parties) in formulating proposals (Cormick, 1982b). It may also involve explaining and interpreting settlement agreements to the community at large (Susskind, 1981:18).

Unmitigatable Effects

Because some environmental effects of large-scale developments are irreversible, they are not as susceptible to mitigation through repeated negotiations to correct deficiencies in earlier agreements, as are labor-management contracts (Cormick and Patton, 1980:77; Baldwin, 1978:2–3). The information and foresight required to anticipate consequences and specify mitigation measures is therefore greater in environmental mediation than in labor-management relations.

Discontinuous Relationships
Because there is generally no prior relationship between many of the parties, and no expectation of a future relationship (as there is in labor-management relations), there is often no perception of a common purpose or shared objectives, no perceived need to cooperate, and little willingness to negotiate environmental disputes (Baldwin, 1978:2–3). Convincing potential participations that negotiation is desirable may be a difficult initial task requiring executive leadership, in addition to stalemate.

Lack of Accepted Framework
Unlike labor-management bargaining, there is no established framework for negotiation of most environmental disputes in legislation or tradition. Consequently, a context and framework for environmental mediation must be created as an integral part of each dispute settlement effort (Cormick and Patton, 1980:77). This allows considerable procedural flexibility to mediators in structuring a context for negotiations (McCrory, 1981:55–56), but does little to shape expectations of other participants.

Similarly, because there is neither a previous nor expected future relationship between participants, and because there is no single institutional framework for implementation of agreements, a process for joint implementation and monitoring must be specified during negotiations and incorporated into the settlement agreement (Cormick and Patton, 1980:78). This has resulted in establishment of joint committees (Mernitz, 1980:77) to monitor and resolve unanticipated difficulties which may arise during implementation of agreements, and innovations in the use of contracts, permits, and court orders as vehicles of implementation (Cormick, 1984:20).

The need for ratification of settlement agreements by government officials (Lake, 1980:61–62) may make their implementation more difficult and uncertain than that of labor-management contracts (Baldwin, 1978:3). Bureaucratic rigidity, standard operating procedures, and the institutional imperative of survival may inhibit participation in unconventional decision making processes by regulatory officials concerning environmental controversies (O'Conner, 1980:250; Susskind and Weinstein, 1980:350–354). Thus, clear statements of support for mediation efforts by agency heads or chief executives are needed to encourage participation by public officials in negotiated settlements (Cormick, 1982a:38).

These situational characteristics strongly suggest a need for institutionalization of environmental mediation in a manner which does not impair the neutrality of the mediator or unduly reduce flexibility in design of mediation efforts, yet provides a framework for participation of all affected parties.

Participation in Mediation Negotiations

Mediation theory presumes interests are organized and articulate. But as a practical matter, the mediator and parties to a dispute share a responsibility of ensuring that any settlement agreement represents "a workable solution—one that is politically, physically, and financially feasible" (Cormick and Patton, 1980:78). This implies that all identifiable interests capable of rendering an agreement unworkable must be represented during negotiations, if a settlement agreement is to have a realistic chance of being implemented. It also suggests the parties must consider potential impacts of the settlement agreement on foreseeable concerns of unrepresented interests, if they wish implementation to be successful.

Number of Participants

Theoretically any number of persons can participate in negotiations, and some writers have suggested it is better to include too many than too few (Susskind and Weinstein, 1980:337). However, Lake argues that a large number of participants "should be avoided because of the greater difficulty in reaching consensus" (Lake, 1980:68). It seems clear that direct participation by every individual with an interest in negotiations over large-scale development projects would be impractical, so specification of criteria for selection of representative negotiators is a significant practical issue.

Selecting Participants

A variety of methods have been used to select representative negotiators. They share a common principle of "keeping the number of face-to-face participants small while maintaining a balance among competing interest groups" (Lake, 1980:68). Lake looks to administrative law for selection criteria:

> Participants must be "responsible" and "representative spokesmen" and should not be involved if their interests are already represented. . . . (Lake, 1980:65)

This shifts the focus of representation from group *affiliations* to categories of *interests* of participants in negotiations. This focus is consistent with the body of negotiation theory which sees an emphasis on the underlying interests of parties as a means to encourage discovery of mutual gains, or non-zero-sum settlements (Fisher and Ury, 1981). Categories of interests which might be represented include developers, local persons concerned about socioeconomic impacts, others concerned with environmental impacts, or consumers of commodities or services to be produced.

While mediators have often selected representatives, this may undermine their neutrality. Lake maintains negotiators should be selected by those they will represent in the future (Lake, 1980:68). Negotiators will need to validate the support of those they represent periodically so as to avoid "getting too far out in front," or leading constituents to compromises they will later repudiate.

Government Participants

Public officials are often reluctant to participate directly in mediation efforts, yet their commitment to implement settlement agreements is usually essential (Cormick and Patton, 1980:80, 88). Difficulties during implementation of settlement agreements have been found to be much more likely when an agency which is a project proponent does not participate in mediation efforts (Bingham, 1986: 103).

Susskind and Weinstein maintain that direct involvement of federal and state regulatory agencies in the bargaining process would make successful implementation of settlement agreements more likely because agencies: (1) often control the means of implementation; (2) can assist in identification of all affected parties and assure their participation; (3) can introduce an element of cyclical bargaining over time; and (4) "can add to the bargaining process a party whose mandate is to serve the general public interest rather than a particular interest group" (1980:350–351). Participation of public officials in negotiations may protect them from the possibility an agreement might be reached which is not legally or financially possible for them to implement (Cormick and Patton, 1980:94). Mediation is authorized by statute for annexation disputes in Virginia (Richman, 1983) in bilateral negotiations involving public officials.

Accountability

Lack of an established institutional framework for environmental mediation efforts and implementation of settlement agreements raises questions concerning who should be accountable for integrity of the process and content of agreements reached. Who looks out for the public interest in environmental mediation efforts?

Susskind advanced a controversial answer to this question, arguing the mediator should be legally liable for the fairness of both the mediation process and output.

> Environmental mediators ought to be concerned about: (1) the impacts of negotiated agreements on underrepresented or unrepresentable groups in the community; (2) the possibility that joint net gains have not been maximized; (3) the long-term spillover effects of the settlements they help to reach, and (4) the precedents that they set and the precedents upon which agreements are based. . . .
>
> An environmental mediator should be committed to procedural fairness—all parties should have an opportunity to be represented by individuals with the technical sophistication to bargain effectively on their behalf. Environmental mediators should also be concerned that the agreements they help to reach are just and stable (Susskind, 1981:46–47).

Susskind maintained mediation should be institutionalized by attaching mediators to government agencies or courts, so they might be effectively chastized, sued, or fired for failing to live up to the above standards (Susskind, 1981:4, 43, 47). Others have asserted that mediators bear much of the responsibility for protecting interests of weaker or unrepresented parties, as well as the public interest (Blackburn, 1988:568).

Such proposals would undermine the conceptual basis for mediation by substituting a presumably near-omniscient public advocate for the impartial third-party intervener. A requirement that the mediator be responsible to ensure maximization of joint net gains would impose a standard of Pareto optimality on the negotiated settlement, implying a necessity for comprehensive information gathering and processing abilities. This would be more akin to asking a philosopher king to solve problems, than asking a mediator to assist parties in settling their disputes (Stulberg, 1981:114–115).

Each modification of the mediator's role proposed by Susskind undercuts the mediator's neutrality. Requiring a mediator to assume responsibility for protecting the public interest converts mediation to arbitration (Stulberg, 1981:107–112). This would also undercut voluntariness of negotiations, as weak or distrustful parties would have less hope of influencing outcomes (McCrory, 1981:80–81). It would undermine mutuality of outcomes, lessening commitment of the parties to implementation. The possibility of litigation alleging procedural unfairness would encourage mediators to emphasize form over substance, severely curtailing flexibility of mediation efforts, and might discourage many individuals from serving as mediators (McCrory, 1981:81–83).

Alternatives

Alternative measures may serve as checks on fairness of environmental mediation efforts, without drastically altering the role of mediator. The personal ethics of mediators, when based on a principle of self-determination for all parties to a dispute, are a powerful check on their behavior (Cormick, 1982b). Similar arguments have been persuasively applied to public officials in general (Friedrich, 1940; Armstrong and Graham, 1975:6).

The requirement for a workable agreement implies it is necessary to secure participation of all identifiable interests in mediated negotiations—and the reputations of mediators will rest largely on their success in mediating settlements which are successfully implemented. Therefore, it is likely mediators will, for purely practical reasons, press parties to consider the legality and acceptability of their proposals to the community before reaching a settlement agreement.

Participation in mediation efforts by public officials whose responsibility it is to advance the public interest is more appropriate than attempting to hold the mediator accountable for the content of settlement agreements. Mediation is not a substitute for regulatory proceedings, which provide opportunities for public scrutiny of settlement agreements before they are incorporated into permit requirements.

Ultimately, it must be the parties to a dispute, not the mediator, who are responsible for the content of a settlement agreement. Accountability is enchanced when public officials are participants in mediated negotiations, must be relied upon to incorporate settlement agreements into required permits, or must implement the terms of such agreements.

Requirements for Institutionalization

If mediation is a potentially useful process for settling some but not all environmental controversies, and if—as the foregoing discussion suggests—there is a need to establish an institutional framework for its use, what are the fundamental requirements for public policy?

Proposals for institutionalization of environmental mediation, if they are to produce effective and equitable settlement agreements, must contain the following seven elements:

1. *Full disclosure of development proposals before regulatory proceedings begin.* This will allow time for interested parties to organize, develop the issues and represent their interests.
2. *Conflict stalemate.* Intervention before stalemate occurs may inhibit development of sufficient power by weaker parties to ensure true mutuality of outcomes (Cormick, 1982b:5), or may foster premature settlement of disputes before some affected groups have organized to represent their interests. Stalemate may occur either during or before regulatory proceedings begin.
3. *Mediation assessment.* Stalemate provides a recognizable trigger for any affected party to request an assessment of the dispute by an independent consultant to ascertain whether mediation may be appropriate. Such assessments require the judgement of an experienced mediator, usually after interviews with interested parties (Cormick, 1984; Bellman, Sampson and Cormick, 1982). Environmental disputes are not frequent enough to warrant hiring permanent full-time staff with this expertise. Assessment should be related to the first regulatory proceeding for a disputed development, but may be made available later for late developing disputes.
4. *Impartial intervention.* If a dispute is ripe for mediation, intervention by an independent mediator may be requested by any affected party, with selection of the individual subject to agreement by all interested parties. Provision should be made for payment of compensation to the mediator for services rendered and expenses on a contract basis directly from the state treasurer, regardless of outcome. The mediator should not be affiliated with any interested party, including participating government offices, and should be subject to dismissal by any party. Confidentiality of communications with the mediator concerning the substance of negotiations should be protected by statute.
5. *Self-determination.* Interested parties must be allowed to select their own negotiators and participate voluntarily in negotiations. Representation should be provided on the basis of interest rather than group affiliation, with the total number of participants reflecting diversity of interests. This may require legislation authorizing interagency coordination sufficient to support

a "lead agency" negotiator for each jurisdiction of government participating (e.g., federal, state, local) and exceptions from open meetings laws.

6. *Consensus decision-making.* Settlement agreements must be the product of consensus decision making on an all-or-nothing package of negotiated provisions. Mediation efforts must be terminated on withdrawal of any of the parties or the mediator.

7. *Preservation of conventional remedies.* Legal rights of all parties to intervene in administrative or court proceedings or initiate election campaigns must be preserved in the event negotiations fail or settlement agreements must be enforced. Legal rights of groups not party to negotiations must also be preserved.

Incorporation of these seven elements in policy to institutionalize environmental mediation in state permitting processes for controversial industrial facilities would preserve neutrality of the mediator and establish a framework for participation of all interested parties, including government officials. This would make mediation available on a contingency basis, and might be accomplished through either executive or legislative initiative. Mediation services have been available for several years on an as-needed basis through the Colorado Joint Review Process, which was established by executive action prior to its legislative authorization (Mcrnitz, 1980).

Policy Implications

Institutionalization of environmental mediation on a contingency basis will do much to legitimize the practice and establish an enduring framework for negotiation of environmental disputes. Reduction of the aura of *"ad hocracy"* currently associated with environmental mediation, and establishment of ground rules for parties, including public officials, will help eliminate confusion about roles of participants, and constructively shape expectations about the likelihood of successful implementation of settlement agreements.

Negotiation and bargaining are the preferred forms of dispute handling for most people and organizations because they keep disputing parties in control of the conflict and the terms of its settlement (Christie, 1977). Institutionalization of environmental mediation will allow some conflicts to be channeled into a forum where disputants can maintain control over events, perhaps breaking a stalemate or resolving a no-win political dilemma while avoiding the uncertainty of an all-or-nothing litigated outcome. Rates of compliance and satisfaction are high among participants in mediated civil cases which originate in small claims courts (McEwen and Maiman, 1984). Rates of successful implementation in environmental mediation also appear to be quite high (Bingham, 1986:77), suggesting some social change is possible using this mechanism for conflict management.

Successful mediation efforts may produce settlement agreements which are helpful in resolving regulatory issues during permitting proceedings for major resource development projects. Developing the information necessary to negotiate such agreements may increase organizational costs at an earlier time in the planning process for such projects.

Environmental mediation has often been touted as faster and cheaper than litigation. It is possible, but seems unlikely this would often be the case. The multiplicity of interests and complexity of issues involved in many environmental disputes tends to make mediation difficult and time consuming. Benefits of successful mediation are more likely to be substantive than financial in nature.

Mediation cannot resolve non-negotiable issues and is unlikely to resolve fundamental value differences between contending interests, even if a dispute is settled. Institutionalizing environmental mediation will not end the inequities of interest group competition. It may provide opportunities for interests with unequal political and financial resources to meet on a somewhat more level playing field, knowing that the results of their negotiations will be subject to implementation by persons charged with seeking the public interest, and subject to public scrutiny.

Any policy can be implemented poorly. This fact accentuates the need for conceptual clarity in design of institutions and procedures for environmental mediation, and for recognition of its limitations.

Conclusion

This chapter has reviewed the prospects and conditions necessary for institutionalizing environmental mediation in regulatory processes for controversial public facilities. Environmental mediation is found similar in important respects to mediation of labor-management disputes, but different in its pronounced complexity, uncertainty, and lack of established relationships to support negotiations.

Environmental mediation must be distinguished from techniques of citizen participation, and policy makers must be cognizant of the requirements for successful institutionalization. Far from a panacea for environmental disputes, mediation may be an appropriate ancillary activity to, but is not a proper substitute for either litigation or regulatory proceedings.

REFERENCES

Adler v. Adams. 1979. Case No. 673–73C2. U.S. District Court, Western District of Washington. Filed 3 May.

Alinsky, Saul. 1971. *Rules for Radicals.* New York: Random House.

Amy, Douglas J. 1987. *The Politics of Environmental Mediation.* New York: Columbia University Press.

Armstrong, Dewitt C., and George A. Graham. 1975. "Ethical Preparation for the Public Service." *The Bureaucrat* 4:6–13.

Baldwin, Pamela. 1978. *Environmental Mediation an Effective Alternative.* Palo Alto, CA: RESOLVE, Center for Environmental Conflict Resolution.

Bellman, Howard S., Carl Bingham, Ronnie Brooks, Susan Carpenter, Peter Clark, and Roger Craig. 1981. "Environmental Conflict Resolution: Practitioners' Perspective on an Emerging Field." *Environmental Consensus* (now called *RESOLVE*), (Winter):1–7.

Bellman, Howard S., Cynthia Sampson, and Gerald Cormick. 1982. *Using Mediation When Siting Hazardous Waste Facilities—A Handbook.* Washington, DC: U.S. Environmental Protection Agency.

Bingham, Gail. 1986. *Resolving Environmental Disputes.* Washington, D.C.: Conservation Foundation.

Blackburn, J. Walton. 1988. "Environmental Mediation as an Alternative to Litigation." *Policy Studies Journal* 16(Spring):562–574.

"Calm After the Storm: Grandmother of Environmental Lawsuits Settled by Mediation." 1981. *Environmental Law Reporter* 11:10074–10075.

Carpenter, Susan. 1982. "Environmental Conflict Management Practitioners' Workshop." *Environmental Impact Assessment Review* 3:387–396.

Christie, Nils. 1977. "Conflicts as Property." *British Journal of Criminology* 17:1–21.

Cormick, Gerald W. 1980. "The Theory and Practice of Environmental Mediation." *Environmental Professional* 1:24–33.

————. 1982a. "The Myth, the Reality, and the Future of Environmental Mediation." *Environment* 24(September):15–39.

————. 1982b. "Intervention and Self-Determination in Environmental Disputes: A Mediator's Perspective." *RESOLVE* (Winter):1–7.

————. 1984. "How and When to Mediate Natural Resource Disputes." Paper presented at the Institute on Resolution and Avoidance of Disputes of the Rocky Mountain Mineral Law Foundation, Denver, CO, March 23.

Cormick, Gerald W., and Leota K. Patton. 1980. "Environmental Mediation: Defining the Process through Experience." In Laura M. Lake (ed.), *Environmental Mediation: the Search for Consensus.* Boulder, CO: Westview.

Coser, Lewis. 1956. *The Functions of Social Conflict*. Glencoe, IL: Free Press.

Fisher, Roger, and William Ury. 1981. *Getting to Yes: Negotiating Agreement Without Giving In*. Boston, MA: Houghton Mifflin.

Folk-Williams, John. 1982. "Negotiation Becomes More Important in Settling Indian Water Rights Disputes in the West." *RESOLVE* (Summer):1.

Friederick, Carl J. 1940. "Public Policy and the Nature of Administrative Responsibility." *Public Policy* 1:3–24.

Gusman, Sam, and Verne Huser. 1984. "Mediation in the Estuary." *Coastal Zone Management Journal* 11:273–295.

Lake, Laura M. 1980. *Environmental Mediation: The Search for Consensus*. Boulder, CO: Westview.

Lee, Kai N. 1982. "Defining Success in Environmental Dispute Resolution." *RESOLVE* (Spring):1–6.

Lentz, Sydney S. 1986. "The Labor Model for Mediation and Its Application to the Resolution of Environmental Disputes." *Journal of Applied Behavioral Science* 22:127–139.

Liepmann, Karen L. 1986. "Confidentiality in Environmental Mediation: Should Third Parties Have Access to the Process?" *Boston College Environmental Affairs Law Review* 14:93–129.

Lipsky, Michael. 1968. "Protest as a Political Resource." *American Political Science Review* 62:1144–1158.

McCrory, John P. 1981. "Environmental Mediation—Another Piece for the Puzzle." *Vermont Law Review* 6:49–84.

McEwen, Craig, and Richard J. Maiman. 1984. "Mediation in Small Claims Court: Achieving Compliance Through Consent." *Law and Society Review* 18:11–49.

Mernitz, Scott. 1980. *Mediation of Environmental Disputes: A Sourcebook*. New York: Praeger.

O'Conner, David. 1980. "Environmental Mediation: The State of the Art." In Frank Schnidman and Jane Silverman (eds), *Management and Control of Growth*, vol. 5, pp. 245–251. Washington, DC: Urban Land Institute.

Raiffa, Howard. 1982. *The Art and Science of Negotiation*. Cambridge, MA: Harvard University Press.

Richman, Roger. 1983. "Structuring Interjurisdictional Negotiation: Virginia's Use of Mediation in Annexation Disputes." *RESOLVE* (Summer):1–6.

Rivkin, Malcolm D. 1977. *Negotiated Development: A Breakthrough in Environmental Controversies*. Washington, DC: Conservation Foundation.

Simkin, William E. 1971. *Mediation and the Dynamics of Collective Bargaining*. Washington, DC: Bureau of National Affairs.

Stewart, Richard B. 1975. "The Reformation of American Administrative Law." *Harvard Law Review* 88:1667–1774.

Strauss, Donald B. 1980. "Mediating Environmental, Energy, and Economic Tradeoffs: A Research for Improved Tools for Coastal Zone Planning."

In Laura M. Lake (ed.), *Environmental Mediation: The Search for Consensus;* Boulder, CO: Westview.

Stulberg, Joseph B. 1981. "The Theory and Practice of Mediation: A Reply to Professor Susskind." *Vermont Law Review* 6:85–117.

Susskind, Lawrence. 1981. "Environmental Mediation and the Accountability Problem." *Vermont Law Review* 6:1–47.

Susskind, Lawrence, and Alan Weinstein. 1980. "Towards a Theory of Environmental Dispute Resolution." *Environmental Affairs* 9:311–357.

Talbott, Allan R. 1983. *Settling Things: Six Case Studies in Environmental Mediation.* Washington, DC: Conservation Foundation.

"Update." 1982. *RESOLVE* (Spring):7.

Watson, John L., and Luke J. Danielson. 1983. "Environmental Mediation." *Natural Resources Lawyer* 15:687–723.

CHAPTER TEN

RESOLVING ENVIRONMENTAL CONFLICTS: NEOCORPORATISM, NEGOTIATED RULE-MAKING, AND THE TIMBER/FISH/WILDLIFE COALITION IN THE STATE OF WASHINGTON

Greg J. Protasel

THE RISE of the environment as a public policy issue in the late 1960s and 1970s helped usher in an era of social regulation (Wenner, 1976). Unlike traditional economic regulation which sought to promote efficient market activity, the new social regulation focused on health, safety, and environmental concerns (Fritschler, 1984; Reagan, 1987). One of the most obvious differences between economic and social regulation has been the high level of adversarial conflict in the social regulatory area. Environmental protection, in particular, has been a very conflict-prone area (Congressional Quarterly, 1983).

Although many sources of conflict in environmental regulation have been identified, one source is especially salient—the proliferation of rules by administrative agencies (Bryner, 1987). Through a quasi-legislative rulemaking process regulatory agencies make rules which fill in the gaps in necessarily nondetailed laws. However, final regulations are frequently challenged in court and the level of confrontational litigation in environmental protection affairs is extremely high (Benveniste, 1981).

This chapter explores negotiated rule-making as an approach to environmental protection which is intended to reduce the levels of adversarial conflict surrounding environmental regulations (Harter, 1981:1–118; Susskind and McMahon, 1985:133–165). The first part focuses on policy theory. The distinguishing characteristics of negotiated rule-making as a form of neocorporatism are set forth and contrasted with administrative rule-making as a pluralist mode of policy-making. The ethical dilemma public managers face in choosing between these two different approaches to environmental protection is discussed.

The second part of the chapter evaluates the experience of the state of Washington in using regulatory negotiation to resolve forest policy conflicts. The successful efforts of the Timber/Fish/Wildlife coalition in regulating forest practices without the usual interest-group battles are studied with an eye toward extending the lessons learned to other regulatory situations (Protasel, 1987).

Resolving Environmental Conflicts: Policy Theory

The use of government regulations to protect the environment has generated much conflict—especially in the courts. One of the main ethical dilemmas which the public regulator faces in attempting to resolve the regulatory conflicts involved in environmental protection is how to respond to technical expertise and public participation. Should the public regulator defer to technical expertise and limit citizen participation or vice versa? Discussion of this tradeoff can be found in Shapiro, 1982:18–25; Sunstein, 1984:177-213. The two major regulatory approaches available for protecting the environment—administrative rule-making and negotiated rule-making—offer contrasting solutions to the dilemma of dealing with technical expertise and public participation. As will be explained below, administrative rule-making gives more emphasis to technical expertise and is an adjunct to the pluralist mode of collective decision-making. In contrast, negotiated rule-making places more stress on public participation and has emerged as a form of neo-corporatism.

To assist in resolving the ethical dilemma of making a trade-off between technical expertise and public participation, the different conceptions of rationality which underlie the two regulatory strategies are explored. Traditional administrative rule-making is shown to be a form of instrumental rationality appropriate for solving relatively simple problems that can be readily disaggregated or decomposed for analysis and which involves unambiguous uncontroversial goals (Weber, 1968; Habermas, 1970). In contrast, negotiated rule-making is based on a form of communicative rationality which is well-suited for handling complex, nondecomposable problems that are dynamic and controversial (Denhardt and Denhardt, 1979:107–120; Drysek, 1987:656–679). In view of the different problem-solving capacities of administrative rule-making and negotiated rule-making, the choice of a trade-off between technical expertise and public participation is made easier.

The following *methodological proposition* is proposed to help resolve the dilemma of how much weight to give technical expertise and public participation in environmental protection regulation: Environmental exploitation is best prevented through negotiated rule-making since environmental protection involves complex ecological problems and controversial social issues which are most successfully dealt with by communicative rationality. Thus, the declarative logic of problem-solving offers some assistance to the public regulator. The use of declarative logic to formulate imperative statements is illustrated in Simon (1981). Public participation *should* be emphasized in environmental protection rule-making since negotiated rule-making *is* the best approach for handling complex ecological and controversial environmental issues.

Administrative Rule-Making: The Pluralist-Technocratic Approach

Regulatory policy-making has been most frequently described as a process of coalition building that takes place in the legislative arena (Lowi, 1964:675–715; Lowi, 1972:298–310). It is in the legislative bodies where pluralistic interests contend with one another to eventually forge a winning coalition which enacts regulatory policy. Administrative rulemaking is but an extension of this pluralist coalition-building process. The details of general laws are specified through a quasi-legislative process which further refines the winning coalition's policy decisions by enacting rules which have the full force of law.

The delegation of legislative power to executive agencies has become a much decried fact of modern American political life (Lowi, 1979). To talk about the regulatory arena conjures up images of iron triangles and organizational capture—a crisis of liberal polyarchy. Evidence suggests though that the regulatory arena may be much more pluralistic than previously thought, especially in the area of environmental protection. The administrative rule-making process has been greatly democratized through informal notice and comment procedures which allow citizen participation to ensure due process. This is especially true in the area of environmental and safety regulation (Verkuil, 1984). At these public hearings groups are given the opportunity to comment and rebut the evidence submitted by other groups regarding proposed substantive rules and regulations. Through citizen participation a wide range of views are considered on determining the rules.

The democratization of administrative rule-making, however, has been criticized for being too responsive to the public (Shapiro, 1987). Public involvement in the technocratic arena of administrative rule-making, after all, clashes with the pluralist principle of majority rule which governs the legislature (Pops and Stephenson, 1987:28). The notion is that the losers in the legislature ought not to be allowed in the administrative arena to design instrumental means to achieve policy ends. The expectation is that minority losers can most properly assert their legitimate interests in court.

From this pluralist perspective, public participation in administrative rule-making not only erodes majority rule and legislative sovereignty, but makes for bad regulation (Sunstein, 1984). By relying upon citizen access rather than on techniques of formal analysis to guide rule-making, the substantive elements are pushed into the background. Furthermore, the emphasis on public participation plays into the hands of those groups who would challenge the collective decisions made by winning legislative coalitions in court (Benveniste, 1981; Reich, 1981:82–91). When group access rather than the technical expertise of administrative agencies is the paramount concern, it becomes much easier to use the courts to block the implementation of regulatory policy.

The pluralist-technocratic solution to courtroom controversies which have surrounded environmental protection regulation is, of course, to limit citizen participation in administrative rule-making and to defer to agency experts. The notion is that if the courts would just stop second guessing the technical experts in terms of the adequacy of due process, the number of lawsuits would be dramatically reduced. It is also argued that while adversarial courtroom proceedings are appropriate for settling disputes over traditional economic regulation of marketplace activity, the same adversarial tactics are ill-suited for the newer type of social regulation which seeks to protect the public from harm by focusing on health, safety, and environmental concerns. The belief is that the complex technological matters encountered in social regulation are best left to be resolved by the experts.

The technocratic approach to administrative rulemaking is an instrumental approach to problem-solving. Through the pursuit of objective scientific knowledge and the use of techniques of formal analysis, means are devised and selected to achieve specific ends. Found throughout the hard sciences, social sciences, and policy sciences, instrumental rationality is modernity's dominant conception of rationality. But, before heralding instrumental rationality as the preferred solution to problems of social regulation, the limits to instrumental reasoning must be explored.

It has been demonstrated that instrumental rationality works best when applied to static problems with simple goals. For a good discussion of the limits of analytic techniques in the public sector, see Kraemer and Perry (1983:256–279). Static problems are relatively insulated from their environment and can be readily isolated for technical analysis especially if there is a single, clear objective. But, unless problems are near-decomposable, most analytic techniques cannot be applied. Instrumental rationality can rarely deal adequately with dynamic problems with complex goals.

Since the ecological problems which arise in environmental protection are complex and dynamic, it is unlikely that they are very amenable to instrumental problem solving. What then is a viable alternative to technocracy? This question is explored next as negotiated rule-making is examined as an approach to environmental protection regulation.

Negotiated Rule-Making: The Neocorporatist-Bargaining Approach

The search for a nontechnocratic approach to environmental regulation begins by re-addressing the question, "Does democratization of administrative rule-making produce bad regulation?" Evaluated by the standards of pluralist democracy, the answer is yes. As was pointed out above, democratization of administrative rule-making clashes with principles of pluralist democracy. According to the pluralist model, individuals act as citizens by voting. They do not participate directly in government, but have access to government through interest groups. The groups supposedly aggregate individual interests and articulate them to legislative policymakers who by majority vote pass laws which citizens are obliged to conform to. The pluralist model is described in Truman (1951). Participative administration challenges the concepts of citizenship, legislative sovereignty, and majority rule upon which pluralism is based.

While democratization of administrative rule-making diverges from pluralist principles, another political arrangement has recently emerged in some democratic governments which is compatible with such participative administration. Neocorporatism is a political arrangement which intermediates between interest associations and authoritative decision-makers by organizing and incorporating partial interests into policy-making (Schmitter, 1977:7–38; Lehmbruch, 1979:53–62; Lehmruch and Scmitter, 1982; and Schmitter, 1983: 885–928). Neocorporatism departs from the pluralist standards of legislative sovereignty and majority rule which are the basis for discrediting public participation in technocratic rule-making. Instead, neocorporatism promotes consensual bargaining among co-equal minorities which generates binding policy commitments. The deals worked out by the various incorporated interests are then either routinely legitimized by the legislature or never subject to legislative approval.

Negotiated rule-making is an alternative mode of collective decision-making which is being used in the United States on an experimental basis to develop and implement regulatory programs (Murray, 1978; Sullivan, 1984). Although it has only been used to settle disputes within well-defined policy areas, negotiated rule-making is a nascent form of neocorporatism which might well be extended across many policy areas. During the prenegotiation phase of the negotiated rule-making process, the regulatory agency appoints a neutral third party to convene a meeting of those affected by a particular regulatory controversy. The convening of responsible representatives of the affected parties to the negotiating table is a neocorporatist practice. Rather than simply respond to pluralist pressure politics during informal comment procedures at public hearings, a more formalized neocorporatist forum is created which guarantees more parity in representation.

During the actual negotiation phase, a facilitator—also appointed by the regulatory agency—attempts to move the participants toward consensus. The adversarial win-lose bargaining which typically dominates the pluralist regulatory arena is replaced by nonadversarial win-win bargaining in a neocorporatist decision-making forum. The facilitator develops a timetable and agenda and over the course of several working meetings helps the affected parties confront their different interests. Through neocorporatist interest-based negotiation (as opposed to pluralist position-based negotiation), preliminary draft proposals are developed. For a classic statement of the differences between position-based and interest-based negotiation, see Fisher and Ury (1983). This may be one reason why neocorporatist polities are demonstrably more governable ones. Neocorporatists' collective decisions emerge from consensus, whereas pluralist policies are forged by battles to form winning coalitions. The negotiation phase ends when consensus is achieved. During the postnegotiation phase, the facilitator helps the negotiating parties sell the draft agreement to their constituencies. Once constituency support is won, the agreement is formally signed by the participating parties and takes effect with the full force of the law. This illustrates how neocorporatism not only alters the relative resources of interest groups and the nature of policy-making. Neocorporatism changes the relationship between interest groups and their members as well. In the pluralist mode, interest groups aggregate individual interests and articulate them before policymakers. But, in the neocorporatist mode, interest groups are more than a conduit for citizen preferences. They are committed to delivering the troops—that is, securing member compliance with negotiated decisions.

In this context, it is interesting to speculate that the proliferation of single-purpose organizations concerned with environmental and resource policy is a factor which has contributed to the growth of negotiated rule-making as an approach for resolving environmental conflicts. The consensual nature of bargaining with privileged minorities in a neocorporatist forum has allowed single-purpose groups which are normally intransigent in a pluralist forum to hammer out deals. Furthermore, the central focus and homogeneous clientele of the single-purpose groups ensures that their leaders can mobilize support for the commitments made during regulatory negotiations. In short, instead of generating conflict and creating compliance problems in a pluralist-technocratic arena, single-purpose group activity facilitates agreement and governability in a neocorporatist-bargaining arena.

Having pointed out that negotiated rule-making is compatible with democracy is likely to attract the suspicions of those opposed to neocorporatist practices. The term "corporatist" is often used as an epithet directed against those who would threaten freedom and democracy. Undoubtedly neocorporatism does change the character of democracy. The image of public policy as the outcome of contests between interest groups which have arisen naturally in civil society, is replaced by the vision of public policy codetermined by interest groups which have been incorporated by the state. Leaving the neocorporatist solution to interest group conflict aside for a moment though, it is possible to make a case for negotiated rule-making as a viable alternative to traditional administrative rule-making by analyzing its problem-solving capabilities.

Negotiated rule-making operates in a world of social interaction and encourages reflective understanding by the relevant parties who codetermine the content of social consensus. Negotiated rule-making is thus rooted in a conception of communicative rationality which encourages intersubjective discourse and policy dialogue

(Dryzek, 1987:668–670). The potential of communicative rationality to contribute to the resolution of complex, dynamic, and controversial environment problems can be recognized as a positive feature of negotiated rule-making. This is reason enough for endorsing negotiated rulemaking as an approach to environmental regulation.

To choose negotiated rule-making over traditional administrative rulemaking as a form of environmental regulation implies following a social interaction rather than a technocratic problem-solving strategy. Social interaction invites participation in the public sphere and creates a consensus about mutual expectations. Through the creation of shared images of the future, regulatory conflicts are avoided. Just how negotiated rule-making incorporates public participation to build a consensus about complex environmental policies and regulatory decisions is examined in the next section. The recent experience of the Timber/Fish/Wildlife coalition in the state of Washington with negotiated rule-making is evaluated.

Resolving Forest Policy Conflicts: Evaluating the T/F/W Experience

In July 1986, a coalition of groups was formed in the state of Washington which reached agreement in December 1986 on how to manage forest practices. What made the coalition remarkable was that it was a cooperative effort by former battle-weary adversaries. After more than sixty work sessions, representatives from the timber industry, environmental groups, Indian tribes, and government agencies were successful in negotiating a Timber/Fish/Wildlife (T/F/W) agreement designed to regulate forest practices on private land. This consensual negotiated rule-making process was in marked contrast to the conflict-laden scramble to regulate which accompanied the passage of the Washington Forest Practices Act of 1974 (Northwest Renewable Resources Center, 1987:1–2).

The state board charged with regulatory policy-making under the Washington Forest Practices Act of 1974—the Forest Practices Board—formally accepted the T/F/W agreement in February 1987 (Northwest Renewable Resources Center, 1987). Rules and regulations reflecting the T/F/W agreement were then developed by the state Department of Natural Resources (DNR) and reviewed by the public during the summer of 1987 (Washington State Forest Practices Board, 1987). The final rules and regulations for the T/F/W agreement were published in October 1987 (Washington State Forest Practices Board, 1987). The Forest Practices Board, in one of its shortest meetings ever, formally adopted the rules and regulations on November 2, 1987. The changes to the Forest Practices Act were then unanimously approved by both houses of the Washington state legislature without a single word being altered. The T/F/W agreement went into effect on January 1, 1988.

In this section, the T/F/W process is analyzed as an innovative approach to regulatory policy-making. What began as a conflictual process of administrative rule-making was replaced in July 1986 by a consensual process of negotiated rule-making. Just a few months later, in December 1986, the T/F/W coalition reached agreement on a new framework for managing forest resources. The shift from administrative to negotiated rule-making is examined below.

The Traditional Technocratic Approach: Administrative Rule-Making

The Washington Forest Practices Act of 1974 created a new state agency—the Forest Practices Board (FPB)—to promulgate regulations that would establish minimum standards for forest practices (Protasel, 1980). Six of eleven members of the FPB are members of the general public appointed by the governor. The governor also appoints an elected member of a county legislative authority. All appointed members serve staggered four-year terms. The remaining four members are heads of state agencies (the Commissioner of Public Lands, the Director of the Department of Commerce and Economic Development, the Director of the Department of Agriculture, the Director of the Department of Ecology). The Commissioner of Public Lands serves as chairman of the FPB.

To assist in administrative rulemaking, the Forest Practices Act established an eleven-member Forest Practices Advisory Committee (FPAC) appointed by the governor. The FPAC must consist of representatives from: the College of Forest Resources of the University of Washington; the Department of Forestry and Range Management of the College of Agriculture of Washington State University; the Washington Soil and Water Conservation districts; the Department of Fisheries; the Department of Wildlife; three private forest land owners and timber owners regularly engaged in forest operations; and three members of the public at large with no direct financial interest in the forest products industry. It is the FPAC which holds public meetings and takes testimony to prepare proposals for forest practice regulations for submission to the FPB.

In addition to providing for administrative rule-making through the Forest Practices Board and Forest Practices Advisory Committee, the Forest Practices Act also created the Forest Practices Appeal Board to handle disputes through formal judication. The Forest Practices Appeal Board consists of three members who are qualified in environmental matters. They are appointed by the governor with the advice and consent of the Senate. At least one of the members must be a practicing attorney in the state. The Forest Practices Appeal Board has exclusive jurisdiction to hear appeals stemming from any action or determination by the Department of Natural Resources. Any person aggrieved by the approval or disapproval of an application to conduct a forest practice has thirty days to seek review from the appeals board.

Less formal administrative adjudication routinely occurs whenever there are applications to conduct forest practices. The Forest Practices Act requires that forest operators wishing to engage in particular types of on-the-ground forest practices secure permission from the Department of Natural Resources before starting operations. A significant number of agency adjudications have been settled informally. Forest practices which were determined to have less than ordinary potential to damage a public resource have been routinely verbally approved in the field after the operator notified the Department of Natural Resources of his intent to start operations. In other cases, agency adjuciations have been more formal. Applications rather than notifications have been required for forest practices which have a potentially more severe impact on the environment. Formal applications have sometimes required a detailed environmental impact statement (EIS) and have been approved by the Department of Natural Resources only after allowing for comments from the departments of Ecology, Fisheries, and Game.

Despite the institutional framework for administrative rule-making and agency adjudication established by the Forest Practices Act of 1974, the Forest Practices Board found it increasingly difficult to modify regulations to accommodate new knowledge about the cumulative effects of forest practices on riparian ecosystems. Riparian zones along rivers and streams contain extremely important wildlife habitat. These strips of land also frequently contain highly productive timber sites. Yet, for the most part, the laws governing public and private forest management (e.g., the Multiple Use, Sustained-Yield Act of 1960, the Forest and Rangeland Renewable Resource Planning Act of 1974, the National Forest Management Act of 1976, and the state Forest Practices Act) do not expressly mention riparian zones. Nor do they specify how wildlife habitat is to be managed in these areas (Protasel, 1987). The state Forest Practices Act was primarily intended to cover different categories of forest practices (e.g., harvesting, road construction, reforestation, slash disposal, applications of chemicals) rather than different types of forest ecosystems (e.g., riparian zones, upland zones). With the exception of riparian areas containing wildlife protected by the Endangered Species Act of 1973, riparian wildlife habitat is not distinguished from other forest ecosystems in legislation.

The issue of how to manage riparian ecosystems was brought before the Forest Practices Board in 1982 during forest practices rules revisions (Washington State Forest Practices Board, 1987:5–8). The FPB decided that they didn't have enough information to act, so they authorized the Department of Ecology to conduct a riparian habitat study which was completed in April 1985. The Department of Natural Resources staff used this study to prepare draft rules for regulating forest practices in riparian ecosystems. In February 1986, the FPB accepted the draft rules and ordered the preparation of a draft environmental impact statement covering the proposals.

Just as previous revisions of forest practices regulations in 1975, 1977, and 1982 had touched off conflicts among the forest products industry, environmental groups, state agencies, and Indian tribes— the 1986 round of revisions proved to be no exception (Northwest Renewable Resources Center, 1987:1). Environmentalists called the proposals inadequate. Industry declared the proposals an economic disaster. It was against this background of dissatisfaction and recurring interest-group conflict that leaders of the various affected parties began to search for a better approach to regulating forest practices.

The T/F/W Bargaining Approach: Negotiated Rule-Making

Several of the combatants involved in the conflict over regulating riparian ecosystems approached the Northwest Renewable Resources Center for help in arriving at a negotiated solution to the many issues arising from the interaction of timber, fish, and wildlife in riparian zones (Northwest Renewable Resources Center, 1987:8). The Center had been created in 1984 by industry, environmental, and tribal leaders to help the Washington Department of Fisheries and the treaty Indian tribes resolve their disputes over salmon management outside of federal court. Talks hosted by the Center between state and tribal leaders eventually led to a Joint Management Project and a number of cooperative management agreements.

The cooperative problem-solving approach facilitated by the Northwest Renewable Resources Center reduced the number of times the state and tribes went to court on salmon season management issues from sixty-six in 1983 to zero in 1984. Since 1984, the number of court cases per year has been kept below double digits. In light of these successful negotiations, the natural resource agencies, timber industry, Indian tribes, and environmentalists concerned about regulation of forest practices in riparian zones hoped that the Northwest Renewable Resources Center could convene and facilitate a series of equally productive negotiating sessions.

With the consent of tribal chairmen, industry executives, state agency directors, and environmental leaders, the Northwest Renewable Resources Center assembled a group of some forty individuals in July, 1986 for a two-and-a-half day retreat at Port Ludlow, Washington to see if the battle adversaries could learn to work together (Washington State Forest Practices Board, 1987:7). Representatives from the following organizations attended: the state Departments of Natural Resources, Ecology, Fishers and Game; several Indian tribes; the Northwest Indian Fisheries Commission; the Columbia River Intertribal Fish Commission; the Washington Environmental Council; the Audubon Society; the Washington Forest Protection Association; the Washington Farm Forestry Association; and Weyerhaeuser, Georgia Pacific, Plum Creek and Simpson Timber companies. This association became known as the Timber/Fish/Wildlife group.

It was at the Port Ludlow meeting that the state natural resource agencies, the timber industry, the Indian tribes, and environmentalists adopted new ground rules for doing business with each other. They agreed that the state of Washington needs a viable timber industry and that the state needs to protect and enhance its fish, wildlife, water, and cultural/archaeological resources. Furthermore, they agreed that these needs are compatible, not mutually exclusive (Northwest Renewable Resources Center, 1987:1). With these simple win-win ground rules, the participants felt that there existed a genuine opportunity to negotiate a new system of forest practices management.

Because the Forest Practices Board was still considering pending changes in the Forest Practices Act that failed to reflect a consensus, members of the T/F/W group felt the urgency to come up with their own series of recommendations for regulatory forestry that all the T/F/W participants could live with. November 1986 was set as a self-imposed deadline to reach consensus (Northwest Renewable Resources Center, 1987:1). Normally, one would expect that to reach consensus on such a complex set of issues involving so many people would require several months or years to complete. However, because of the impending revisions to forest practice rules, everyone in the T/F/W group agreed to try to reach consensus in just four months time.

The T/F/W group was split into a working group and a policy group by the facilitators from the Northwest Renewable Resources Center (Washington State Forest Practices Board, 1987:8). The working group did preliminary evaluations of all the contentious technical issues that were the bases for conflict. Committees of the working groups met until they managed to reach consensus on how to deal with the issues and problems which confronted them. Especially difficult issues were brought before the entire working group for resolution. The policy group then reviewed the proposed agreements and provided policy guidances.

After four months and over one hundred meetings, in the early morning hours of December 3, 1986, the members of the T/F/W group reached a consensus. With no votes taken, the T/F/W group adopted an agreement in principle containing recommendations designed to improve the regulation of forest practices throughout the state. At the December 15, 1986, meeting of the Forest Practices Board, the T/F/W Agreement was reviewed and accepted in principle. The proposed rules which the FPB had previously accepted in February 1986 were withdrawn from further consideration. The Forest Practices Board then directed the Department of Natural Resources staff to begin drafting rule language to implement the T/F/W proposal.

In February 1987, the Forest Practices Board reached formal final agreement on the T/F/W proposal. In March 1987, the new proposed rules drafted by the Department of Natural Resources staff to reflect the T/F/W agreement were approved by the FPB. In May 1987, the FPB approved the draft environmental impact statement on the revised set of new regulations. Public hearings on the proposed regulations and draft environmental impact statement were held throughout the state during Summer 1987. The final draft of the new rules and regulations was published in October 1987. The Forest Practices Board adopted it in less than an hour at its November 1987 meeting without too many changes. The state legislature which was stunned by the absence of interest group conflict which historically had surrounded forest policy-making, officialized the changes in the Forest Practices Act without a single dissenting vote and without a single word being changed.

Summary and Conclusions

During the early phases of the pluralist policymaking process, winning coalitions are forged through competitive bargaining in the legislature to formulate and adopt general policy. Administrative rulemaking is then used to begin to implement policy and develop programs. Frequently, as the implementation phase begins, conflict again erupts over the enforcement of the new administrative rules.

Through agency adjudication or courtroom litigation, specific cases or controversies are resolved by taking into consideration facts relating to the specific parties involved.

To be sure, technocratic rule-making and formal adjudication are necessarily interrelated. Rules often do not become operative until they are further defined in adjudicative proceedings. However, while a moderate amount of adjudication is usually necessary for rules to take effect, a great deal of adjudication interferes with policy implementation. It has been the desire to produce better rules that are more likely to be implemented and less likely to be litigated, that has led to the growing popularity of negotiation as a mode of conflict resolution (Kettl, 1987:46–47).

The T/F/W agreement "developed because the Forest Practices Board was considering changes to the forest practice regulations that were unacceptable to many interest groups" (Washington State Forest Practices Board, 1987:iv). Faced with the prospect of not being able to successfully implement forest policy, the FPB sanctioned the negotiated rule-making process. In this neocorporatist fashion, the semi-public T/F/W coalition of coequal minorities was created (for example, the timber industry which had fought and lost to the Indian tribes sixteen times in court was put on equal footing with them). The notion is that by incorporating interest groups into the negotiated rule-making process, the affected parties will be given ownership in the rules and will be less likely to challenge them.

By bringing together representatives from the state regulatory agencies, the timber industry, the Indian tribes, and environmental groups, a remarkable degree of consensus was achieved on how to better protect the environment while at the same time meet the forest operating needs of individual private landowners. This seems to substantiate the proposition that the communicative rationality of the negotiated rule-making process is well suited for solving the controversial issues and complex problems that arise when protecting the environment. Regulatory negotiation among the incorporated interests resolves regulatory conflicts because through communicative action it creates consensus on the content of regulations that is sensitive to real-world conditions.

REFERENCES

Benveniste, Guy. 1981. *Regulation and Planning: The Case of Environmental Politics.* San Francisco, CA: Boyd and Fraser.

Bryner, Gary C. 1987. *Bureaucratic Discretion: Law and Policy in Federal Regulatory Agencies.* New York: Pergammon Press.

Congressional Quarterly. 1983. *The Battle for Natural Resources.* Washington, DC: Congressional Quarterly Inc.

Denhardt, Robert B., and Kathryn G. Denhardt. 1979. "Public Administration and the Critique of Domination." *Administration and Society* 11(2):107–120.

Dryzek, John S. "Discursive Designs: Critical Theory and Political Institutions." *American Journal of Political Science* 31(3):656–679.

Fisher, Roger, and William Ury. 1983. *Getting to Yes: Negotiating Agreement Without Giving In.* New York: Penguin.

Fritschler, A. Lee. 1984. "The Changing Face of Government Regulation." In Howard Ball (ed.), *Federal Administrative Agencies.* Englewood Cliffs, NJ: Prentice-Hall.

Habermas, Jurgen. 1970. *Toward a Rational Society,* trans. by Jeremy J. Shapiro. Boston, MA: Beacon Press.

Harter, Philip J. 1981. "Negotiating Regulations: A Cure for Malaise." *Georgetown Law Review* 70:1–118.

Kettl, Donald F. 1987. "Performance and Accountability: The Challenge to Public Administration." In Donald F. Kettl (ed.), *Third-Party Government and the Public Manager: The Changing Forms of Government Action.* Summary of Proceedings and Commentary on the 1986 Spring NAPA Meeting. Washington, DC: National Academy of Public Administration.

Kraemer, Kenneth L., and James L. Perry. 1983. "Implementation of Management Science in the Public Sector." In James L. Perry and Kenneth L. Kraemer (eds.), *Public Management: Public and Private Perspectives.* Palo Alto, CA: Mayfield.

Lehmbruch, Gerhard. 1979. "Consociational Democracy, Class Conflict, and the New Corporatism." In Philippe C. Schmitter and Gerhard Lehmbruch (eds.), *Trends Toward Corporatists Intermediation.* Beverly Hills, CA: Sage.

Lehmbruch, Gerhard, and Philippe C. Schmitter (eds.). 1982. *Patterns of Corporatist Policy-Making.* Beverly Hills, CA: Sage.

Lowi, Theodore J. 1979. *The End of Liberalism: The Second Republic of the United States,* 2d ed. New York: Norton.

———. 1972. "Four Systems of Policy, Politics, and Choice." *Public Administration Review* (July/August):298–310.

———. 1964. "American Business, Public Policy, Case-Studies, and Political Theory." *World Politics* (July):675–715.

Murray, Francis X. (ed.). 1978. *Where We Agree: Report of the National Coal Policy Project,* 2 vols. Boulder, CO: Westview.

Northwest Renewable Resources Center. 1987. "From Conflict to Consensus." *Timber/Fish/Wildlife: A Report from the Northwest Renewable Resources Center* 1(1) (Summer):1–2.

———. 1987. "Timber/Fish/Wildlife: A Better Future in Our Woods and Streams." Final Report. Northwest Renewable Resources Center.

_____. 1987. "Unique Approaches to Natural Resource Issues." *Timber/Fish/ Wildlife: A Report from the Northwest Renewable Resources Center* 1 (Summer):1, 8.

Pops, Gerald M., and Max O. Stephenson, Jr. 1987. *Conflict Resolution in the Policy Process: Teaching Material for Public Administration and Public Affairs.* West Virginia University, Dept. of Public Administration.

Protasel, Greg J. 1987. "Cooperative Natural Resource Management: Negotiated Rulemaking by the T/F/W Coalition in the State of Washington." Paper prepared for the Pacific Northwest Political Science Association Convention, Spokane, WA, October 16–17.

_____. 1987. "How Institutional Laws, Rules, Policies, and Objectives Influence On-the-Ground Riparian Forest Management." Paper prepared for the Interdisciplinary Symposium on Streamside Management: Riparian Wildlife and Forestry Interactions, University of Washington, College of Forest Resources, February 11–13.

_____. 1980. *Forest Policy Institutions and Organizations: Forest Policy Project.* Springfield, VA: National Technical Information Service.

Reagan, Michael D. 1987. *Regulation: The Politics of Policy.* Boston, MA: Little, Brown.

Reich, Robert B. 1981. "Regulation by Confrontation or Negotiation?" *Harvard Business Review* 59, (May-June):82–91.

Schmitter, Philippe C. 1983. "Democratic Theory and Neocorporatist Practice." *Social Research* 50(4) (Winter):885–928.

_____. 1977. "Modes of Interest Intermediation and Models of Societal Change in Western Europe." *Comparative Political Studies* 10(1):7–38.

Shapiro, Martin. 1987. "Rules, Discretion, and Reasonableness under the Constitution." In Gary Bryner and Dennis Thompson (eds.), *The Constitution and the Regulation of Society.* Provo, UT: Brigham Young University.

_____. 1982. "On Predicting the Future of Administrative Law." *Regulation* (May/June):18–25.

Simon, Herbert A. 1981. *The Sciences of the Artificial,* 2d ed. Cambridge, MA: MIT Press.

Sullivan, Timothy J. 1984. *Resolving Development Disputes Through Negotiations.* New York: Plenum Press.

Sunstein, Cass R. 1984. "Deregulation and the Hard-Look Doctrine." In Philip B. Kurland et al. (eds.), *Supreme Court Review.* Chicago, IL: University of Chicago Press.

Susskind, Lawrence, and Gerald McMahon. 1985. "The Theory and Practice of Negotiated Rulemaking." *Yale Journal of Regulation,* 133–165.

Truman, David B. 1951. *The Governmental Process.* New York: Knopf.

Verkuil, Paul A. 1984. "Administrative Procedure." In Howard Ball (ed.), *Federal Administrative Agencies.* Englewood Cliffs, NJ: Prentice-Hall.

Washington State Forest Practices Board. 1987. *Proposed Forest Practice Rules and Regulations Draft Environmental Impact Statement.* Washington State Department of Natural Resources.

————. 1987. *Proposed Forest Practice Rules and Regulations Draft Environmental Impact Statement.* Washington State Department of Natural Resources.

Weber, Max. 1968. *Economy and Society* (Guenther Rother and Klaus Wittich, eds.) New York: Bedminister.

Wenner, Lettie M. 1976. *One Environment Under Law: A Public-Policy Dilemma.* Pacific Palisades, CA: Goodyear.

CONTRIBUTORS

J. Walton Blackburn is currently Assistant to the President for Planning and Institutional Research at Creighton University in Omaha, Nebraska. He has a BA from Earlham College, a Master of City Planning from Ohio State, a Master of Professional Studies from Cornell, and a Ph.D. from Virginia Polytechnic Institute. He has worked in planning in Tennessee, Iran, and New York, and taught college courses at Virginia Tech, the University of Nebraska at Omaha, and Creighton. He has also worked in Mexico, Paraguay, and Costa Rica.

Paul F. Clark is assistant professor of labor studies and industrial relations at Pennsylvania State University. Professor Clark received his Ph.D. in public administration from the University of Pittsburgh. His research interests include union government and administration, public sector labor relations, and survey methodology.

Richard C. Feiock is an assistant professor of public administration at Florida State University. His recent publications have appeared in *American Politics Quarterly, Journal of Urban Affairs, Policy Studies Journal, Public Administration Quarterly,* and *State and Local Government Review.*

Daniel G. Gallagher is professor of management at James Madison University. Professor Gallagher received his Ph.D. in labor and industrial relations from the University of Illinois. His research interests include dispute resolution and behavioral aspects of human resource management. Professor Gallagher is a member of the labor arbitration panels of the Federal Mediation and Conciliation Services and the American Arbitration Association.

Michael S. Hamilton is associate professor of political science, University of Southern Maine, Portland. He is a specialist in environmental regulation of industrial facilities; his research on power plant siting, state and national energy policy, public land management and ocean policy has appeared in numerous professional journals. He is principal coauthor of *Environmental, Legal and Political Constraints on Power Plant Siting in the Southwestern United States* (1981) and *Nuclear Weapons in the University Classroom* (1990), and contributing editor of *Regulatory Federalism, Natural Resources and Environmental Management* (1990). Dr. Hamilton is a member of the governing board of the American Society for Public Administration and has chaired its Section on Environmental and Natural Resources Administration.

Vern Hauck is professor of industrial relations and management at the School of Business, University of Alaska at Anchorage. His most recent work is a book involving the application of the integrated Project Planning and Management Cycle model to strategic decision making.

Douglas M. McCabe is professor of industrial and labor relations at Georgetown University's School of Business Administration in Washington, DC. He is the author of numerous articles in the field of labor-management relations. He has served as a member of the Board of Governors of the Industrial Relations Research Association and the Society of Professionals in Dispute Resolution, Washington, DC, chapters. Professor McCabe holds a Ph.D. in industrial and labor relations from Cornell University and is a member of Phi Beta Kappa.

Miriam Mills is professor of management at the New Jersey Institute of Technology. Among other books, she is co-author of *Multi-Criteria Methods in Alternative Dispute Resolution* (1990) and editor of *Conflict Resolution and Public Policy* (1990). She has written extensively on labor relations and the social impacts of technology. Professor Mills is a labor arbitrator and mediator with the Federal Mediation and Conciliation Service and state agencies in Illinois and New Jersey. She earned her doctorate in public administration from New York University.

Thomas J. Pavlak is professor of public administration and director of the Public Administration Institute at Fairleigh Dickinson University. Professor Pavlak received his Ph.D. in political science from the University of Illinois. Among his research interests are performance evaluation, organizational effectiveness, and administrative justice. He has been a visiting scholar at the National Institute of Justice, the U. S. Department of Housing and Urban Development, and the Navy Personnel Research and Development Center.

Gerald M. Pops is professor of public administration at West Virginia University. He received a law degree from the University of California, Berkeley, and a doctoral degree in public administration from the Maxwell School at Syracuse University. He has taught and published widely in the fields of administrative law, justice, and ethics, public sector labor relations, and conflict management. His books include *Emergence of the Public Sector Arbitrator* (1976) and *Conflict Resolution in the Policy Process* (1987, with M. O. Stephenson, Jr.).

Greg J. Protasel is an associate professor of public administration in the School of Public Affairs at the University of Alaska at Anchorage. His Ph.D. is in political science from the University of Michigan, Ann Arbor. One of his research interests is environmental policy-making. He has written about forest policy, riparian wildlife and forestry interactions, and nonpoint source pollution control. He became interested in environmental dispute resolution while studying Washington State's Timber/Fish/Wildlife Agreement. He hopes to extend this interest to the other side of the Bering Strait and compare the way Alaskans and Soviets resolve their environmental conflicts.

Barry G. Rabe is an assistant professor of health politics in the School of Public Health and an adjunct assistant professor in the Department of Political Science at the University of Michigan—Ann Arbor. He is the author of *Fragmentation and Integration in State Environmental Management* (1986) and co-author of *When Federalism Works* (1986). He is currently completing books on the politics of hazardous waste facility sitings in Canada and the United States and on the politics of cross-media pollution in the Great Lakes Basin.

Matthew Silberman is professor of sociology at Bucknell University. Much of his work is on the role of coercion in the legal system. He has published articles on the administration of social welfare, the deterrence of crime, and violence in correctional institutions. His work also focuses on dispute resolution in the legal arena. His book *The Civil Justice Process* (1985) concerns the transformation of everyday disputes into legal claims. Professor Silberman is currently writing a book on the production of violence in the American correctional system, past and present.

John C. South is professor of organizational behavior and management at the School of Business and Administration, Duquesne University in Pittsburgh. A graduate of Ohio State University, he holds a Ph.D. in industrial psychology and worked for a number of years as a personnel psychologist in a major corporation prior to teaching. Dr. South has done research and published articles in the areas of employee performance appraisal, motivation, and morale, and personnel development.

Max O. Stephenson, Jr., is assistant professor in the Department of Urban Affairs and Planning at Virginia Polytechnic Institute and State University. He is the author of a number of articles and book chapters in the area of conflict resolution.

Jonathan P. West is professor and chair of the Department of Political Science at the University of Miami. His most recent research has appeared in *Policy Studies Review, Polity, Public Personnel Management, Public Productivity Review,* and *Review of Public Personnel Administration.*

Name Index

SUBJECT INDEX